Trust, Ethics and Human Reason

BLOOMSBURY ETHICS SERIES

Bloomsbury Ethics is a series of books written to help students explore, engage with and master key topics in contemporary ethics and moral philosophy.

Autonomy, Andrew Sneddon
Ethics Without Intention, Ezio Di Nucci
Intuitionism, David Kaspar
Moral Principles, Maike Albertzart
Moral Realism, Kevin DeLapp
Reasons, Eric Wiland
Value Theory, Francesco Orsi
Virtue Ethics, Nafsika Athanassoulis

Forthcoming in the series:
Character, Jay R. Elliott
Climate Ethics, Sarah Kenehan
Luck Egalitarianism, Kasper Lippert-Rasmussen
Moral Psychology, Jay R. Elliott
Moral Skepticism, Basil Smith

Series Editors:

Thom Brooks is Reader in Law at Durham Law School. He is the founding editor of the *Journal of Moral Philosophy* and runs a popular Political Philosophy blog called *The Brooks Blog*.

Simon Kirchin is Senior Lecturer in Philosophy at the University of Kent, UK. He is President of the British Society for Ethical Theory and co-editor of *Arguing About Metaethics* (Routledge, 2006).

Trust, Ethics and Human Reason

OLLI LAGERSPETZ

Bloomsbury Academic
An imprint of Bloomsbury Publishing Plc

B L O O M S B U R Y
LONDON • NEW DELHI • NEW YORK • SYDNEY

Bloomsbury Academic
An imprint of Bloomsbury Publishing Plc

50 Bedford Square	1385 Broadway
London	New York
WC1B 3DP	NY 10018
UK	USA

www.bloomsbury.com

BLOOMSBURY and the Diana logo are trademarks of Bloomsbury Publishing Plc

First published 2015

© Olli Lagerspetz, 2015

Olli Lagerspetz has asserted his right under the Copyright, Designs and Patents Act, 1988, to be identified as Author of this work.

All rights reserved. No part of this publication may be reproduced or transmitted in any form or by any means, electronic or mechanical, including photocopying, recording, or any information storage or retrieval system, without prior permission in writing from the publishers.

No responsibility for loss caused to any individual or organization acting on or refraining from action as a result of the material in this publication can be accepted by Bloomsbury or the author.

British Library Cataloguing-in-Publication Data
A catalogue record for this book is available from the British Library.

ISBN: HB: 978-1-44116-977-8
PB: 978-1-44118-487-0
ePDF: 978-1-44114-609-0
ePub: 978-1-44110-919-4

Library of Congress Cataloging-in-Publication Data
A catalog record for this book is available from the Library of Congress.

Series: Bloomsbury Ethics

Typeset by Fakenham Prepress Solutions, Fakenham, Norfolk NR21 8NN

*Dedicated to Lars Hertzberg and the philosophical
community at Åbo*

CONTENTS

Acknowledgements x

1 **Trust and our worries with it** 1
   Trust and reason: Friends or foes? 2
   On how to write about what trust 'is' 6
   The need for reflexivity 8
   Current issues 12
   Trust and reliance 15
   Normative and non-normative conceptions of trust 18
   What happens next? 21

2 **Trust and Hobbesian reason** 25
   The Hobbesian dilemma 26
   Trust as risk management 29
   A game-theoretic solution 31
   Critique of game theory: The need for a social framework 35
   Trustworthiness and encapsulated interests 37
   Is this trust? – A caveat 39

Trust and strategic reason, and where to go from here 40
The metaphysics of interests 42

3 **Vulnerability and entrusting** 47
Baier's ambiguous critique of rationalism 48
The theory of trust as entrusting 50
Entrusting and simple trust 51
Factual and ethical vulnerability 54
The notion of possibility 56
Vulnerability revisited 60
A Novel from the 21st Century 60
Trusting and being trusted 65

4 **The time dimension** 69
Methodological timelessness 70
Prisoners' Dilemma revisited 74
Timelessness in non-formal treatments of trust 77
Assessing probability 78
Trust as an interpretative activity 81
Normality in ongoing interaction 87
Methodological timelessness and methodological individualism 88

5 **'Trust' as an organizing tool** 91
Is trust a psychological state? 92
The 'dys-appearance' of trust 95

First- and third-person perspectives 100
The need for challenge 103
Conclusion 105

6 **Communication, truthfulness, trust** 107
Communication as manipulation and mind-reading 108
The testimony debate 112
The norm of truthfulness 116
Løgstrup: Trust in conversation 120
'Image' vs real presence 123
The place of 'trust' in different ideas of language 126

7 **Basic trust** 131
Trust as a response to scepticism 133
A self-deception theory of basic trust 136
Paranoia and scepticism 139
'The substratum of all my enquiring and asserting' 142
Meeting the other in trust: Weil and Løgstrup 147
Ideas of basic trust in context 153

8 **Conclusions** 155

Notes 159
Bibliography 191
Index 199

ACKNOWLEDGEMENTS

This book was mainly written during the two years 2013 and 2014, but its prehistory is much longer. I spent the academic year of 1990–1 studying moral and political philosophy with Peter Winch at the University of Illinois at Urbana-Champaign. He helped and supported me in many ways at this philosophically and personally formative time of my life. It was then that I decided to write my doctoral dissertation on the concept of trust. Lars Hertzberg, my supervisor at Åbo, was immediately and consistently supportive of the project, as he has always been of my work. The dissertation was finished in 1996 and published as a book two years later.

Having finished that book I consciously turned my attention to other philosophical topics. Later developments, however, made me take up the philosophy of trust again. When I was occasionally asked to contribute with papers on the concept of trust for conferences and anthologies I grew aware of the shortcomings and blind spots of the earlier book. To put it briefly, it had the good as well as bad qualities of a young person's philosophical profession of faith. Moreover, the philosophical field itself has developed rapidly in the last few years. Forms of contractarianism and rationalism are less predominant than they used to be in English-speaking moral philosophy; there is a new kind of openness towards the philosophy of emotions and the philosophy of language, including the current philosophical debate on testimony. The time seems ripe for a new overview.

My educational and work history squarely places this book within the philosophical tradition known as Swansea Wittgensteinianism. More specific philosophical influences stem from Peter Winch and (especially) Lars Hertzberg – of all philosophers now living or dead, the two who have influenced me most. I hope some of their impact shows through everywhere in the book, not only where I explicitly cite them. Moreover, Hertzberg's work on the philosophy of trust belongs as a matter of course to the sources of the current philosophical trust debate. Some years ago we also wrote a paper together, and some arguments from that paper have found their way into the present book.

My colleagues, students and friends at Åbo Akademi University, Finland, have helped me above all by commenting on various parts of the book at our weekly seminars. Among those at Åbo who have stimulated my work on this theme I now only mention a few: Jonas Ahlskog, Antony Fredriksson, Martin Gustafsson, Ylva Gustafsson, Markus Kananen, Camilla Kronqvist, Tage Kurtén, Yrsa Neuman, Hugo Strandberg and Göran Torrkulla. Outside Åbo, the comments and encouragement of David Cockburn (of the University of Wales, Trinity St David), Richard H. R. Harper (of Microsoft Research in Cambridge) and Christopher C. Robinson (of Clarkson University, Potsdam, NY) have stimulated this book or earlier work leading up to it. I want especially to mention that Ahlskog and Robinson took the trouble to read and comment on the entire manuscript draft. The Finnish Society of Sciences and Letters has supported the work with a grant.

All this is, however, not to say I expect any of the persons mentioned here (or anyone else) to agree with everything in this book. Disagreement is the lifeblood of philosophy; not because philosophy has not yet found the secure path of a science, but because a philosophical perspective on things is always *someone's* perspective on things.

Given this background history, I have found it natural to dedicate this book jointly to Lars Hertzberg and the philosophical community at Åbo.

Åbo, Finland, 31 December 2014

CHAPTER ONE

Trust and our worries with it

If one were very briefly to describe the life of the human being as a species, one characteristic would easily spring to mind: our dependence on other people. It is the very fabric of our lives. At times such dependence results from considered choices, but on the whole the life that involves mutual dependence and trust is not something we have planned or chosen. To start with the obvious, learning processes take time and require instruction by others. Consequently the human young still remain dependent on the previous generation long after they physically reach maturity. Once in the full enjoyment of our rational faculties, we make decisions about engaging in cooperative ventures or withdrawing from them. But all this takes place in society – within a massive network of mutual dependence that can hardly be surveyed, even by experts. Dependence on others is constitutive of important human practices, which is perhaps best seen in situations where for some reason help is *unavailable*. Many of us would be prepared to ask complete strangers for directions in a foreign city. But consider those who do not feel safe to do so: such as, perhaps, the very young and the very old, women in some situations, and members of minority groups routinely treated with suspicion. Where we cannot trust and be trusted, we are shut out of society at large – not only because our contacts with others turn difficult and unpredictable in a practical sense, but because we are divested of our very capacity as a social agent.

David Hume has remarked: 'The mutual dependence of men is so great that scarce any human action is entirely complete in itself, or is performed without some reference to the actions of others, which are required to make it answer fully to the intentions of the agent.'[1] Hume's observation is apt, but he perhaps did not see its full implications. He was mainly thinking of cooperation for specific, limited undertakings – things that we can plan to do or not to do. Our involvement with each other clearly goes deeper than that. The very possibility of reasonable distrust depends on a huge body of knowledge, thinking patterns and accepted patterns of action that we take on trust from others.

In English-speaking academic philosophy, most of the work concerning trust has been published in the 1980s or later. The work published in the 1980s is still widely cited and used as a starting point for research. Today trust is no longer a neglected subject but more or less well-defined central questions and approaches have emerged. Hence the time seems ripe for an overview.[2] Surveying the philosophical trust literature, one question comes across as central. How does the inescapability of trust square with rationality – another feature agreed to be central in the life of *Homo sapiens*? For isn't there a tension between these two characteristically human conditions: (1) the overwhelming fact of our mutual dependence; and (2) the character of rational thinking as the *independent* exercise of reason? Ever since Descartes, if not earlier, we are constantly told that knowledge rests on evidence and reasoning, not trust; for, as John Hardwig formulates the point, 'trust, in order to be trust, must be at least partially blind'.[3] It seems that trust involves going beyond or against what is accessible or justified merely on the basis of our own reasoning from available information. If we refuse to trust someone or something (a person, a source of information) more than they have demonstrably 'earned', we just do not trust them. Yet it is difficult to imagine human life where no such trust is involved. A considerable part of the philosophical discussion concerning trust involves various attempts to overcome the apparent conflict between trust and reason.[4]

Trust and reason: Friends or foes?

In his brief book on trust and rationality, Martin Hollis argues that trust and even cooperative action in general seem in the last analysis to be incompatible with the individualist bent of what he calls 'Enlightenment reason'.[5] His analysis, to which we will return later,[6] seems convincing with regard to a specific view on practical rationality, defined as the individual pursuit of utility. No formal argument seems to be available for convincing a rational agent (of the kind implied in Hollis's discussion) to trust another agent known to be similarly motivated. An analogous case for the incompatibility of trust and rationality has been made in the epistemological realm. According to standard views on the rational justification of knowledge claims, it is problematic, at least *prima facie*, to accept knowledge claims by others on trust.[7] These are views generally associated with the Enlightenment, implying individualism and emancipation from tradition. However, a somewhat different picture arises if we turn to that pivotal document of the Enlightenment, Immanuel Kant's 1784 essay on the concept of enlightenment.[8] As is well known, Kant coins the Enlightenment dictum, '*Sapere aude*! Have courage to use your own understanding!'[9] But he wants to find out exactly what using one's 'own understanding' amounts to. Kant stresses the importance of an informed general public. The progress of reason depends on the possibility of *shared* reflection and cannot be imagined to occur in social isolation.[10] It would thus be more fitting to describe the target of Hollis's criticism as a specifically *individualist* and *rationalist* idea of reason and autonomy, and it is not quite obvious on whose side 'Enlightenment' would finally stand in the dispute. This individualist tradition, of which Thomas Hobbes is an important pre-Enlightenment representative, assumes suspicion as the default stance; for him it is the obvious position that human beings in a Hobbesian world need rationally to overcome. Kant may be rather seen as saying that the enlightened public needs, in a certain important but limited range of cases, to overcome the natural human default stance of *trustfulness*. But regardless of its historical roots, a large part of our philosophical tradition both in political philosophy and epistemology has involved focus on the individual agent. This is an agent supposedly only using his or her strictly personal resources to arrive at rational conclusions.

Let me consider some features of this individualist and rationalist picture of human life which of course has been dissected in detail by others.[11] Philosophically its most important feature is the privileged position it gives to scepticism. Believing *nothing* is the initial position which the individual agent supposedly must overcome with the help of experience and rational thinking. Elizabeth Wolgast accordingly refers to the ideal launched in the

Renaissance as one of 'do-it-yourself science and theology'.[12] The consequences of this general stance are shown, in epistemology, in the difficulty of accommodating knowledge by testimony as a legitimate source of knowledge.[13] In political philosophy, the sceptical legacy surfaces as problems about explaining how cooperation can be rationally justified at all.[14] And it is expressed in both political and moral philosophy in an explicit or implicit view on the proper place for trust, vulnerability and dependence. On that view, mutual dependence is not the natural environment for human thought and action. At least in a perfect world populated by fully rational adults, dependence should be treated as something we may either do without or *choose* because of some prudentially or morally justified end. The philosophical debate on trust in the last few decades, especially in English-speaking philosophy, has largely consisted of attempts to engage with that tradition.

The focus of that debate lies in attempts to *justify* trust and other forms of interpersonal dependence. At the same time there is perhaps something inherently self-defeating in the idea of justifying trust, or at least *fully* justifying trust.[15] For isn't the problem precisely that we must trust because there is no certainty? Thus it seems that any reason for trusting that might be brought up *must* fall short of a complete justification. On the other hand, if we already trust the other, the need to look for a justification does not even arise. In other words, it appears that the force of argument as such could never move a person from an initial stance of distrust to that of trust or *vice versa*. This is not to claim that such shifts do not take place in real life, but the role of argument in them is not very clear-cut. In sum, reviewing the literature on trust from the 1980s onwards, the ubiquity and perhaps irreducible character of trust are mostly recognized, but these features are often taken to imply a *prima facie* difficulty. Trust is something that in a sense rationally 'ought not' to be there, but which nevertheless clearly *is* there; something which moreover seems inescapable and which calls for rational explanation and justification.

Barring the conclusion that trusting simply *is* irrational and should be avoided, three strategies seem available. One is to argue that trust, despite appearances, consists of justified beliefs that only seemingly conflict with received ideas of rationality.[16] Another is to maintain that trust as a human tendency is neither rational nor irrational, but has beneficial (prudential, ethical, psychological) consequences that make it reasonable and justified.[17] The third possibility is to argue that trust is not external to human reason in the first place but an important aspect of it. Thus, on that last view, our conceptions of rationality must be revised in order to accommodate the role of trust in it.[18] On the whole I side with the last view in the present book. The growth and employment of rationality are not inimical or extraneous to sociality. Even what we recognize to be 'informed decisions' are influenced by our engagements with people; as I will later argue, also our ideas about 'evidence' speaking in favour of one conclusion or other reflect our relations with other people.

In the opening chapter of his book on testimony, C. A. J. Coady describes his trip to Holland, pointing out that at every step his reasons for believing he actually *is* in Holland depend on what others are telling him.[19] But his dependence on testimony goes even further. His conviction that there is a country called Holland, and indeed the very idea that there are such things as 'countries', is something he has accepted as true from others. We are happy with this state of things because, as Ludwig Wittgenstein puts it in the notes published as *On Certainty*, 'we belong to a community which is bound together by science and education'.[20] One might see this as a problem because it implies that our lives, in their great outlines, are dependent on a general pattern of behaviour not rationally chosen by us; rational decisions appear only as tiny islands in a huge sea of irrationality or non-rationality. But Wittgenstein's work here and elsewhere may just as well be taken as suggesting that 'rationality' just *is* the way (or ways) in which humans organize their lives. 'Reason' does not stand for a philosophical or political *programme* of any kind, but it describes how human beings in the course of their lives invoke ideas of the 'reasonable'. Not all suggestions of what is reasonable are equally plausible and philosophers who look at human discourse are under no obligation to accept them all. But disagreements of this kind also belong to the general framework of a life where certain forms of interpersonal dependence are self-evident.

The present book has two main objectives. It aims to present a general outline of the philosophical trust debate of the last few decades. In the course of doing so it moreover hopes to develop a view that does justice to interpersonal dependence and trust as central aspects of reason itself. The analysis will necessarily include an idea of our life with 'reason' as one involving moral relations. By 'moral relations' I do not now mean '*good* moral relations' but generally relationships where the moral vocabulary is available. For instance, I will argue that the applicability of notions of truthfulness and being committed to one's words as elements of possible praise or criticism is essential to understanding what a person means by what he or she is saying.[21] Epistemological and moral concepts are tightly intertwined here.

Given the nature of the present inquiry, one should not expect it to result in definitions of what trust or reason 'really' are. Concepts are made for use, and the advisability of adopting certain definitions of 'trust' or 'reason' depends on the issue that they are meant to illuminate. For instance, technical and stipulative definitions may be used when needed. Moreover, this kind of flexibility is itself an important part of our use of these concepts. I do insist on one thing, however. We will end up with a very limited understanding of the place of both trust and rationality in the human form of life if we think that their relation is only external.

On how to write about what trust 'is'

A fellow philosopher,[22] in considering the concept of trust, remarked to me that he is reminded of St Augustine's observation about time: we know what it is when no one asks us, but once they do we don't know what to answer. He would probably also agree with me about a chief reason for Augustine's perplexity. If the question is, 'What is time?', not only the answer, but the question itself eludes us. Who is asking the question, for what purpose? Almost each and every human activity or concern involves what may be called a time dimension. But the ubiquity of 'time' in our pursuits does not make the question easier, quite the contrary. For it also means that, before the context of the inquiry is settled, there is no *privileged* way to approach it. To put this another way, the meaning of 'What is time?' is not settled simply by uttering the question.

'What is mustard gas?' almost always invites an answer either in terms of the chemical makeup or the devastating effects of this forbidden substance – unless some unusual circumstance indicates the need of other kinds of discussion. The question typically surfaces along with rather obvious topics about warfare and war industry. In contrast, given the practically unlimited range of possible contexts for our talk about 'time', the appropriate response to every purported general answer to 'What is time?' might be, 'Yes, but ...'. This is compatible with the fact that hugely important things have been said about time both in philosophy and in empirical research.

Something similar is true of the question 'What is trust'. The meanings that the philosophical question can take on board will be dependent on the specific worries that give rise to it. In an overview of the debate in 2001, Martin Hartmann claims that, in comparison with most academic research, authors of theoretical treatments of trust have been unusually keen to specify their key concept by way of analytical definitions of some kind. He hints at an 'overabundance of definitions'[23] that 'rarely leave the dry atmosphere of theoretical abstraction'.[24] But he also suggests that the definitions on offer in these works do not necessarily conform to their subsequent illustrations and further analyses.[25] This is symptomatic of the difficulty of surveying a thoroughly familiar concept. We cannot hope to find an all-purpose definition of 'trust' and it would not help us anyway, because an all-purpose definition would not help us with the context-sensitive questions that arise.

Consider the suggestion, 'To trust is to place a bet'. To someone unfamiliar with the literature it may come as a surprise that this is perhaps the most usual way to describe trust. For shouldn't we say the very opposite? Saying of someone, 'To trust her is like placing a bet' would plausibly come across as the claim that she is a person *not* to be trusted. Nevertheless, philosophical ideas arise from somewhere. Clearly there are social practices (for instance, economic practices) that may for some purposes profitably be described as forms of betting. We may be of different minds about how to extend our uses of the concept of trust, but nothing is gained by simply asserting that uses such as this one must forever be excluded.

The philosophical task cannot be to create a definition that would explain the meaning of 'trust' to someone who does not know. The chances are that a person like that would not understand the explanation either. Nor should the ambition be to find out whether trust in general is a good thing. Comparing with 'time' again, on the whole it is certainly better to have time than not to have any, but that would not be an answer to the 'question' whether a time-and-space universe is a good thing. Human life is social, and social life implies a complicated network of explicit and tacit expectations and relationships of dependence. To ask whether *that* in general is a good thing is to ask whether we should not prefer to be something else instead of belonging to the human species.

In philosophy, to study what trust 'is' is to see what is *meant* by 'trust' in various circumstances. The way to approach trust is consequently this: describe the context in which the concept is *invoked* and study the contribution of *that* back to the context. In other words, what are the worries to which the vocabulary of 'trust' is invoked as a solution? And how does the solution perhaps add new complications? The fact that human life involves mutual dependence is easily seen. For the most part we do not even notice it and have no need to do so. In some cases of dependence, however, we feel the need to single out a relationship or an action and describe it as one of 'trust'. Our applications of the word 'trust' and related concepts like 'betrayal' are our ways to bring the situation into perspective. Thus it seems to me that what trust 'is' is best seen, not by looking for the psychological and behavioural phenomena the relevant words stand for, but by looking at situations where 'trust' is raised as an issue. We should focus on what prompts us to apply this kind of vocabulary in certain problematic situations, and on how those applications contribute to solving, creating or transforming those situations.

The need for reflexivity

One may want to close in on trust by way of examples. Paul Faulkner writes:

> Trusting someone to do something is an action. Leaving one's closed diary on one's desk where one knows one's partner will see it. Not asking for a second quote when a mechanic says one's car needs a lot of work. Shaking on a deal. Following a stranger's directions. Purchasing a good that will be delivered later. These are examples of trust, and we trust in these cases by acting one way rather than another.[26]

This quote from Faulkner's recent book serves well to illustrate that questions about trust may turn up in all kinds of everyday occasions. However, at this point it will be useful to call for reflexivity on the part of the philosopher or social theorist. We need not only take note of the examples themselves but also consider what *we* do in describing them. All the quoted cases can certainly be construed as instances of trusting; but this is partly because they are not offered as *factual* descriptions in any clear-cut sense. The author's claim is not that, in engaging in these actions, we always explicitly or implicitly think that our actions involve trust. (Some of the examples in a sense do not need to count as 'actions' at all insofar as they only involve carrying on with a set pattern of behaviour.) What we learn from Faulkner's descriptions is that also actions that one might see as simple matters of routine can legitimately be described as involving a leap of faith. This involves persuasive re-descriptions of our practices.

Consider the remark that I must trust my wife if I leave a diary on my desk. It is – here, anyway – not offered as a claim about what I am personally thinking, or what anyone else in that situation must be thinking. It is a point about the general implications of leaving a private document in plain view; ones already inherent in describing a document as 'private'. The situation may moreover be understood in different ways. One way to think of it is to argue that I trust my wife to refrain from reading my diary. Another possibility is that I trust she will not think ill of me regardless of what she finds in it. A third possibility would be that I 'trust' her to have so little interest in me that she simply would not bother. Moreover, there is a better way for her to find out what I have been doing and thinking, namely, asking me. As another kind of reaction to Faulkner's suggestion, I might reply that we share a household anyway: it would hardly be practicable for us to keep hiding objects from each other. The latter response would in effect remove the focus from the issue of trust. Sharing a household may be said by definition to imply trust, but perhaps this particular example does not stand out. In *theory*, there is no end to the mischief my wife might do if she set her mind to it, but it has not been explained why any of these theoretical possibilities must be raised and singled out as *problems*. Finally, the discussion would take a different twist and leave philosophy behind if someone were to make the concrete suggestion that my wife – that is, a specified person – wants to spy on me, a specified person. I come home and discover my diary lying open on the desk. Did I leave it that way or has someone touched it? What are the situations in which that question starts to worry me and what do my reactions tell you about my relations to other people in the house? And what does it tell us about *philosophers* if they maintain that the situation must be obviously worrisome?

To say in *this* context that my behaviour implies trust is more or less to draw the listener's attention to the fact that one might imagine my wife – or rather, quite unspecified, *someone's* wife in a similar situation – to take advantage of the chance to read her husband's diary. To 'imagine' this is to take a perspective where certain kinds of scenario are invoked. In this context it is important to ask why these things are said. In other words, whence the need to consider a distrustful scenario? To cite an extreme example, Annette Baier claims that a wife who goes to bed next to her husband trusts that a brain disease will not unexpectedly turn him into a mad aggressor.[27] This remark is 'true' in the sense that married couples do not usually take precautions against this sort of imaginary development. On the other hand, it will take very special circumstances for anyone to *make* a remark like this except as a joke.[28] Still, we should not think of it as a *false* remark, but look for the background that motivates it in a debate. My problem with these descriptions does not concern their 'truth' but our reasons, if any, for stating them. We need reflexion about what would make someone, in a real situation, describe an example as a case of trusting.[29] In other words: what are those troubling circumstances one would be bringing up? And how does *voicing* the troubles contribute towards solving or aggravating them?

It might be thought that we need to look for no reason for making a factual assertion over and above the fact that the assertion is true. But here two things must be remembered about human communication. First of all, communication does not merely consist in the fact that we go around telling each other things that are true (or false, as the case may be). These things are said for a reason, by someone, to someone. Suppose I tell you I am hungry and that there is a café after the next junction. Presumably among the reasons for my saying this figures the fact that it is true[30] and presumably I want to inform you about this truth. Nevertheless you would not catch my meaning unless you understood my suggestion that we stop at the café.

Secondly, it is not clear that our talk about trust has an independent reference in the same way as here. When I feel hungry and there is a café nearby, I may still choose not to bring it up, while facts about physiology and geography nevertheless remain the same. But when I say, 'I trust you', I am not merely reporting my thoughts and hoping for a response – even if these things are important too. I am, in a sense, creating new interpersonal reality. 'I trust you', uttered in the right circumstances (notably, ones where you are in a position of control), conveys something more than does a mere description of *my* state of mind. It indicates that I expect you to assume the responsibilities of someone who is trusted.[31] In one possible situation, I am confronting you with a commitment that I take you to have made at an earlier date. You now have either to take your commitment back or to reassure me.

The general methodological point I am now making is this: When an example is described as a case of trusting, we should consider what kinds of commitments, suspicions, complexities, worries, etc. are invoked when it is so presented. Thus the main question to be addressed to an example is not *whether* it is a true case of trust but, instead, what kinds of worries are suggested *if* the example is so presented. This has quite important consequences to our initial question 'What is trust'. In the light of the points just made, the general question dissolves itself into context-sensitive issues about particular cases. If it is taken to be a unitary question, it can only be stated from a starting point that was shown to be false.

The methodological point also needs to be applied to the philosophical debate itself. One thing we discover from looking at the debate is the way in which specific theoretical concerns are reflected in the various theories of trust on offer. Trust is not obviously problematic in itself any more than time is, but it can become a focal point for issues that arise for specific perspectives on human agency. This is true even though the authors that I have been looking at – certainly a majority of them – do present their theories of trust as answers to what they take to be a unitary question about how to define 'trust'. Hartmann emphasizes that the different definitions have been developed as responses to specific challenges. What 'trust' is expected to accomplish is determined by the needs of the theoretical frame of reference.[32] Thus we should not expect agreement, and using one theory to criticize another always carries the risk of not appreciating the concerns behind the theory originally under scrutiny.

Current issues

Much of the recent trust debate has been dealing with a conundrum that historically can be further traced back to Hobbes. According to Hobbes, trust is necessary whenever there is exchange of goods or services and there is a time gap between the first performance and the equivalent return. However, as is well known, Hobbes maintained that the natural state of humankind is one of universal war.[33] Stable trustful relations between agents can only be established insofar as it is not up to the agents themselves to decide when an action should count as keeping or breaking faith. They can escape the condition of war only if they agree to set up a coercive authority that can pass judgement on breaches of trust and impose penalties. However, the Hobbesian description of human psychology on the whole invites the question of how humans in the state of nature could possibly agree on *anything*.

Such internal problems of contractarian approaches lie behind the currently renewed philosophical interest in the necessary conditions for trusting. The main question addressed there concerns *risk taking*: how to account for cooperative relations between rationally self-interested agents in conditions of uncertainty. The connection of these issues also to economic theory is obvious. The volume *Trust: Making and Breaking Cooperative Relations*, a collection edited by Diego Gambetta[34] (first published 1988) was influential in establishing the parameters of the present debate. The emerging consensus was to think of trust in terms of predictability and lack thereof. The main interest was to find out what kinds of consideration would induce agents to act in a cooperative manner. Game theory and rational choice theory were employed as tools.

Several authors regard the Hobbesian dilemma as unsolvable in its own terms. For instance, Hollis claims that all the available options had been fully explored and found wanting already by the end of the eighteenth century.[35] That has encouraged some philosophers and political scientists to look beyond rational choice theory to the 'soft' cultural variables explored by sociologists.[36] The idea is that social cohesion implies or presupposes generalized trust. Such cohesion cannot be explained by strategic rationality but it is rather a condition of the latter.

But the trust debate has also included voices that questioned the contractual view on trust.[37] The most influential of these contributions was no doubt Annette Baier's essay 'Trust and Antitrust', first published in 1986 and followed up by some subsequent work of hers. Contractarianism at least ideally assumes rationally motivated exchanges between agents roughly equal in power and resources. Baier pointed out that this is not the usual case in family relations, i.e. the kinds of everyday human relation where the presence of trust and the need thereof are especially marked. On the other hand, as I will argue later, Baier's paper is more helpful in raising questions than in following them through. On some key points, she retains the view on trust as pertaining to the mutual exchange of goods and services. On the whole – as also Martin Hartmann argues – the theoretical starting points of contractarianism, rational choice theories and game theory have been widely accepted, also tacitly by authors who profess scepticism of those theories.[38] Mainly this is shown in the characteristic question addressed by a large number of writers: 'Whom should I trust, and why?' The implicit assumption is the game-theoretical one of initially unconnected rational agents *looking for* other agents on whom to 'place' their trust.

One challenge to this approach comes from the philosophy of emotions, which has seen a renaissance in the last few decades. It has involved the questioning of any neat distinction between cognition and emotion. Emotions involve an aspect of cognition because they involve the perception of their objects in particular kinds of way – for instance, as friendly, hostile, valuable, important and unimportant. Notably, Karen Jones has described trust as an 'affective attitude' whereby we tend to interpret the available information in the light of trust and distrust.[39] This implies criticism of rational choice approaches. Rational choice would presuppose that decisions to trust need to be compatible with reasonable interpretations of available information. But what Jones's view on trust suggests is that the question of what the information implies – and indeed what we should be prepared to accept as information in the first place – is always already addressed in some context of trust and distrust. If the context of trust and distrust is there from the outset, it seems to follow that trust is in an important sense *not* subject to decision.

A more thoroughgoing critique of rationalism is voiced by Wittgensteinian philosophers, building especially on Wittgenstein's *On Certainty*. In his essay 'On the Attitude of Trust' (first published 1988) and some subsequent work, Lars Hertzberg has challenged the sceptical bias of mainstream ethics and epistemology.[40] He argues that *On Certainty* develops a pronouncedly social and ethical view on knowledge and reasoning. Reasoning means that we take certain facts or reasons to speak in favour of a conclusion. But this cannot be divorced from the fact that certain *people* – parents and teachers, friends, research communities – represent ideas of what should count as reasonable in the circumstances. In that sense, trust is not a judgement we make, but the form of our judging.

There seems to be some convergence between Wittgensteinian views and some ideas voiced in the recently revived debate on the role of second-hand information – even if those ideas still represent a minority view. The debate started with John Hardwig's paper 'The Role of Trust in Knowledge' (1991) and C. A. J. Coady's book *Testimony: A Philosophical Study* (1992). Mainstream views, based on Empiricist starting points, had tended to privilege direct observational knowledge over knowledge accepted on trust (or 'testimony'). It was argued that that presented an unrealistic picture of the growth of knowledge, both in science and in everyday life. As Hardwig pointed out, the standard Empiricist view would warrant only a very limited idea of what it is possible for us to know at all. Looking at the things we are generally agreed to know, it seems on the contrary to be a mark of rational agency to be prepared freely to use the intellectual resources available in one's environment. It is possible to conclude that intellectual maturation generally results in the ability to use more, rather than less, second-hand information.

In sum, the philosophical debate on trust in the last decades has largely consisted of attempts to come to grips with the theoretical scepticism inherent in the philosophical tradition of modernity. But some of the work has also been directly triggered by concrete social changes. Social scientists generally maintain that modernity, implying urbanization and enhanced division of labour, has created social contexts no longer surveyable to their individual participants. With the increase of functional differentiation in society, 'we know constantly less about a constantly larger number of others' and hence we need to take more and more about them on trust.[41] Completely new arenas of interaction have emerged, including the internet, public health services, food safety and international terrorism.[42] But generally speaking, 'trust' within these specific areas is not a unitary issue but an avenue to tackling specific problems (e.g. of accountability and privacy) that arise within them. These works mainly fall outside the scope of the present book, except insofar as they engage with the general philosophical debate. Also the long and thriving traditions of discussing trust within theology, sociology and psychology will only occasionally be touched upon.

Trust and reliance

Philosophers generally recognize a distinction between two trust-related concepts: trust and reliance. The distinction was introduced in Baier's paper of 1986 and by Hertzberg in 1988.[43] It is not suggested that it maps a distinction consistently made in language use. Nevertheless it should highlight a contrast between two different, even opposed human attitudes. To rely on someone is to take account of that person's expected behaviour in planning; relying on a person is somewhat similar to relying on the weather or on a watch. Baier mentions 'the comedian, the advertiser, the blackmailer, the kidnapper-extortioner, and the terrorist, who all depend on particular attitudes and reactions of others for the success of their actions'. But the blame for disappointment in these cases always lies with the agent, not with those whose responses he or she was counting on. Unlike those who engage in such manipulative relationships, '[t]he trusting can be betrayed, or at least let down, and not just disappointed'.[44] Trust has a moral aspect that is absent in reliance.

Hertzberg also describes the trust vs reliance distinction in another way. Reliance is defined in terms of expected performance. In other words, it consists in relying on a person – or a gadget, an institution, etc. – to carry out something specific (or to refrain from something specific). Reliance thus implies a three-place relation, as in 'A relies on B to φ'. In contrast, Hertzberg would characterize trust as a two-place relation: A trusts B. While reliance is conditional on performance, trust is not. It is directed at a person, and A's trust of B cannot be reduced to a description of *what* A expects B to do. Trust is, as it were, open-ended in a way that reliance is not:

> [T]he grammar of reliance [...] can, I believe, be briefly characterized by saying that to rely on someone is to exercize one's judgment concerning him. [...] Reliance has a more or less specific content: one relies on a person *for particular purposes*. This means that there is a more or less definite range of things concerning which I am prepared to take her word, or a more or less definite range of things I expect her to do or not to do. Correspondingly, relying on someone involves the thought of independent standards by which it is to be judged whether or not my reliance on her was misplaced; reliance is conditional on those standards being met.[45]

An obvious objection to this formulation would be that if trust indeed is a relationship that can be betrayed, it should also be possible to specify *what expectations* are betrayed, i.e. what kinds of action would count as betrayals of trust. Trust cannot be completely open-ended. But as I see Hertzberg's point, it is not really one about the criteria for the proper use of the words 'trust' and 'reliance' but a way to demarcate trust from cases where the other is treated as a means to an end only. To trust is to invite the other to a relation where the goals are set *jointly*. The contrast with reliance does not lie in my complete absence of expectations but in the fact that I am responsive to the other's alternative understanding of the good. Perhaps my expectations are not met, but I may nevertheless accept that what my friend did was all for the best. To trust her is to open up oneself to the possibility that she may bring in a fresh perspective. Deeply engaging with another person changes our outlook on the world and thus our very way of thinking about reasons for action.

That there *are* such cases is sufficiently demonstrated by trust in child–parent relations. A child's trust in its parents can hardly be described exhaustively in terms of specific expectations. This is because in important respects it falls upon the parents to form the child's ideas about what kinds of thing *may* generally be expected in a relationship. Compare this with a remark by Onora O'Neill:

> When we trust we know – at least when we are no longer small children – that we could be disappointed. Sometimes we place trust in spite of past disappointment, or without much evidence of reliability. [...] Trust is needed not because everything is wholly predictable, or wholly guaranteed, but on the contrary because life has to be led without guarantees.[46]

O'Neill's quip about children invites the following response. As a matter of fact, it is not true that small children are never *disappointed* by what their parents do. As any parent can testify, small children are constantly disappointed and frustrated by the mere fact of their parents not being at their beck and call day and night. But their trust is not betrayed or annihilated as soon as there is disappointment. Children's trust in their parents rather seems to consist in openness, a generally natural relation with them without second thoughts. We let them down not by failing to satisfy their every whim, but by manipulating them and closing ourselves to them. O'Neill equates betrayal of trust with disappointment. Trust is the reasonable hope that some specific expectation of ours will be honoured. But on the whole it seems to me that this moves the focus in the wrong direction, at least insofar as intimate human relations are concerned. She contrasts reasonable trust with the blind idea that the other party is *wholly* predictable. To maintain reasonable trust (as opposed to blind trust) is, by her reckoning, to assume only that the other party is *sufficiently* predictable. But against this suggestion it may be argued that the contrast between strong trust and weak trust is not the same as that between the assumptions of complete and only partial predictability. When we turn to a trusted friend for help and advice, we often hope for the unpredictable, the second opinion, the creative thinking that helps us forward.

While the importance of childhood trust is widely acknowledged, authors differ on the role that they would give to it in their general accounts. If the distinction between reliance and trust is emphasized, childhood trust will come across as a 'pure' form of trust. The *more* the relation contains elements of rational betting, the *less* trust-like will it be. If instead the rational core of trust is taken to lie in this very idea of betting, the relationship will approach fully fledged trust only to the extent that elements of betting can be found in it. Also the distinction between trust and reliance must be seen differently depending on general approach. From the point of view of rational choice theories, the distinction must be negligible. At most one might maintain that expectations based on the assumed goodwill of the other person are less vulnerable to risk than expectations based on their fear of reprisal or other self-regarding motives.[47] In some areas of social interchange that is perhaps all that needs to be said. On the other hand, in a recent paper Evan Simpson takes the failure to do justice to this distinction to demonstrate the limitations of rational choice.[48]

Normative and non-normative conceptions of trust

To discuss whether the expectations directed at someone should be called 'trust' or 'reliance' is also to discuss what kinds of reaction would count as appropriate in the case of nonfulfilment. In the rough division just presented, 'trust' is contrasted with 'betrayal', while 'reliance' contrasts with 'disappointment'. The introduction of the concept of betrayal squarely locates the discussion of trust in a sphere of moral relations. Hertzberg uses the contrast between trust and reliance as a way to open up a perspective on trust, *not* from the point of view of an agent who decides to 'place' certain expectations on someone or something, but from that of the person who *receives* trust. Once we recognize that someone else trusts us, we implicitly *agree* that deliberately letting her down would amount to betrayal and expose us to blame.[49] The ethically important question is not how to minimize the risks of trusting but how to respond to the implicit demand of trust. This perspective strikes me as absolutely central to an adequate understanding of trust, and it will be further discussed later.[50]

It will be a good idea, however, already to address some objections. Insisting that trust implies an ethical demand may look like an attempt to introduce normative views under the guise of conceptual analysis. Thus Annette Baier, Russell Hardin and Trudy

Govier have all reacted to what they perceive as a Wittgensteinian normative argument in favour of less reflection and more trust.[51] In contrast with what she sees as idealizing descriptions, Baier states that '[o]nly if we had *reason to believe* that the most familiar types of trust relationships were morally sound would breaking trust be any more prima facie wrong than breaking silence.'[52] Hardin for his part is critical of 'purely normative accounts' of trust, 'in which it is commonly asserted that trust is a moral notion'. He describes those accounts as claiming that '[i]t is moral to trust and immoral not to trust'.[53] Such a claim would be open to the obvious objection that we cannot be required to trust those who would not think twice about taking advantage of us. However, *pace* Hardin, the idea that trust is 'a moral notion' does not need to imply any stance concerning a general obligation to trust. The implication is not that trusting is *a priori* always a good thing, but rather that considerations about moral obligation necessarily enter the stage once it *is* established that someone trusts us. We are moving into a space of moral reasoning where notions like betrayal, steadfastness and conscientiousness make sense. Thus, normativity is not brought in by philosophical theory; it is already there when someone chooses to describe a relationship as one of trust.

That last clause is important. The faith that I perhaps pin on you may be described as trust, but that is often not the only description available. People rely on others for many reasons, not all of which stand up to scrutiny. You may instead want to describe my attitude as naïve, unthinking, reckless or – in a different kind of case – manipulative. Thus you may well understand I am counting on your future behaviour in some way or other but you refuse to think of it as implying a valid claim on you. The question of whether my expectations should rightly be described as implying trust can only be answered by considering the general relation between us. For instance, we may need to ask whether you are my parent, teacher or friend; whether through promises or through your past behaviour you had permitted me to count on you; or, for instance, whether what I was counting on was something that anyone could count on from another in the circumstances. When a gang of kidnappers tell the distraught parents they 'trust' them not to go to the police once their child is released, the parents may refuse to think of the case as one of trust. Their relation to the criminals is not of the kind to give the latter a moral right to expect compliance even though there may be prudential reasons for complying.[54]

Linus Johnsson has discussed the objection that trust does not always create obligations because it can be foisted on someone against his or her will.[55] For instance, a patient goes to a doctor with unrealistic expectations that apparently cannot be swayed. This can be a case where trust is unwanted and where the doctor has no duty to fulfil the patient's expectations. However, Johnsson points out that, by the same token, to *see* this as an awkward situation forced on the doctor *is* precisely to recognize that the doctor is aware of having incurred an obligation. The situation is problematic exactly because the doctor now has to find a way forward, dispelling illusions without violating the patient's trust. Thus, 'trust implies a normative expectation – a demand – which can be both burdensome and unwelcome but also morally appropriate in the circumstances'.[56] This is not to say that when I trust you, you must fulfil my expectations whatever happens; but if you recognize our relationship as one of trust you also commit yourself to *somehow* respecting them. Perhaps you later find out that despite your intentions it is simply impossible for you to live up to your obligations. In addressing such cases we will need to consider questions such as: Is the difficulty a real one, or are you simply trying to wriggle out of your commitments? If you have given me a promise, should you have let me understand at once that there would be difficulties? Is there a way for you to make it up somehow? The answers will determine whether you can be released from your obligations without blame.

There is one critical point, however, that must be heeded. While some uses of the word 'trust' are normative in the way just described, there are others that surely are not. Some of these instances of 'trusting' are simply predictive beliefs with no clear moral implications, as when I trust that the weather will stay warm or that the Euro will not fall in relation to Pound Sterling. The crucial question is how plausible it would be to construe nonfulfilment as betrayal. However, I am not suggesting that these other cases are not 'really' instances of trust after all. That I leave to the reader to consider. Differentiating between cases is philosophically important, but legislating about language use is not.

Still, for many reasons it will be important for philosophy to focus on the moral aspects of trust. Morally significant trust is an emotionally and personally important part of our lives. Research concerning relations of this kind is consequently of particular relevance to human self-understanding. Moreover, the existing research on the whole – at least in English-speaking moral and political philosophy – has definitely underplayed the moral dimension of trust. This explains the layout of the following chapters. I will discuss a number of more or less reductionist accounts of human relations (explicitly or implicitly so), with the aim of showing how those accounts cry out for correction when applied to real cases. Trust as a moral relationship pervades human life more than usually acknowledged.

What happens next?

The present book is organized as a series of local contributions to issues that have emerged in the trust debate. As a unifying concern, I have tried to show the limitations and internal contradictions that follow from assuming scepticism as the rational default stance in human relationships. This critique repeatedly takes me back to issues connected with Hobbesianism. My frequent use of the work of Wittgenstein is another unifying theme. Wittgenstein's ideas are relevant here at several levels. In part he puts forward a conception of human thinking where trust plays a central role. And in part he works with a view of language that allows us to ask the right questions about what it means to invoke the vocabulary of trust and distrust. What we need to realize here is that our descriptions of action are themselves actions. By applying a certain vocabulary to behaviour, we propose to see it in a certain light. Thus the question to ask is not, 'what are the proper criteria for applying the word "trust" to psychological or behavioural phenomena?' but instead, 'what is the role, in human interaction, of speaking about trust?'. The work of Wittgenstein ought to be central to any philosophical study of trust.

In the philosophical debate, the issue of trust has been taken up in response to various theoretical conundrums, each with its own logic of success. On the other hand, it seems to me that each of the issues in one way or other involves ideas about how some understanding of rational agency ends up in conflict with fundamental facts about human dependence and vulnerability. This calls for a more holistic understanding of reason – reason not merely as a technique aimed at securing certain ends such as correct information or preference satisfaction. What emerges is instead a 'normative' conception of rationality. Rationality includes the entire web of practices and ways of thinking that constitute human agency – including our ways of speaking about them, or what Wittgensteinian philosophers often call 'grammar'. We are always already embedded in relations of trust; we are committed to each other as beings that trust and receive trust.

The next chapter, 'Trust and Hobbesian reason', aims to relate the game-theoretical discussion to what is identified as the Hobbesian dilemma. How is rational cooperation possible *at all*? While these considerations are interesting in their own right, and important for understanding the trust debate, I believe they are of limited relevance for understanding trust in some key areas of human life. Thus the chapter ends not in a rejection of Hobbesian arguments as such, but in a questioning of the relevance of their starting points.

Chapter 3, 'Vulnerability and entrusting', deals specifically with Baier's paper. Baier defines trust as 'accepted vulnerability', especially as expressed in acts of entrusting. She raises important issues, but I conclude that she cannot address them successfully because she retains too much of the conception of agency that she professes to criticize. The later part of the chapter develops other ways in which 'vulnerability' may be understood. Some of the surface appeal of Baier's essay owes to our implicit understanding of vulnerability as an ethically significant condition. I discuss some of this significance with the help of Karin Boye's Dystopian novel *Kallocain*, dealing with the marriage of the two main characters.

The central idea of Chapter 4, 'The time dimension', is to suggest that we should think of trust not as a one-off decision, but as part of an ongoing flow of human relations. This connects to the way in which we do not perceive 'evidence' in favour of trust (or distrust) from a neutral point of view but from a point of view already embedded in human relations. In particular, this is seen if we consider Jones's treatment of the concept of evidence in trustful relationships.

Chapter 5, '"Trust" as an organizing tool', presents my main point insofar as the psychology of trust is concerned. 'Trust' should not be seen as a word with a stable reference (referring to a psychological state) but as an organizing tool for human relations. 'Trust' is most obviously seen when problems arise. Using an expression by Drew Leder, trust, like health, 'dys-appears'. We are made conscious of both trust and health when problems arise.

Chapter 6 is entitled 'Communication, truthfulness, trust'. Connecting with the recent debate on testimony, I am discussing the idea of a 'norm of truthfulness' as a necessary condition of language. Linguistic communication in a full sense presupposes a web of moral relations where we commit ourselves both to what we say and to the people to whom we say it.

Chapter 7, 'Basic trust', is similar to some of the previous chapters in that it tries to identify the meaning of a certain idea of trust by considering its *appeal* in the various contexts where it has been brought up. The existence or nonexistence of basic trust is not a strictly empirical issue, because the meaningfulness of attributing basic trust to someone (or to human beings universally) is tied up with particular perspectives. The point of assuming basic trust may simply lie in attempts to patch up a rationalist conception of agency, but it may also be an attempt to voice an ethical perspective that focuses on human vulnerability.

The final Conclusions chapter does not bring in new material but looks back at some main themes that run through the book.

CHAPTER TWO

Trust and Hobbesian reason

The impact of Thomas Hobbes's *Leviathan* on Western political philosophy is perhaps only rivalled by that of Plato's *Republic* and Aristotle's *Politics*. In his book, first published in 1651, Hobbes aimed to outline a vision of politics based on thoroughly scientific principles. Like his great predecessors he saw the need of a worked-out conception of human motivation. The conception he did present is still with us, but few later thinkers working with it have presented a picture equally comprehensive and explicit.

The source of human voluntary action lies in physiological processes manifesting themselves as appetites and aversions.[1] When these interior forces conflict a balance is struck and the stronger impulse is carried out; Hobbes calls this *deliberation*. Following a folk etymology, he derives the word from the fact of 'putting an end to the *Liberty* we had of doing, or omitting, according to our own Appetite, or Aversion'.[2] The usually accepted etymology, connecting the word with *libra* or balance, is even more fitting for Hobbesian purposes because he thinks of deliberation literally as a process of balancing between physical forces. By connecting deliberation with causal processes Hobbes accentuates it as a process ruled by natural necessity; the agent is caught in a balance of forces that quite physically determine the outcome. The agent's will equals his or her final motivational balance and, as Peter Winch has put it, the Hobbesian man can exercise self-restraint no more than he can fly.[3] Ultimately for Hobbes, as for his later fellow Empiricists, reason is purely instrumental, a slave of the passions: without changing the fundamental role of appetites and aversions it introduces more orderly ways of pursuing pleasure and avoiding pain.[4] The effect of rational thinking is to introduce order in the deliberative process by manipulating symbols. What distinguishes human beings from brutes is that humans can form ideas of the long-term consequences of their actions. This is for good and ill: reason makes strategic thinking possible, creating possibilities for both cooperation and deception.

The Hobbesian dilemma

The question of trust arises at this juncture. Hobbes does not give trust a central place in his description of human psychology, but this very lack of prominence makes the need for it all the more conspicuous. Famously, the Hobbesian state of nature is a destructive milieu where life is bound to be 'solitary, poore, nasty, brutish, and short'.[5] The individuals can escape this anarchic state only by means of stable cooperative relations, which need to be instituted by a social contract or Covenant. The question that arises is: Can they trust each other to keep the Covenant? In the state of nature, force and *fraud* are the main methods in the fight for survival.[6] In *Leviathan*, Hobbes defines 'trust' concisely as a belief: 'To *have faith in*, or *trust to*, or *beleeve a man*, signifie the same thing; namely, an opinion of the veracity of the man'.[7] In a related work, 'Human Nature', he includes a formulation that perhaps captures more adequately its role in his overall vision:

> *Trust* is a Passion proceeding from the *Belief of him* from whom we *expect* or *hope* for Good, so *free* from *Doubt* that upon the same we pursue no other Way to attain the same Good: as *Distrust* or Diffidence is *Doubt* that maketh him endeavour to provide himself by other means.[8]

This passage links trust with the act of choosing between available strategies for pursuing one's interests. It is a dispositional state, the importance of which lies in the fact that it makes the use of help from others both plausible and possible. In the state of nature, however, it must be an exception. It is precisely because humans on the whole are not to be expected naturally to trust each other that stable cooperative relations cannot be established in the absence of a coercive power. The individual can never trust the other to perform his or her part if the latter can reap short-term gains by defection and get away with it. In this situation, he that performeth first, has no assurance the other will performe after; because the bonds of words are too weak to bridle mens ambition, avarice, anger, and other Passions, without the feare of some coercive Power; [...] And therefore he which performeth first, does but betray himselfe to his enemy; contrary to the Right (he can never abandon) of defending his life, and means of living.[9]

This situation generates the particular kind of dilemma that defines Hobbes's entire approach to social life. He expects individuals in the state of nature to be rational enough also to see the dilemma for themselves. Stable cooperative relations would clearly lie in their *long-term* interest, but given the short-term benefits of defection such relations cannot be established before the onset of the Covenant. At the same time, the very character of the situation they are facing forces Hobbes to consider how the Covenant can get off the ground at all.

According to Hobbes, in the state of nature human thinking is ruled by certain 'laws of nature', maxims based on the simple principle that individuals would not do anything that would endanger their survival.[10] Among them Hobbes includes the law *'That men performe their Covenants made'*, i.e. 'the keeping of Faith'.[11] But in the state of nature, that law can hardly amount to more than a rule of thumb: 'Covenants of mutuall trust, where there is feare of not performance on either part [...] are invalid'.[12] In that situation it is not possible for anything like a *moral* obligation to exist:

> Therefore before the name of Just, or Unjust can have place, there must be some coercive Power, to compell men equally to the performance of their Covenants, by the terrour of some punishment, greater than the benefit they expect by the breach of their Covenant [...]. Therefore where there is no Commonwealth, there nothing is Unjust.[13]

As Peter Winch has pointed out, the issue has both a 'sociological' and a 'philosophical' aspect.[14] There is the question what kinds of consideration might persuade rational agents to honour their mutual promises in the absence of coercive authority. And there is the philosophical question of how the *concept of* being 'bound' by one's past commitment could conceivably exist at all in Hobbesian psychology. How can the Hobbesian individual have a sense of being obliged to do something not because of one's current inclinations but because of something one has said in some past situation? If 'deliberation' always means striking a balance between the agent's present appetites and aversions, a past utterance can carry weight with the agent only insofar as fulfilling the promise appears somehow conducive to the agent's interests as he or she *now* perceives them.

Hobbes's solution to the 'sociological' problem consisted in the introduction of a Sovereign as an enforcing agency, after which penalties for non-performance introduce a change of the agent's motivational balance. The subjects' motivation to keep their promises would presumably be enhanced in this way. However, as long as their reasoning simply reproduces the current balance of strategic considerations, they would still not have any conception of the independent value of keeping their word as long as they can get away with defection.[15] And this means that while the possibility of binding promises is something needed for the Covenant to be possible, it is also, at the same time, rendered unintelligible before the Covenant is in place. The human capacity for rational planning is both the feature that makes the state of nature unacceptable for humans *and* the chief reason why it appears impossible for them to escape it. The impasse seems unescapable, and it seems that Hobbes has not found a way out of it in the confines of his own theory.

It is, on the other hand, difficult to see how Hobbes could have significantly revised any of his presuppositions about human motivation without bringing the whole of his system out of balance. The Covenant is described as necessary exactly because of the impossibility of stable human cooperation without coercion. Comparisons in the *Leviathan* between human beings and naturally cooperative animals like ants are meant to drive home that point. Should we instead decide to paint the state of nature in less sombre colours and imagine human beings as naturally cooperative, establishing the Covenant would no doubt appear easier;[16] but Hobbes's other main point, the *necessity* of the Covenant, is weakened to a corresponding degree. Summing up the dilemma as understood in Hobbesian terms, he proposes that we must think of organized social life as a system built up of 'bare' individuals, each motivated by the need for personal survival. In order to make long-term cooperation possible, trust must be induced into the system, but the question is whether this can be done while keeping inside the system. Trust is required by the system, but can it be created by it?

At present, I have outlined a form of argument that recurs in political philosophy but which found an early and unusually lucid expression in Hobbes.[17] Modern political theory and philosophy have to a large extent consisted in attempts to respond to the Hobbesian dilemma. Speaking quantitatively, probably the most important strand in the philosophical research about trust belongs to this tradition. This research has, however, focused on trust in a fairly limited sense, because it has little to say about the emotional aspects of trusting. It has been addressing what many writers would think of as the rational minimal core of trusting: *the preparedness to cooperate under uncertainty about the other's intentions.*

Trust as risk management

Can the kind of trust required for stable cooperative relations be rationally induced in terms of strategic reason alone? The main question addressed here has concerned *risk taking*: how to account for the rationality of cooperative relations between parties not predictable to each other. Trust is made necessary by the freedom of action of the other party. Thus our need for trust will increase with the decrease of our chances actually to coerce and monitor the other.[18] This of course gives rise to the main problem. By this definition, we need to trust only when there is some uncertainty about how the other will behave. But if we are *uncertain*, rationally speaking it seems we should *not* trust, and perhaps by definition *do not* trust as long as our state of uncertainty continues. At most, we might engage in tentative cooperation. Trust now appears either as redundant (when we already have assurance) or ill-advised (when there is none).[19] But this is not a conclusion that those writing on the subject generally want to embrace. It is easy to see that organized social life would be impossible without some more robust form of trust. The point of trusting, from the point of view presented in this debate, is that it makes it possible for us to act *as if* we could monitor the other party even under uncertainty. As Niklas Luhmann puts it, '[t]rust rests on illusion. In actuality, there is less information available than would be required to give assurance of success. The actor willingly surmounts to this deficit of information'.[20] Guido Möllering concludes:

> The problem of trust therefore arises due to the other's principal freedom to act in a way that benefits or harms the trustor [...] By definition enacting trust means that the trustor increases her vulnerability towards the other's uncertain actions [...] We might now say that the essence of trust is to overcome this dilemma by placing trust *nevertheless*.[21]

The task is to show how this kind of *acting-as-if* can be rationally defensible. The volume *Trust: Making and Breaking Cooperative Relations*, edited by Diego Gambetta[22] (first published 1988), presents the collective fruit of efforts in this direction by a group of scholars mainly working within the Rational Choice paradigm. Gambetta outlines a broad agreement on the definition of 'trust':

> In this volume there is a degree of convergence on the definition of trust which can be summarised as follows: trust (or, symmetrically, distrust) is a particular level of subjective probability with which an agent assesses that another agent or group of agents will perform a particular action, both *before* he can monitor such action [...] *and* in a context in which it affects *his own* action [...]. When we say we trust someone or that someone is trustworthy, we implicitly mean that the probability that he will perform an action that is beneficial or at least not detrimental to us is high enough for us to consider engaging in some form of cooperation with him.[23]

This definition locates 'trust' in situations where a choice must be made between 'cooperating' and 'defecting'. The criteria of ascribing trust are expressed in functional terms: as in the Hobbesian definition previously quoted, trust equals readiness to rely on the other, based on one's assessment of the probability of performing. Gambetta adds:

> This definition [...] tells us that trust is better seen as a threshold point, located on a probabilistic distribution of more general expectations, which can take a number of values suspended

between complete distrust (0) and complete trust (1), and which is centred around a mid-point (0.50) of uncertainty.[24]

How far on the axis between distrust and certainty should the threshold of cooperation lie? In the first of the two quoted passages, Gambetta speaks of probability 'high *enough*'. What counts as 'enough' here is dependent on the balance of rewards and risks involved in the operation. As James Coleman formulates the point in his book, the agent will 'place' his or her trust in exactly the same way as 'a rational actor [...] in deciding whether to place a bet'.[25]

For this reason, several authors writing on the subject converge in recommending a kind of Pascal's Wager.[26] In his *Pensées*, Blaise Pascal had argued that if reason alone cannot be trusted to judge, it is a wiser choice to believe in the existence of God than to deny it. This is because if God does exist, the reward for believing is immense. The believer has everything to win and nothing to lose.[27] In analogy with Pascal's reasoning, the choice between cooperation and withdrawal should be a function of the value of what is at stake. The advisability of cooperating will chiefly depend on two variables: the probability of a beneficial outcome and the value of what we stand to gain or lose. Trust should be placed if the probability of cooperation relative to the probability of defection is greater than the ratio of potential loss to potential gain.[28] Of course we almost never have precise assessments of the probabilities in a real situation. A degree of abstraction is natural here, however. The model is presented as a general formulation of what is taken to be a central feature of rational cooperative behaviour.

A game-theoretic solution

For many, game theory offers a concise way to formulate the reasoning just described. The game known as *Prisoners' Dilemma* is widely employed for this purpose.[29] According to the standard description, the players are two prisoners accused of committing a crime together. Each prisoner must either turn Queen's evidence and plead guilty (labelled 'defection') or deny the charges ('cooperation'). In the latter case, the prisoner refuses to confess, thus keeping his or her implicit alliance with the other prisoner. But the prisoners must make their choices individually, as no contact is allowed between them. The payoffs from the prisoners' choices are usually described as lengths of prison sentences. If neither informs on the other they can only be sentenced for a minor offence (say, one year in prison).[30] If *one* of them turns in the other, he or she will be freed in return but the other will receive the full prison term for the crime they have supposedly committed (20 years). If *both* inform on the other, both are sentenced for the crime, receiving a somewhat reduced prison term (10 years).

Crucially, with the players A and B, the individual payoff from any decision by A will also depend on what B chooses to do and vice versa. The best outcome for A and B *taken together* would be for neither of them to confess (i.e. 'cooperation' for both A and B), but the best outcome for A individually would be for A to confess ('defection' for A) when B does not ('cooperation' for B). Thus the payoffs for player A are, in descending order of desirability: A *defects, B cooperates* > A *cooperates, B cooperates* > A *defects, B defects* > A *cooperates, B defects*. Or, in terms of their respective prison sentences, if the first number of each pair stands for the payoff for A: $\{0, -20\} > \{-1, -1\} > \{-10, -10\} > \{-20, 0\}$. (The numbers are negative because they stand for years in prison.) The implication is that it pays for A to defect whenever B cooperates. But it also pays for A to defect whenever B *defects*. In other words, it pays for A to defect in *every* possible combination of moves. Since the same thing holds *mutatis mutandis* for B, and both know it, and both are expected to try to maximize individual payoff, any cooperation seems doomed from the start. The prisoners will end up with the suboptimal result $\{-10, -10\}$ instead of the optimal aggregate payoff $\{-1, -1\}$. If the scenario is left standing it offers a concise formulation of the Hobbesian dilemma. The agents' lack of mutual trust leaves them with outcomes less desirable than what they might achieve through cooperation.

My question now is: What must we assume in order to see the situation as a dilemma? First of all, there must be some conception of a shared interest. Assuming a purely antagonistic state of nature, there would be no dilemma to start with. This is why we do not expect cooperation normally to develop between predators and their prey and we do not see their mutual relations as puzzling for rational observers. Unless cooperation is somehow expected it would hardly be reasonable even to use the word 'defection' for the non-cooperative move. On the other hand, we might instead want to think of the scenario as a realistic depiction of a situation facing two partners in crime. But, taking this attempt at realism seriously, the scenario would not *necessarily* constitute a dilemma. That would have to depend on the prisoners' motivational background. If they have already agreed to cooperate and do not consider betrayal an option, they can simply go ahead and keep their agreement. The two-prisoner scenario is not inherently puzzling but it becomes so by virtue of the additional assumptions of possible cooperation and lack of mutual trust.

One seemingly obvious solution would be to introduce penalties for defection – a move analogous to the introduction of the Sovereign in Hobbesian theory. Penalties would change the payoffs and hence the rational order of preferences for the individual agents. But this suggestion would not really solve the dilemma. While cooperative relations can be imposed by means of coercion and surveillance, the crucial question was how to ensure the rationality of *free* cooperation. The dilemma could only be overcome if the agents could rationally disregard the risk of defection by the other party and cooperate *nevertheless*. The question facing game theoretic research in 'rational trust' is consequently how cooperative choices could fail to be irrational or imprudent.[31]

Since an appeal to the participants' short-term interests will not do, might cooperation be secured by appealing to their *long-term* interests? Social life characteristically involves repeated interaction and not only one-off choices as in the classical Prisoners' Dilemma. For instance, a salesman not only wants to make a profit but also hopes for customers to return; he must show himself worthy of long-term trust.

The *iterated* Prisoners' Dilemma was studied in a well-known experimental work by Robert Axelrod, who pitted different computer programmes against each other.[32] The game was continued for a large number of rounds in order to assess the long-term performances of the programmes, each representing a different strategy. The 'players' thus had the chance to respond to each other's moves in the next round. The computer programme representing the simple strategy of tit-for-tat with a cooperative first move emerged with the best overall score. In other words, cooperate in the first round and subsequently do whatever the other player did in the previous round. In the winning strategy, defection was met with a 'punitive' response and cooperation was 'rewarded' with cooperation in response. The interesting indication of this experiment was that, for agents striving for individual payoff maximization, a reason to cooperate can be introduced by simply assuming repeated transactions but without introducing any change in the players' basic order of preferences. No 'altruistic' tendencies had to be assumed.[33]

Axelrod illustrates his thesis with a real-life example: the informal system of 'live and let live' on the Western Front during the Great War. After the initial offensive phase, the war was fought as a war of attrition. Soldiers in trenches facing each other developed daily routines of unofficial ceasefires, which sabotaged the war effort but made life more tolerable for the men in the trenches. Treating the situation as an iterated Prisoners' Dilemma, for each military unit, defecting (shooting to kill) while the enemy cooperates (keeps the truce) represents the most favourable outcome (i.e. *A defects, B cooperates*). However, assuming repeated encounters, mutual cooperation (both units keeping the implicit truce; or *A cooperates, B cooperates*) emerges as the most advantageous strategy. Diego Gambetta takes Axelrod's result to suggest:

> a powerful set of reasons why [...] a basic disposition *to trust* can be perceived and adopted as a rational pursuit even by moderately forward-looking egoists. [...] [I]t can be rewarding to behave *as if* we trusted even in unpromising situations.[34]

Cooperation 'as if' one trusted may later give rise to proper trust. According to an interpretation, tacit truces on the Western Front started as a simple strategy of survival. The stability of the interaction over time allowed for the soldiers' mutual perception of each other later to develop beyond the 'as if' and turn into real trust. Imagining a parallel development on the level of the evolution of the human species, Marek Kohn writes in his book:

> Taking the long view of the evolution of cooperative behaviour, trust is a recent and inessential development. As long as B scratches A's back if A scratches B's, A and B can cooperate without trust, or the brains with which to trust, or without backs, for that matter. Trust arises relatively late in the evolutionary

day, when animals become able to make predictions based on the experience about the behaviour of others.[35]

Kohn presents the development on the Western Front implicitly as the transformation from a kind of state of nature (where nothing can safely be predicted) via strategic cooperation to mutual trust. The role of trust as a psychological phenomenon would, on this model, be secondary. Rationality favours cooperation, and trust emerges as a mental and emotional by-product. Thus the game-theoretic model does not motivate or rationally explain the psychology of trust, but it indicates that its emergence is rationally *compatible with* strategic considerations.[36]

Critique of game theory: The need for a social framework

My objection to this attempt at solving the Hobbesian dilemma is that the main element of the solution is completely unaccounted for. Arguably the chief distinguishing feature of any game is the presence of rules. The existence of the game and its rules must be taken as given: the game does not explain *itself*. If we now think of a game as a model for collective action, we will explicitly or implicitly be assuming a background that includes social structures stable enough to uphold the game. This means that, at a more general level, the game presupposes cooperation rather than explaining it.

Rules not only exclude impermissible moves; they also define the game as a 'space' for possible action, outside which its moves and payoffs have neither purpose nor meaning. While it may be said of games that we play in order to win, and that we need skill, luck, dexterity and such, the particular forms that those notions take are game-specific. In Prisoners' Dilemma, the game-specific accomplishment of 'rationality' is defined in terms of moves that maximize payoff on a fixed scale. We may, however, imagine human beings exhibiting their rationality in other ways; for instance, a mother allowing her children to win because she thinks of the game in the larger context of socializing in the family. In this sense, game-theoretic 'rationality' is an artefact generated by the given game and *its* space for meaningful action. How does it relate to rationality in the outside world? That is a question the game itself does not answer. The applicability of Axelrod's solution can thus be questioned because it tacitly presupposes a framework for the game-specific rationality rather than explaining it.[37]

Even though game theory alone does not explain how social life as such is possible, it may still be maintained that it is useful for modelling specific dilemmas once social life is in place. It seems fair to say that this will be an empirical matter, by and large boiling down to the question of predictive power. In his book *After Virtue* Alasdair MacIntyre, however, points to complications that must be taken into account when game theory is used in real-life prediction.[38] Unlike the players described in any simple model, human agents will almost always be involved in several 'games' at once, and what might look like a bad move in one game may simultaneously improve one's score in another. At any given occasion we cannot be entirely sure *which* games are being played, on the one hand because our opponent may perceive the game differently from us, and on the other hand because the scope and duration of the 'game' will be perceptible only in retrospect. Moreover, since human subjects are to some degree opaque to each other – sometimes deliberately so – their motives are in part left in the dark. In many cases, it is only after the event that we can be sure of the informative value of a specific model.

Largely thanks to the institutional constraints of a war situation, Axelrod's real-life example from the Western Front does, however, have features that make it amenable to treatment in game-theoretic terms. It involves antagonistic players and a choice between 'cooperation' and 'defection'. On the other hand, as I previously argued, seeing a two-prisoner scenario as a dilemma implies additional assumptions about the motivational background of the players. Speaking empirically, one may wonder whether the British and German soldiers indeed had the specific order of payoffs that would correspond to those presumed in Prisoners' Dilemma. Kohn cites an exchange between two British soldiers:

> One British soldier told a brigadier that there was an 'elderly gentleman' with a long beard who often showed himself above the German parapet. The brigadier demanded to know why

the soldier had not shot the German. 'Why, Lor' bless you sir', replied the soldier, "e's never done me no harm'.[39]

This passage describes the culture of cooperation that had gradually emerged across the front line. According to Kohn's interpretation, a more benign view of the enemy had developed from strategic choices in the initially antagonistic situation. However, it seems to me one might plausibly see the attitude expressed in the quote as a *return* to normality: an attempt to rebuild a sense of decency in the profoundly alien situation temporarily imposed on the soldier by his superiors. The soldier's response to his superior implicitly questions the identification of the opposite party as an enemy. In game-theoretic terms, this may indicate that his individual best choice was from the very start not *A defects, B cooperates*, as in classical Prisoners' Dilemma, but *A cooperates, B cooperates*. That is, not to kill *B* and live, but for *both* to live until a peace settlement is reached. It is plausible to surmise that the culture of implicit truces developed so quickly partly because of already existing, often class-based, patterns of solidarity.

Axelrod's work is a constant point of reference in research on 'rational trust', which indicates that it might be the best available general attempt to ground trust in strategic considerations. Axelrod's results support the rather plausible hypothesis that there are incentives for cooperation when both parties know that their relationship will continue in the future. However, to sum up the argument in this section: the continuity in question relies on institutional arrangements and/or cultural patterns. The game needs a framework that goes beyond what it can explain.

Trustworthiness and encapsulated interests

The political theorist Russell Hardin, while accepting the game-theoretic approach on the whole, has advanced a somewhat modified interpretation of it. He argues that most attempts to ground trust in strategic rationality have concerned themselves with trustworthiness rather than trust; with rational motivations for keeping one's promises, or generally for maintaining a cooperative attitude, but not for *believing* that the opposite party is trustworthy. Axelrod's argument is assumed to show why it is rational for the agent to choose cooperation instead of defection. But it does not give a reason to the agent to trust the other player, i.e. believe that the other is trustworthy. Similarly, Pascal's Wager might at best give us reasons to act *as if* we trusted the other.[40]

Hardin argues that belief in the other's trustworthiness must be founded on considerations about likely motives. Rationally justified trust involves the belief that the trustee has reasons of his or her own to honour the expectations of the trustor; for Hardin this equals simply saying that it lies in the perceived *interest* of the trustee. But arguments for trustworthiness indirectly function also as arguments for trusting insofar as they allow the trustor to draw conclusions about the likely reasoning of the trustee. Thus while Hardin's analysis of trust is presented in terms of beliefs rather than mere strategies, his view on human motivation is firmly rooted in strategic considerations. He proposes to analyse rational trust on the model of 'encapsulated interests'.[41] When I trust you, I believe you will act in ways that lie in my interest, because it lies in *your* interest to promote mine.

Hardin chooses an example from Dostoevsky's *The Brothers Karamazov* for illustration. The story concerns economic dealings between an officer and a merchant in a small garrison town.[42] Colonel Verkhovtsev, who is in charge of regimental funds, is in the habit of lending money from it to Trifonov, the local merchant. Otherwise the funds would be just lying idle, for the profit of no one. Trifonov does business with the money and then always returns the sum to Verkhovtsev with a commission that the latter puts in his own pocket. The arrangement is completely illegal, and both parties would be at fault before the law. If Trifonov were to defect, Verkhovtsev would have no legal recourse. On the other hand, the latter knows that it lies in Trifonov's interest to continue the relationship, where both parties stand to win. Things take an unhappy turn one day, however, when Trifonov simply keeps the money and denies there has ever been business dealings between them. Verkhovtsev's embezzlement is discovered; he makes a suicide attempt and dies soon afterwards.

The Brothers Karamazov, as Dostoevsky's work in general, is a goldmine of examples of trust and betrayal, but most readers would not jump at this particular example. It looks more like one of those shady manipulative relations that Dostoevsky was also fond of describing. One might perhaps call it a case of mutually distrustful cooperation, coloured by ideas of 'cunning'. But it conforms to a game-theoretic understanding of 'trust' because of course it *is* a case of expectations based on rationally grounded ideas about risk and gain, although the wisdom of the scheme may be questioned. By choosing an example of this kind, Hardin wants to get hold of what he sees as the minimal rational core of trust relationships regardless of value judgements and psychological considerations. On his reckoning, trust appears when I have reason to believe that the other person will attend to my interests because of his or her interest – of whatever kind – in continuing the relation.[43]

However, Hardin's model has the same obvious limitation as do the others based on game theory. A stable social framework (at least for the time being) must be presupposed. While the model may helpfully illustrate certain kinds of cooperation once a framework of social trust is in place, it does not address the Hobbesian question of how the latter is initially possible.

Is this trust? – A caveat

Before moving on, I should put on record my immediate general reaction to the analyses I have presented. I would say they are hardly about trust at all – at least if we stick to a widespread ordinary usage. A peculiar feature of the analyses is that they make trust redundant as normally understood. The need for trust disappears if cooperation can be expected anyway because of other reasons; for instance, if the other person has a strong financial interest in the scheme we are proposing, or might get into trouble if she refuses, or is too naïve, lazy or uninformed to object. The presence of such considerations in our reasoning marks a manipulative and suspicious frame of mind that seems the very opposite of trust. On the other hand, following ordinary usage, the kind of strategic thinking that occupies the centre stage for the game theorists rather falls out of the picture altogether if we already trust.

Game-theoretic accounts, of course, present quite a different idea: precisely the *presence* of manipulative features is supposed to qualify the case as one of trust. The relation between mutually suspicious conmen would be a case in point, as long as both men think they can outwit the other. The surer they are of their ability to manipulate their adversary, the more *trustful* would they apparently be if the theories on 'rational trust' are to be believed. As Hertzberg puts his objection, however, '*the more explicitly* those external considerations enter into the relation, *the less* it comes to have a character of trust. This means that the more a relation conforms to the philosophers' conception of rational trust, the less trust-like it becomes.'[44]

Having made these objections, I nevertheless see a point of view from which they might be treated as simply irrelevant. From the perspective of the present debate on strategic reasoning, one may still want to define 'rational trust'[45] as a form of strategic stance on the basis of self-interest. One may want to investigate whether such strategic reasoning would be enough to allow social life to develop. And it is possible to examine the conditions under which strategic cooperation might arise between rational agents motivated by self-interest. Thus while I would say the approaches I have considered illuminate a very limited aspect of what we usually call trust, they have a use within that sphere. Moreover they are interesting precisely as illustrations of the scope and limits of strategic reason. Hence I will simply go ahead to consider the debate in its own terms and see what conclusions may be drawn. The question there is: Does strategic reasoning support a sufficiently robust 'rational trust'? If not, a basic human tendency *to trust* must somehow be imagined as being induced into the system in the very beginning from the outside. Then the further question will be: If strategic reason cannot create trust, what is the relationship between *strategic* reason and reasoning in general?

Trust and strategic reason, and where to go from here

In this chapter I have to some extent wanted to address Hobbesian questions within their own frame of reference. The original question was whether trust, either as a behavioural tendency or as a predictive belief, might be justified from the point of view of strategic reason; i.e. whether one could imagine trust arising when rational agents act exclusively on individual payoff-maximizing considerations. My answer was negative on the whole, and something like it seems to be accepted by many authors writing about the matter.[46] Some tendency to trust must be presumed as a given already before strategic relations develop. Since the maximization of individual payoff requires trust, Hobbesian reason contains an inherent tension which it cannot solve if left to its own devices. Martin Hollis concludes:

> if prudence, speaking a language of homogenised utility and forward-looking reasons, is the voice of reason itself, then there is no trust within reason and critics will be right to say that the progress of Enlightenment destroys the bond of society.[47]

Hollis argues in his book that the available candidates for a solution in Hobbesian terms had been largely explored and found wanting already at the close of the eighteenth century. But where should we go from here? According to Hollis, the result calls for a revision of the Enlightenment, individualist understanding of reason. Social games cannot be expected to maximize the players' payoffs unless the players can trust one another to play as a team – that is, in the spirit of generalized reciprocity among members.[48] How can team spirit be achieved? Hollis believes socially rational agents need to be anchored in a community local enough to foster mutual trust and universal enough, for instance, to endorse 'the UN declaration of human rights'.[49] It can be claimed that strategic rationality points outside its own domain, to a necessary non-rational background in culture, psychology or biology. The limitations of strategic rationality will, of course, be all the more enhanced if we turn to the 'warm', moral and emotional aspects of trust.

The intellectual predicament I have outlined is the outcome of a certain way of thinking of the relation between reason and sociality. I would also say it is in part a cultural product. With the omnipresence of market economy, asking for reasons for action is easily interpreted as a question about why the action in question is rational, and questions about the rationality of action are assumed to call for only one kind of answer, namely in terms of payoffs. The paradigm is only slightly modified by allowing for, for instance, *affective* payoffs. We should in fact be wary of the introduction of such concepts, because they also serve to insinuate the economic paradigm even further into our lives. As a mark of our present cultural predicament, we now read of parents' emotional 'investment' in their children. And we may feel the need to justify our actions in terms of the payoff-maximizing paradigm even when it does not describe our thinking as we would spontaneously understand it.[50]

It has been frequently pointed out that we need a new and more inclusive conception of rationality.[51] However, the contours of that new conception appear unclear. The last section of this chapter considers some reasons why Hobbesian reason is so difficult to leave behind.

The metaphysics of interests

At the heart of Hobbesian reason lies the idea of *interests*. Interests define the values of payoffs, and the task of practical reason is to maximize payoff. The individual is defined as the carrier of interests. When this model is applied to bargaining between collective agents – say countries or businesses – collectives are in this respect treated as individuals. Interests are mostly defined in terms of what is desired or preferred, and sometimes in terms of what is conducive to survival. While the relation between interests, desires and preferences can be described in different ways, at the bottom there is an idea of a basic motivational source to which rational explanations of action must be deferred. All this might appear quite self-evident and we might ask: How else could it be? Why *would* a rational individual act against his or her perceived interests, preferences or desires? But we should note that a sense of self-evidence is often the mark of a *metaphysical* conception. 'Interests' have gained a status as the *only* thing not questioned in explanations of behaviour. In this sense they lie behind the rational explanation as a transcendental presupposition.

What we, however, need to see is that questions of what a person wants or prefers are not *unitary* questions: what they mean is highly context-sensitive. Sometimes, of course, we raise simple unproblematic questions concerning someone's present desires – such as asking a guest, 'Tea or coffee?' If nothing else hangs on the answer, we have hit the relative rock bottom when you say

'Tea, please'. You want tea and you ask for it because you want it. The fact that this is your desire is a sufficient justification for your choice. However, even apparently simple exchanges of this kind often involve more than just the straightforward expression of desire. The starting point is that you have tacitly accepted the limited choice I am offering. After that, you may have to strike a balance between conflicting wishes and considerations. Perhaps you would spontaneously prefer coffee, but do not want to make a fuss as everyone else is having tea. You may also be taking a stand in an ethical or political question: my coffee is Nescafé and should be boycotted. In this kind of context it is not, for instance, obvious you would always give more weight to *your* desires than to those of others.

In formulating your desire you are then not simply expressing a 'raw' impulse, as perhaps an animal would when it runs for one food item but leaves another untouched. You take a stand by *letting* certain wishes count. Desires are something that we learn to understand and represent as reasonable or unreasonable.[52] This is all the more obvious in the case of more momentous choices than that between tea and coffee. I may ask you *why* you want something and you tell me a story about your life, your ideas and plans. Or you cut me short and say you simply desire it. In that latter reaction, you question my right to challenge your choices. 'I (do not) desire it' often has the function of a discussion-stopper in this way, but that is no sufficient evidence for the fundamental status of desires as the rock bottom of motivation. What makes philosophical discourse on desires metaphysical is precisely the assumption that there is The One rock bottom somewhere. We should rather say that your expressions of your desires, and the exact point where you decide to cut me short, are expressions of our relation as speaker and addressee. After you have indicated your desire, there may be room for me to ask whether it is what you *really* want. Such a question may function as an invitation to self-reflection: I hear your words but I refuse to take them as your final position on the matter. The conclusion will sometimes have to emerge in a dialogue where the interlocutors are expected honestly to reflect on the nature of their commitments and perhaps to revise them. Like every other human tendency, desires are informed, accepted and rejected in the context of our daily give-and-take with others.

A superb instance of such dialogical reflection is portrayed in Plato's *Gorgias*. The protagonists are brought to air their views on the nature of human excellence, welfare and ambition.[53] Callicles maintains that the superior or admirable kind of man is one who skilfully and ruthlessly pursues *whatever* gives him pleasure.[54] In the dialogue, Socrates makes him see that he, Callicles, would still distinguish between acceptable and shameful pleasures and find the latter contemptible.[55] Callicles is forced to admit that the mindless pursuit of pleasure without distinction is not the kind of life he would admire, which leads to the collapse of his initial a-moralist position. The conclusion is not reached merely thanks to Socrates' skill in finding logical loopholes in the assertions of his opponent. The crucial point is that Callicles is made to see, dimly at least, the manner of person he would become by fully endorsing each of the two things he claims he wants. He is torn between two impulses: he aspires to human excellence *and* he is fascinated by the pursuit of success as conventionally understood. Socrates makes the further claim that everyone who understands the choice between an ethical life and the pursuit of pleasure would choose the former above the latter. That generalization need not concern us here. The main point is that the question of what we *want* is something we need to settle for ourselves, in person. Nor is it a question to be settled simply by attending to our appetites of the moment: we are expected to take a stand.

The exchange between Socrates and Callicles implies it may sometimes be necessary to think of indications of desire as starting points for further probing, not as the speaker's final word on the issue. Sometimes our lives show that we act on motives (e.g. feelings of inferiority or the need of love) that we seldom or never express in words and which we might disavow if made conscious of them. We may come to dismiss a possible motive as a temptation. We may also harbour contradictory desires, in which case we need to make choices and to get clearer about the implications of those we do make.

These complexities about the concept of desire also imply a view on rationality different from that of the game theorists. The latter would see rational deliberation as a kind of neutral machinery, the task of which is to process desires and background information into choices. Rationality is instrumental rationality and 'desire' is whatever impulse is fed into the machinery. On the alternative view just sketched, rationality is other-directed, ultimately a question of working out conceptions of reasonableness in dialogue with others. These considerations do not invalidate Hobbesian reason lock, stock and barrel. It is not as if there are *no* situations where it is applicable – because there are some, perhaps especially in economics, partly due to conscious efforts by institutional agents to uphold the 'mechanisms' of economic life. However, the Hobbesian conception of reason turns metaphysical when it is no longer seen for what it is: the end point of a process of regimentation for a limited purpose.[56] Attempts at resolving the Hobbesian dilemma in its own terms amount only to wriggling in the grip of a metaphysical picture of human agency.

CHAPTER THREE

Vulnerability and entrusting

Annette Baier's work represents an attempt to break loose of the framework of instrumentalism and rationalism[1] that dominated English-speaking ethics in the late 1900s. In her 1986 paper she defined trust as *accepted vulnerability* which is expressed in acts of *entrusting*. The concepts of trust and vulnerability are connected in important ways, but it may be difficult to see exactly what their relation is. The first part of this chapter will discuss Baier's views on the matter, whereas the second part outlines an alternative way to understand vulnerability in this context. I will argue that, while helpfully drawing attention to interpersonal dependence and vulnerability, Baier remains too close to the rationalist understanding of human relations she wants to criticize. By equating vulnerability with *risk* she opens the door once more to the questionable game-theoretic idea that trust should best be seen as a species of risk management.

I would formulate the main point of this chapter as follows. Baier, in what she thinks of as the paradigm case, treats trust as an undertaking for the sake of a goal. But this – or so I will argue – prevents her from developing insights that she does put forward in her work. She associates trust with a sense of vulnerability, but does not explore the way in which speaking of 'vulnerability' must in this context be understood as a way of articulating a relationship that is ethical rather than merely practical or strategic. The *factual* claim that trust involves increase of vulnerability is simply false in many of the cases that we normally describe as trust. On the other hand, thinking of vulnerability as an ethical notion leads the analysis beyond the rationalistic scenarios typical not only of game theory but also of many normative treatments of trust. My criticism of Baier is then *not* based on the fact that her definition of trust is quite demonstrably at odds with the use of 'trust' in everyday speech. Rather, I will look into how *she* defines 'vulnerability' and ask whether trust defined as accepted vulnerability in *her* sense is helpful in capturing the moral features of life that she feels to be important.

The idea of trust as accepted vulnerability has a surface appeal that may be captured by Baier's description of trust as entrusting. But it also has a deeper appeal: it connects with our longing for authentic human encounters beyond considerations of power relations or utility. It involves an important change of perspective, because the ethical power of vulnerability is best seen not from the standpoint of the person who, by an act of risk-taking, makes herself vulnerable, but from the point of view of the person who receives trust and recognizes the vulnerability of those whose trust he receives.

Baier's ambiguous critique of rationalism

In 'Trust and Antitrust' Baier looked for a theory of trust which, as she saw it, should deliver guidelines for distinguishing between morally sound and unsound cases of trusting. The main question would be, 'Whom should I trust in what way, and why'.[2] The question as such is not very different from those addressed in the Hobbesian theories discussed in the previous chapter. However, as Gloria Origgi points out in her book on trust, Baier's approach differs from that of the game theorists because of her emphasis on the 'warm', emotive aspects of trust.[3] According to Baier, mainstream ethics has been hostage to what she describes as 'male fixation on contract'.[4] Ethical relations, she submits, have been construed on the model of quasi-contractual arrangements between parties roughly equal in power.[5] But our most important human relations belong to family life. Those relations inescapably involve trust, dependence and vulnerability. They are in many cases not something we have explicitly undertaken to engage in. Our motives, if any, for entering such relations and maintaining them are not necessarily based on self-interest.[6] Also, very typically, relationships of trust within the family and between intimate friends are not relations between partners equal in power, unlike the favoured cases in contract theories. According to Baier, ethics needs to address questions about the soundness of our various forms of dependence and vulnerability.[7]

Despite these important openings, Baier's position vis-à-vis some main tenets of rationalist ethical theory seems ambiguous – perhaps, indeed, one reason why her essay has gained sympathies in rather different quarters.[8] Benjamin McMyler, who distinguishes between 'cognitivist' and 'non-cognitivist' approaches to trust, counts Baier among the non-cognitivists, while Hertzberg describes her account of trust as 'cognitive'.[9] Onora O'Neill has for her part described Baier's views on trust as 'nostalgic' – 'not really a good model for thinking about trust in a complex social world' – because of Baier's alleged overemphasis on intimacy.[10]

Baier's position comes out as ambiguous mainly because of her take on the role of deliberation. On the one hand, she does emphasize that trust, in many important cases, occurs quite unplanned and unnoticed.[11] This looks like a psychologically more realistic view than the strategic interaction models by game theorists. On the other hand, in her analysis Baier still shows a definite preference for the explicit case. She wants to think of cases where considerations of our well-being motivate conscious decisions to trust.[12] Her idea is that unself-conscious cases can be profitably construed and assessed *as if* they might be outcomes of explicit rational deliberation. This way of going about things is in some ways analogous to the contractarian idea of testing the acceptability of specific political arrangements by asking whether they might be rationally accepted in an unbiased choice situation. The claim is not that existing societies trace their origin to a social contract, but only that their success in securing justice can be assessed by using an idealized contractual arrangement as a point of comparison. The tacit assumption is that the individual can, at least in theory, pull back from his or her existing web of social relations and look at it with the cool gaze of an outsider.

A certain tendency towards voluntarism no doubt fits in with Baier's overarching goal of working out a normative position. If the main task for a theory of trust is to identify appropriate objects and motives for trusting, we are rather naturally brought to think of situations where we might exercise choice in the matter. The idea of looking (or shopping) for worthy objects of trust implies a presumption in favour of distrust: distrust is the default stance until an assessment of the reasonableness of trusting has been produced. One might perhaps want to describe this initial attitude as neutral, but 'suspicious' might be the more apt description insofar as the agent is supposed to perceive the situation as implying that it is *just as possible as not* that the other has hostile designs.

The theory of trust as entrusting

Working her way towards a theory of trust, Baier proposes that trust should be analysed on the model of entrusting. Fully fledged trust would be of the form, 'A entrusts B with valued thing C'.[13] The 'piece of goods' represented by 'C' might be a physical object – such as a letter which B has agreed to post for A – but it may also consist, for instance, of A's safety, autonomy, or personal well-being. In trusting, we grant the other with discretionary powers to look after something that we care about. Baier states that we now should ask what reasons we might have for accepting or rejecting such dependence.[14] Thus the formula 'A entrusts B with C' can be complemented with, 'because p', where p stands for a reason of some kind. Baier's general answer to why we would be wise to entrust B with C is that 'C' will be better safeguarded or enhanced if we accept the help of 'B'. In many cases, the goods that we care about are of such kind that they cannot be created or sustained single-handedly by one agent.[15]

It seems that the three-place entrusting relation has the role of a kind of Weberian ideal type in Baier's theory. Her suggestion is that it will be easier for us to see what is at stake also in 'inarticulate and uncritical or blind trust'[16] if we keep the formula of 'A entrusting B with C because p' firmly in mind. An infant can be construed as entrusting its well-being to a parent, even though the infant obviously will not be thinking of their relation in such terms, if indeed at all. Baier believes that the development of trustful relations in human life must psychologically and empirically start from 'primitive and basic trust' between infant and adult.[17] When we grow up these relationships unfold, they become more diversified and articulate in the process, many of them approaching the ideal type. The consciously sought and rationally underpinned three-place relation comes across as the natural end point as our degree of self-awareness increases:

It is not a Hobbesian obsession with strike force which dictates the form of analysis I have sketched out but, rather, the natural order of consciousness and self-consciousness of trust, which progresses from the initially unself-conscious trust to awareness of risk along with confidence that it is a good risk, on to some realization of why we are taking this particular risk, and eventually in some evaluation of what we may generally gain and what we may lose from the willingness to take such risks. The ultimate point of what we are doing may be the last thing we come to realize.[18]

The natural conclusion to be drawn from these considerations is, first of all, that our reasons for trusting are derivative of our attachment to the 'goods' that we wish to safeguard or promote. Secondly, the self-conscious and rationally underpinned decision to entrust is to be treated as an ideal type for analysing real-life cases. The touchstone for the acceptability of a less than fully articulated case of trust is the question of whether one's trust would survive even if its ultimate motivation were fully spelled out.[19]

Entrusting and simple trust

Baier's theory of trust as a three-place predicate calls for the rather natural response that not all trustful relations seem to be goods-related in this way. One may feel that it involves an unfortunate focus on *things* instead of people. Is our understanding of a trustful relationship always incomplete until we can point to some entrusted object that explains what the relationship is valuable for? Or should the starting point of the analysis lie at 'simple trust', considering that we are unlikely to trust people *with* anything unless we trust *them*?[20]

In a marriage, trust is supposedly sought for its own sake, not only as a way to safeguard ready-made interests. It will admittedly be possible in some sense to identify pieces of metaphorical goods that bride and bridegroom entrust to each other; thus a husband might trust that his wife will not betray him with other men. Marital loyalty would count as an interest, a piece of goods that must be protected. That description would be particularly apt for arranged marriages in patriarchal societies, where the discovery of (the wife's) infidelities would be ruinous for the man's social standing. But the description does appear insufficient in a modern world. The progress of our understanding here seems to be the opposite of what Baier has in mind. The value of maintaining trust between husband and wife, and the sense of hurt that we may experience at betrayal, are not *explained* by pointing to the advantages of one's spouse not having affairs with others. On the contrary, we typically see fidelity in marriage as emotionally important precisely because we see the *independent* importance of trustful relations between husband and wife. Sexual fidelity is a token of love and trust, not the motive for love and trust, as Baier's theory would seemingly have to imply. Having affairs with others tends to undermine and violate the relationship, but not because it does harm to a ready-made piece of goods.

In response to this point, Baier has explained that the entrusted 'goods' may, in this case, simply consist of the trustful relation itself.[21] Apart from the question whether such an analysis would be circular or otherwise logically flawed,[22] the only obvious reason in favour of it seems to be Baier's preference for the analysis in terms of entrusting to be applicable across the board.[23] In the present case, the entrusted 'goods' look like a mere theoretical placeholder for whatever it is that would be harmed or destroyed in the case of betrayal. Baier argues at this juncture that a trustful relation is always a *particular* trust relation, and so in each case of trust some description will be available of exactly how it was betrayed (e.g. 'she lied to him', or 'she turned his children against him').[24] In this way she suggests that the specification of a breach of trust always also specifies the entrusted thing that was harmed.[25] But it seems to me that this would beg the question. The fact that the wife's breach of trust takes a particular form – say of adultery – does not prove that the married couple's original trustful relation was 'about' adultery. On the whole, marriages consist of more than the mutual promise not to commit adultery.

One implication of what I just said is that marriages are not about just one thing or a few things, but about a huge or even endless range of things. It is possible that Baier would agree with me here. We can never produce a full list of what kinds of action might be understood as breaches of trust in a marriage – and in many cases we have no clear idea of whether a specific action would strike us as a betrayal until we are faced with it. But there is a deeper objection here, because there is also a sense in which marriages are not 'about' any particular thing as such. The meaning that a given 'thing' – for instance, (not) having an affair with someone else – acquires in a marriage can only be appreciated in the context of the marriage as a whole. The ethical and emotional significance of the case turns not on a specific entrusted thing, but on the extent to which this breach of mutual trust comes across as a rejection of closeness as such. I imagine that the married couple, in mature and self-conscious reflection of what has passed between them, would naturally progress *away* from the vindictive focus on violations of this or that 'thing', *towards* an understanding of their actions as part of their relationship as a whole. They might conclude, for instance, that an instance of sexual infidelity was merely a symptom of some more serious flaw in their marriage. Or it may turn out that they manage to see each other in a more forgiving perspective.

Baier herself is aware, in her seminal paper, that her focus on 'goods-relativized or "fancy" trust'[26] may invite the objection that she has not sufficiently distanced herself from the contract theorists.[27] The question is whether Baier's theory does not, in the last analysis, assimilate trust to the sort of risk taking described in rationalistic approaches to behaviour. Does it represent a new take on ethics or just more of the same, only with more willingness to acknowledge psychological complexity?

It can certainly be said that entrusting an item to a person or agency is a decision that by definition results in a kind of 'trust relation' being created. When I post a letter, I can be said to trust the mail to forward my letter as promised. The act of entrusting, given institutional facts such as my property rights and the obligations incurred by the mail service, creates a legal situation that may, at least formally, be described as a relation of trust. This is quite regardless of details about how I arrive at my decision. I can decide to post the letter either *without considering* whether the mail service is reliable – perhaps I take that to be self-evident – or I can do so even though I have my doubts; for instance, because I do not think the letter is important and I have no other easy way of dispatching it. The latter case would indeed fit Baier's description of sensible trust as involving 'consciousness of risk'. A borderline case might appear when someone – a politician, an employer, employee, etc. – or something – a political body, a form of public service – is expected by virtue of a social role to enjoy my 'trust' while I personally distrust them. When the trustee fails to carry out the relevant obligations I may describe the situation as betrayal, all the while also maintaining that I personally never had any trust in them. Recognized public responsibilities thus by definition make the relevant official a recipient of trust, and in this formal sense, public trust can be construed as a case of entrusting.

But it should be obvious by now that the model of trust as entrusting is rather far removed from the personal, emotionally charged relations that originally caught Baier's attention. The question is not whether entrusting exists, but how far it can be extended as a paradigm.

Factual and ethical vulnerability

Baier's definition of trust contains a formulation that several authors have found inspiring. This passage has in the last twenty years or so become the *locus classicus* among English-speaking philosophers writing about the topic:

> When I trust another, I depend on her good will toward me [...] Where one depends on another's good will, one is necessarily vulnerable to the limits of that good will. One leaves others an opportunity to harm one when one trusts, and also shows one's confidence that they will not take it. Reasonable trust will require good grounds for such confidence in another's good will, or at least absence of good grounds for expecting their ill will or indifference.[28] Trust then, on this first approximation, is accepted vulnerability to another's possible but not expected ill will (or lack of good will) toward one.[29]

Trust is, then, *accepted vulnerability*. By trusting I expose myself (or rather the goods I care about) to the other's good or ill will. Speaking generally, 'vulnerability' might be understood simply as a physical condition, as when soft parts of the body are described as vulnerable. It is clear from the context that that is not what Baier has in mind. As Linus Johnsson has remarked, it is not true as a rule that I *physically* run greater risks by relying on the help of others rather than acting alone – as you might know if you have ever moved heavy furniture in a stairwell.³⁰ A similar point seems to hold generally. The question of whether the risks of trusting are greater than those incurred by distrust is empirical, to be settled from case to case.

However, it does seem right to assume a necessary connection between the ideas of trust and vulnerability at a conceptual level. The kind of 'vulnerability' implied here is vulnerability to *betrayal*, and vulnerability in this particular sense is internally related to what is usually meant by 'trust'. This simply implies that 'vulnerability' consists of the *logical* possibility of betrayal. Whenever a relation qualifies as trust, there is logical space in it for something that would count as betrayal. Rather in the same way, if a living being can be described as *healthy*, it is logically possible that it might fall ill. This is not to imply that health creates a risk of illness, or that increased health implies increased risk of illness.

One may speak of the sense of betrayal as a feeling, but the main difference between betrayal and merely surprising or disappointing behaviour is not captured by the empirical question of how I feel about my frustrated expectations.³¹ It seems to me instead that, in our everyday understanding of personal trust, the idea of vulnerability to betrayal enters as an expression of the *ethical* significance of intimate human relationships. The concept of betrayal is not applicable in a situation where my reliance on the other person's good behaviour is merely based on prediction. If she behaves contrary to my expectations I am, properly speaking, not betrayed, just as in trusting that the weather will stay warm I am not prepared morally to condemn anyone or anything in case of a sudden drop in temperature. For this reason, in the standard game-theoretic scenario it would be strained to say I am making myself vulnerable to betrayal, unless 'betrayal' is just a technical term for 'unexpected behaviour'. Linus Johnsson writes:

> If the scenario is better described as a case of risky reliance or a gamble, what we would call 'betrayal' is merely a particularly strong move in whatever game is being played. [...] Given such a description, the anger and indignation that follows will be nothing but a natural (though childish) reaction to losing.³²

Even to call my reaction 'disappointment' would perhaps be too closely tied up with ideas of moral blame if my relation to the other party is assumed to be purely predictive or instrumental. My failure to predict a natural occurrence should direct my feelings of disappointment towards myself and not towards nature. And when, for instance, a household appliance refuses to work properly it is perhaps misleading to describe my frustration as disappointment, unless the implication is that *someone* – perhaps the manufacturer – is to blame.

The question is how best to capture the sense of ethical and emotional urgency that the notions of vulnerability and betrayal should convey in the context of a personal relationship. Does Baier succeed in moving the scenario beyond the simple gaming situation? As we have seen, she explicitly claims that when I trust a friend – at least, supposing my trust is 'reasonable' – I believe there is some risk that she may wilfully let me down.[33] But can this be right? If I merely believed that my friend is *probably* not hostile or indifferent – if I believed there is a *risk* she will let me down – shouldn't I say I am suspicious of her? In that situation, it would of course be natural for me to adopt precisely the procedure that Baier recommends: to look for good grounds for judging how far the relation is likely to promote the interests that make the relationship worthwhile for me in the first place. But then one might object that Baier is not describing trust at all, but only a kind of cautious reliance on the other's good behaviour. A more benign interpretation would be that her description fits a form of behaviour that may *also* be called trust – namely some cases of deliberate entrusting – but not the kind of trust typical of the intimate human relations that initially interested her.

The notion of possibility

On hearing Baier's description of trust as accepted vulnerability, I might naturally protest that I am not making myself vulnerable: I trust my friend fair and square. In a relationship involving trust I am likely to feel less, not more, vulnerable than with people whom I do not trust. If an enemy carries a knife he can harm me, but if a friend has a knife I might feel safer because it affords me protection in a hostile environment.[34] Perhaps our friendship makes me willing to face new risks that I might otherwise avoid, but that is not to say that my friend herself is a risk to my safety. We may suppose that, in this case, no question has arisen for me about my friend's trustworthiness. If challenged I might respond that I *know* her and have no reason to think she has hostile designs.

This formulation might invite the reply that if I know my friend I have apparently *already* considered whether she is a risk. My answer to this is, first of all, that there seems to be no necessity in claiming that we undertake this sort of security screening of our friends. Perhaps you respond to me that we indeed do this – only it is a *subconscious* operation. But the sole reason for believing in the subconscious operation is that it seems to be something required by the theory of trust as risk taking. However – what is even more damaging to Baier's position – her analysis entails not only that I have carried out a risk assessment concerning my friend. She must also assume that, if I have asked whether my friend might be hostile, I have also answered the question in the *positive*; because precisely that is the implication of her definition of trust. My friend *is* a risk, but one I am willing to take because of the benefits I am anticipating. A friend is for Baier essentially someone *with power to harm us*; '[t]hen we can look at various reasons we might have for wanting or accepting such closeness to those with power to harm us, and for confidence that they will not use this power'.[35]

When is it that we think like that of our friends? If I let a friend into my home, I would typically not say I am leaving her an opportunity to harm me, any more than I would if she was a locksmith and I failed to have safety locks installed to keep her out. And if in fact she tries to harm me, from my reaction it will be obvious that I do not regard her behaviour as something I had *accepted*.

Here I must, however, address an obvious objection. Granted that I do not *think* of my friend as someone with power to harm me, is it not nevertheless true that I *objectively* make myself vulnerable to harm? After all I am not taking measures to protect myself. If we are to think of my friend as a free agent – surely a precondition for speaking of trust here at all – we must assume that the *possibility* of defection exists.

In response to this we need to recognize that risks, probabilities and possibilities are not entities that exist out there on their own; they are something we invoke in the context of practical reasoning.

We have aspirations and fears, and we understand that certain obstacles and prohibitions stand in the way of our action. The meaningfulness of speaking of possibilities and risks depend on what kind of a point might be made by invoking a scenario in a context.[36] In one sense it will be theoretically 'possible' for my friend to try to harm me, just as it will be 'possible' for her, in the abstract, to do other completely unexpected things – for instance, attacking some other friend with her knife or taking *her own* life with it. No logical contradiction is involved, nor is there anything physically to stop her. But clearly, no one could challenge a person's trustworthiness merely by bringing up considerations of what is logically conceivable or physically feasible. Any such discussion would be relevant in the first place only if there were recognizable reasons for suspicion. Thus we do not distrust a person *because* we consider certain things possible for her. On the contrary, the fact that we consider certain things possible for her is *an expression of* our distrust.

The idea that it is at least *logically* possible for my friend to try to harm me may still linger on – namely, if we think of logic narrowly as the formal analysis of propositions; it is in other words possible to formulate a sentence that says this. But if logic is to be more than a fingering exercise it must involve the analysis of what is meant by a sentence when it is uttered. Something is said to me by someone; in order to understand the sentence I have to be clear of my relation, not only to my friend, but also to the person who is talking. I will perhaps find it more natural to see his utterance as a revelation about *his* life, about the bad things *he* has been through. In this way, what I can understand to be a description of a possibility – even of a 'logical' possibility – is dependent on my relation to the person who raises the alleged possibility.

Perhaps there is still an objection. It is true that we cannot and should not constantly harbour suspicions against our friends. But still, it may be objected, bad things do occasionally happen. Friends betray and even physically assault each other. It might not occur to me that *my* friend would do so, but that is not a guarantee. Never to consider the possibility of betrayal is to trust blindly. Blind trust is endearing in a child but, rationally speaking, it is not an attitude that we should try to cultivate in adult age. In response, I would point out that there is simply no form of rationality that rules out disappointment in advance. The fact that unexpected facts about my friend may *later* turn up would not be enough at the present point to convict me of irrationality or naïveté, because in any given situation I can merely act on the information I have at the moment of acting. On the contrary, it would be paranoid – *irrational* – if I were to act on a suspicion that I have no reason to hold whatsoever. We are now considering a situation where the risk, if there is any, still has to materialize. Who *was* right can only be seen afterwards.

The requirement of rationality of course cuts both ways. Suspicion, when not simply pathological, needs a reason. It would be unrealistic to think that friends never betray each other, but it would be equally absurd to claim that, on pain of irrationality, all friendship worth its salt 'logically' ought to include a deposit of constant suspicion. Even though we sometimes rightly think of people as possible sources of harm, on the whole we do not view the people we know in that light. I would, for instance, hardly be referring to my friend as a 'friend', and I would hardly be talking to *you* about my trust in her, if all my human relations were constantly up for grabs in that way.

Baier's reasoning here seems to be based on conflation between the third and the first person. From the fact that trust is internally related to betrayal she draws the illegitimate conclusion that *the person who trusts* must suspect betrayal. But while it is true that an observer typically would not *describe* a relationship as one of trust unless he or she can imagine a risk of some kind in connection with it, it does not follow that *I* must believe I am taking a risk when I trust a friend. While the observer may say, 'OL trusts, but he is taking a risk', in an important kind of case I cannot meaningfully say this about myself. In a real sense I cannot even try to take a third-person perspective on my situation. The distinction between my perspective and that of a real observer is that the observer does not have *my* relations to other people. Because of this, the observer's words about my human relationships will always mean something else than when those words are said or thought by me. The statement about risk that in the one case can be said without contradiction is not the 'same' statement as the one that would be impossible for me to say without contradiction.

Vulnerability revisited

Friendship does, however, introduce a type of 'vulnerability' not present in less emotionally and morally charged relationships. If my friend were to let me down in some serious issue, it would wound me more deeply than similar failures by others. It would add insult to injury and bring home in double measure my helplessness and loneliness when the chips are down. In that sense, it may be said that emotional attachment always involves risk. It involves craving for the other, and indeed it always ends in bereavement because, of two friends, one must die before the other. But my vulnerability in this particular sense is not something that could be understood independently of my initial description of the two of us as *friends*.

The relation between trust and vulnerability is, in sum, the opposite of what Baier suggests. We should not start by introducing an idea of vulnerability, identified in ethically neutral terms in relation to some independently intelligible interest or expectation, in order next to define 'trust' in terms of possible harm to that interest. On the contrary, personal trust creates the logical space within which it is possible also to see terms like 'vulnerability' and 'harm' in a new light. Our 'interest' in friendship – if that is a meaningful phrase – is one *created by* friendship. You understand the sadness of losing a friend once you *have* a friend. Such understanding of trust endows the notion of vulnerability with significance beyond mere risk assessment.

A novel or a story may be the best vehicle for demonstrating how this kind of ethical vulnerability enters our lives. An example is obviously no proof. What it can do is offer ways of looking at things that might otherwise be ignored but are often readily recognized by us when we read the story.

A Novel from the 21st Century

Trust and vulnerability come across as the main theme of *Kallocain: A Novel from the 21st Century* by the Swedish writer Karin Boye (1900–41).[37] Originally published in 1940, the book is a haunting dystopia much in the spirit of H. G. Wells, Aldous Huxley and, subsequently, George Orwell. The plot centres on human relations, especially the marriage of the scientist Leo Kall and his wife Linda. As with most stories in the dystopian genre, the scene is set in a hierarchical, thoroughly militarized surveillance state. Citizens, always addressed as 'fellow-soldiers', go to regular jobs but they also spend several evenings a week on policing and soldiering duties. It goes without saying that the standardized family residences are equipped with surveillance apparatus. Family life is understood in instrumental terms only: the aim is to bring up future fellow-soldiers. At the end of their education young people are resettled in other cities according to a central plan, with no chance of staying in touch with their families. Personal closeness is discouraged as it would interfere with that supreme duty, loyalty to the State. Fellow-soldiers are brought up from early age for the kind of sporty cheerfulness that the World-State needs in order to defeat the other superpower, the Universal State.

We may sum up Boye's anti-totalitarian lesson: functional social life includes not only vertical relations of each individual toward centres of power but, more importantly, horizontal lines of free solidarity between members of society – the sorts of uncontrollable relations that the totalitarian State is designed to stamp out. But despite the obvious political message, at a deeper level the book is about longing for trust and openness, and about the fear of vulnerability that simultaneously pulls us away from openness. In the culture that Boye depicts, any sign of weakness can be used against you; you learn 'to talk with the surface and be on guard under the surface' – and if you manage you will feel 'terribly pleased afterwards, as if having escaped some danger'.[38]

The story is told in the form of a memoir. As the plot starts, Leo Kall, the narrator, is intensely devoted to his soldierly duties and to his career as a chemical researcher. (Either by design or by coincidence, his Swedish name *Kall* means 'calling', 'vocation' – but also 'cold'.) He has initially no critical ideas about the regime. On the contrary, he has invented a substance, Kallocain, that he expects to be of use to the State. It is an unfailing truth drug: anyone under the influence will divulge his or her innermost secrets. The test subjects reveal dreams and fears they hardly dare to admit to themselves. The drug has no harmful side effects, but the subject will remember what was said during the interview. Kall thinks of his drug as the final keystone of the best of all possible communities. From now on no thoughts can be kept private.

The secret police are obviously keen to use the truth drug in their search for internal enemies, but a major complication is discovered at once. Already the first voluntary test subjects reveal an amazing degree of disloyalty and a deep sense of personal despair; all, simply all, walk away full of shame, crushed and unhappy. But the police chief understands that this is not necessarily a problem after all. On the contrary, a comfortable way is now available to get *any* fellow-soldier out of the way via the simple chain of denunciation, injection, confession, court decision and execution. Incidentally, the tests also unfold a real sect of dissidents who dream of love, harmony and authenticity.

While Leo's career makes steady progress, his relationship with Linda is a source of anxiety. Her silences, her penetrating gazes, are a mystery to him.

> When her mouth drew together in a narrow red line – oh no, it wasn't a smile, either of derision or of joy, rather it was tension, as when a bow is drawn – and her eyes meanwhile would be wide open and unblinking – then the same feeling of anxiety filled me through and through, and all the time she held me and pulled me with the same mercilessness, and yet I suspected she would never reveal herself to me.[39]

Linda appears invulnerable and impenetrable, whereas Leo is uncomfortably aware of his own transparency. He has been thinking of love as a pursuit of mutual gain where you sacrifice some of your privacy for the sake of emotional support, sexual gratification and shared projects like children (in Baier's terms: the goods you care about). But as he sees it, he has been simply making himself more and more vulnerable, whereas Linda remains just as much a 'riddle' as before – something that gives her 'a hateful superiority'.

> One might speak of 'love' as an obsolete, romantic concept, but I am afraid it exists anyway, and from its very inception it contains an indescribably painful element. A man is attracted to a woman, a woman to a man, and for every step that they move closer together each one loses something of himself or herself; a series of defeats where victories had been expected.[40]

Leo recalls a nightmare that he associates with Linda, in his dream half-naked 'standing in a great darkness with a strong spotlight on me; from out in the darkness I felt the Eyes directed on me, and I wriggled like a worm to escape'.[41]

Leo might be called distrustful of his wife, but 'clueless' and 'fearful' are better descriptions. He does have a specific suspicion, however. Leo suspects Linda of having an affair with Rissen, his immediate chief at the laboratory. On the other hand, his feelings are not ones of simple jealousy. At bottom he *hopes* to be assured that she is in love with another, because that would release him from asking why their relationship is not working. He might then leave it behind and marry someone else – as he admits in retrospect, 'I wanted an assurance that would put an end to my marriage'.[42]

> Should we also separate and remarry, with the childish notion that the same expectation would be less hopeless with someone else? All my common sense told me it was a deceitful illusion. One single little irrational hope whispered: No, no – your failure with Linda is due to her desire for Rissen! She belongs to Rissen, not to you! Make sure it is Rissen she is thinking of – then everything is explained, and you can still have hope for a new love with meaning to it![43]

Things come to a head when Leo makes off with some Kallocain from the laboratory and administers it to Linda. He wants to know the truth and he also hopes for some confession for blackmail if the need should arise. But nothing works out as expected. Linda is not in love with anyone else. Under the influence, she tells Leo of her grief at their failure to find each other – the absence of 'a lot of small matters – friendliness, coziness, caresses – and when they were impossible then the big and important matters also were impossible'.[44] She reveals her fear of loneliness once the children are gone, something she has never talked with him about because he would despise her. She has been looking for love but now there is only emptiness. She would just want to kill him to be away from it all. '"How can it be so?" she whispered in anguish. "How can it be that one seeks something that does not exist? How can it be that one is sick to death when actually completely healthy, when all is as it should...".'[45] Leo sees now that he has gained nothing.

> The whole time I had been quite convinced that whatever she might say she would be in my power afterwards in a different way from before, that [...] she would divulge secrets not to be divulged, which I could threaten to expose if she were to take a single belligerent step against me. Perhaps she had done so, I was uncertain. [...] It was possible that she was in my hands, it was possible that all had gone according to plan. Except for one point: I would never be able to make use of any advantage. All she had said was said from within myself. I was sick, stirred to the bottom of my soul because she had held herself as a mirror before me. I had not suspected that she, with her tight lips, her silence, and her penetrating eyes was of the same weak timber as I. How could I threaten her, how could I force her, when this was the case.[46]

How can Leo ever force Linda if she is weak? From the perspective of rational choice – and from the perspective that Leo at first believed in – a position of strength is precisely one that would allow him to use force successfully. Linda's losses are Leo's gains. But why does this perspective suddenly appear lifeless and pointless? There are two ways to think of a human relation; in both cases the expression 'accepted vulnerability' might be used. If we think of a relationship in terms of a power balance, we should accept our own vulnerability if it cannot be helped and then set to work in order later to turn the tables. In that situation we would agree with Baier: we need good reasons for 'wanting or accepting such closeness to those with power to harm us'. Boye's novel, however, evokes the opposite idea, presenting vulnerability as something we actively seek at least at some level of our being. It is only in freely offering up ourselves to each other that we find true community.

The following night Linda and Leo sit together and, now speaking freely even without the drug, they talk of their fears, of the children, of their faith, love and hope. And, as Leo reflects afterwards, 'I wished at least to imagine that somewhere in other countries and among other people a new Linda would speak like the first one, voluntarily', – 'I cannot, I cannot erase that illusion from my soul that I still, in spite of all, participate in creating a new world.'[47]

Trusting and being trusted

The change in Leo's thinking is best described as a shift of perspectives. Up until Linda's confession he has been painfully aware of his own vulnerability towards both Linda and others that might want to harm him. Now he comes to think of himself as a recipient of trust, as someone to whom the other is exposed in all her vulnerability. In his paper, 'On being trusted', Hertzberg points out that, with rare exceptions (he mentions the Danish thinker K. E. Løgstrup[48]), the philosophy of trust has adopted the perspective of someone who, as a free choice, needs to decide whether to bestow trust on others. 'Failures of trust' are treated as mainly misperceptions by the trustor, exposing him or her to charges of naïveté. What has not been discussed is the ethical situation we face when we realize we are *the object of* someone's trust. To be trusted by others and deliberately to fail them is by definition[49] to betray them. If I let them down I cannot simply shift the blame on them and think they should have seen it coming (on charge of irrationality), any more than the fact that I have been a scoundrel in the past gives me licence to go on being a scoundrel. To focus on the perspective of the recipient of trust is to treat 'vulnerability' as an ethical concept: our recognition of the other's vulnerability is precisely what makes it 'impossible' for us to take advantage of it. And this is why we may be crushed by the realization of our own betrayals just as much as by those of others against us.

Leo's shift of perspective is also visible in his changing ideas about *physical* closeness. Marriage might be called both the safest and the most vulnerable of adult human relations. Vulnerable, because no two people know each other so intimately and have so unrestricted access to each other as spouses or lovers do. Safe, for the same reason. Sharing the same bed is a potent expression of both. As already mentioned, Baier states that a wife who sleeps next to her husband takes the risk of being physically harmed.[50] In this, Baier is thinking from the perspective of the vulnerability of the trustor, presenting the nuptial bed as an essentially dangerous place to be. In a similar way, during another sleepless night Leo Kall is struck by the fact that he has shared the bed with his wife for years on end without thinking twice about the matter:

Had no one until now actually ever thought of the danger inherent in two people sleeping side by side, with no other witnesses but the [surveillance apparatus] on the wall? And even they were no real security: in the first place, they might not always be in use; and in the second, admittedly they could influence or avenge something that happened but not prevent it. Two people alone, night after night, year in year out, and perhaps hating each other; and if the wife should awaken, what couldn't she then do to her husband ...[51]

It would be too simplistic, however, to think of Leo's night thoughts as just expressing his concern for physical safety. Even daytime activities would furnish Linda with ample opportunities for doing harm. But the exposedness of one person to another perhaps finds its most *explicit* expression in the shared bed. Perhaps Norbert Elias comes closer to the truth when he, in his work on the history of civilization, takes issue with the 'invisible walls' that we erect around ourselves:

> that invisible wall of affects that seems mutually to rise between one human body and the other, pushing back and separating, the wall that today is often discernible already at the approach of something that has been in touch with someone else's mouth or hands; and which shows itself in the form of embarrassment at the mere *sight* of several body functions of the other, often at the mere *mention* of them, or as feelings of shame when one's own body functions are exposed to the gaze of others, and indeed not only then.[52]

Leaving aside the historical theses that Elias wants to advance, he clearly has a point about the general role of physical closeness. Closeness introduces a sense of vulnerability, not because of physical risk but because of the sense of shame associated with exposing one's intimate life to others. (The fact that we call some forms of closeness 'intimate' is one more expression of this sense of vulnerability.) What is exceptional about relations between spouses and lovers is that the wall of affects is missing or modified. They expose themselves in ways they would otherwise not do. But such vulnerability is not something they reluctantly accept as the price of love, loyalty and other valuable goods that family life has to offer.

If this kind of language is to be used at all, shared vulnerability in itself *is* a valued piece of goods, perhaps the most valuable ever available.

How should we philosophically understand this? Is marriage retrogression to childhood bliss? On one understanding of the adult norm, the cautious cultivation of relations between relative strangers for mutual gain constitutes the normal case, with appropriate 'walls' protecting us from one another. In that perspective, spouses and lovers come out temporarily as exceptions. Statistically speaking, that would be correct in the sense that *most* human interaction involves caution in some way or other. On the other hand, it is also possible to think of this kind of openness as something that *to a greater or lesser extent* is discernible in all human relations. What in this perspective calls for explanation are the departures from openness. In real situations, however, neither of the two perspectives always rules supreme; sometimes we are amazed at the openness with which a person relates to others and sometimes, on the contrary, by the fact that a person seems constantly to be on his or her guard. Joel Backström suggests in a thought-provoking work on the idea of openness that 'our normal state' is one of '*tension* between a desire for openness and a fearful rejection of that openness'.[53]

All things considered, the concept of vulnerability may be an avenue to understanding the ethical significance of trust. But the relation between trust and vulnerability may be construed in different ways. On one level of understanding, speaking of trust as accepted vulnerability naturally inclines us to look for ways to reduce such vulnerability, because vulnerability counts prima facie as something to avoid. That is the perspective that both the game theorists and Baier take for granted. We can understand the issue in a different way if we think instead of how to face the vulnerability of the other, a fellow mortal who approaches us with trust.

CHAPTER FOUR

The time dimension

Much of the work reviewed so far has explicitly or implicitly treated trust as a relation that we may decide whether or not to enter.[1] Relationships that develop naturally, without conscious decisions on anyone's part, have also by and large been viewed through the lens of the conscious case. Such privileging of the conscious case is endemic in the favoured normative question of where rationally to place one's trust. But the idea of choosing to trust requires in turn an explanation of how choices of that kind are to be imagined. What is the background that must be assumed for voluntary choices to trust?

Consider what might look like a quintessential 'decision to trust': stepping down from a quay into a tiny boat in moderately rough weather. The decision may further involve small momentary, as it were, sub-decisions such as grasping the boatman's outstretched hand and taking the cue from him for when to make the leap. Perhaps there is a moment of hesitation, an inquiring look into the man's eyes and then the decisive step. On the whole the case might be described in the terms that many studies of trust would favour: as a case of weighing a risk against the perceived trustworthiness of those whom we rely upon. What interests me in this chapter is what else is needed for such decisions to become possible. While the movements in embarking a boat can be understood as expressions of momentary deliberations and decisions, it will be just as important to see what has been going on before that moment. One's perception of the situation is also the outcome of a development. In that process, exactly these operations have been singled out as something that calls for special attention. *This* stage-setting makes it possible to view *those* moves under the aspect of 'decisions'. The impression would probably not be the same for someone who lives on an island and relies on the boat for his or her weekly shopping. The routines of embarking would probably not stand out in such a person's life as more critical than most actions undertaken in the course of a normal day, and she would not think of herself as making a decision. On the other hand, those who would never embark a boat at all in the circumstances would not be making a decision either. They would simply put off the boating expedition because it would lie outside their range of reasonable actions. The act of embarking is singled out as 'a decision to trust' for *some*, given what comes before and after it.

The aim of this chapter is to look into ways in which a time dimension enters our understanding of trustful relations. The main positive thesis is: Trust is usually best understood as a continuation of the normal run of life, not as an exception to it. The negative lesson is that existing debates on trust in many cases involve a misleading approach I propose to call *methodological timelessness*. In other words, the time dimension is abstracted away from the examples treated in the debate, and the focus is placed instead on momentary decisions. This seems to be one natural outcome of certain basic assumptions about human motivation – or perhaps more to the point, of assumptions about what is the proper model for *studying* and *accounting for* human motivation.

Methodological timelessness

Methodological timelessness implies that voluntary action should be treated as the net result of the conditions that *presently* influence the agent. In this perspective, motives of action are to be studied as if frozen in a moment in time. In order to explain or predict an individual's behaviour at a given point, one accordingly needs to consider the beliefs and desires, including motivations, psychological tendencies, etc. that affect her at the moment of acting. The agent's historical past comes into the picture merely in the sense that past events are the causal antecedents of the present situation. Similarly, the future, which by definition does not yet exist, enters only in the guise of the relevant agents' present expectations; both past and future are subsumed under the factors that contribute to the agent's current motivational state. Thus this model of explanation works with what might be called a snapshot conception of the agent. It is committed to timelessness also in the sense that the reasoning employed in it is structurally the same regardless of whether it is worked 'forward' or 'backward'. Statements of the form, 'desire D and belief B will together lead to action A', can be used both for explaining past events, predicting future events and working out instructions for how to achieve some desired end result. The explanatory approach involved here is often known as the Belief-Desire model of motivation.[2]

Hobbes is once more relevant here. In his version of this model, beliefs and desires – or their physiological equivalents – function directly as causes of behaviour. A snapshot conception of the agent appears to be implied in the very structure of the explanatory endeavour. For, given widely accepted views concerning the impossibility of causal action at a distance (physical or temporal), any force that might affect the individual's behaviour must be present at the moment of acting.[3] Hence all one needs to consider for the purpose of explanation is the individual's state at the moment in question. Admittedly, the details of the presumed causal processes are for the most part unknown, and few modern authors, if any, would expect us to have anything like a complete causal account of motivation any time soon. Still, the model is in place in its main outlines once it is agreed that the relation between behaviour and its antecedents is *something like* a causal one.

But the snapshot conception may appear natural, not merely when the relation of desires and beliefs to behaviour is supposed to be causal, but also when it is assumed to have the form of a practical syllogism.[4] If the progression from reasons to action is interpreted psychologically, as a kind of 'causality of the mind' where one state of mind leads to another and further to action, it will be natural to assume that the premises of the syllogism must be somehow present for the individual for reasoning to be possible. It looks once again as if all one needs to consider in the situation are the contents of the individual's mind *at the time* of deciding.

The snapshot conception of the acting individual follows, in other words, from a range of widely held ideas about the explanation of behaviour mainly stemming from the Empiricist tradition. But its appeal is easily seen to rest on a seriously simplified view of the role of beliefs and desires in action. In one sense, Belief-Desire models may be considered trivially true, given sufficiently broad definitions of 'belief' and 'desire' (defined as the totality of the motivational and cognitive conditions that underlie an individual's action). The model would simply indicate that the explanation of voluntary action should be sought in a combination of the agent's beliefs and desires at the time of acting. However, even in this rather relaxed variety, this model of motivation tends to redirect the focus of the explanatory inquiry in a rather unfortunate way. For if 'explanation' means 'considerations that make the action intelligible', it would be an oversimplification to think that all one ever needs to know about an individual's motivation can be discovered by looking at the present contents of her mind and taking them at face value. One may also put my objection in another, only apparently opposite way and say that identifying 'the present contents of an individual's mind' is a more complex and ambiguous matter than might initially appear.

At this juncture, I offer two counter-suggestions which look superficially different but really come down to the same thing. First I would suggest that, as a rule, an individual's decisions are seldom outcomes only of those beliefs and desires that literally occupy her mind at the moment of deciding. Decisions are no doubt sometimes completely improvised on the spur of the moment, but that is hardly the usual case. It is quite possible, for instance, to undertake an action in the absence of any desire at the moment to do it. My second suggestion is the following. One might concede that our decisions in *some* sense depend on 'our present states of mind', given a sufficiently inclusive understanding of that phrase. This would give the idea of presence quite a new degree of complexity. A fully fledged description of what is 'present' will have to include its past and future in order to make the 'present' visible in its full complexity. There is certainly a sense in which 'other times' are present in the here and now.[5]

Still one way to describe the contrast here is to see it as one between two ways of understanding what it means for the past to explain someone's action. The Belief-Desire model implies that events in the past *give rise* to the agent's present desires and beliefs, which in turn give rise to the action. The contrasting view that I am proposing implies that to explain the action is to make it intelligible; 'motives for action' are not motivating psychological forces, but instances of reasoning connected with justification.[6]

The explanation of why something was done takes the form of describing *what* was done, where the latter is a way of presenting the action as meaningful, (apparently) justified or the like. Thus the answer to the question, 'Why are those people assembled on the street?' may be 'It is a demonstration'; and the answer to 'Why did Brutus stab Caesar?' may be 'He was trying to save the republican constitution'.[7] The agent's action is in part identified by making claims about the beliefs and desires expressed in it. Conversely, the beliefs and desires are themselves identified by looking at the action. Thus the relation of *explanans* to *explanandum* is not causal but an internal one; each is made sense of in the light of the other. Descriptions of the agent's reasons for a decision are in part also descriptions of what the decision was and vice versa. Also, the identification of something *as* a decision as opposed to, for instance, a case of following up an earlier decision implies that the agent's reasons for action are viewed in a certain light. This was seen already in the case of embarking a boat: we may say of a passenger that she decided to step into the boat, but also that she followed up on her earlier decision to go to the village for shopping. Somewhat similarly, taking out a loan and repaying it are in one sense two actions, each the outcome of a separate decision. In another sense one may see the whole thing as only one extended action, because by borrowing I have already agreed to pay back. The choice between the two descriptions may have implications concerning motivations. To say that I took out a loan and later *made the decision* to repay is perhaps to suggest I had entertained plans not to pay.

These general points about the interpretation of action will of course have to be substantiated in the specific cases to be considered below. I will argue that many discussions about trust in current mainstream theory involve the questionable assumption of methodological timelessness in the sense just described. My suggestion will be that, if the descriptions of trust that they present are taken at face value, we are left with ambiguities and dilemmas that can only be resolved by giving up the implicit assumption of timelessness.

Prisoners' Dilemma revisited

Methodological timelessness is probably most easily recognized in game-theoretic approaches to trust and cooperation. To see the point more clearly, consider the following remark from the collection on trust edited by Gambetta. This is the economist Partha Dasgupta analysing reputation for honesty as a capital asset. He argues that commitments – for instance, promises – motivate trust because they alter our perception of the incentives, and hence of the likely behaviour, of the opposite party. When an agent issues a promise, he or she knows that failing to perform carries a penalty.

> You do not trust a person to do something merely because he says he will do it. You trust him because, knowing what you know of his disposition, his information, his ability, his available options and their consequences, you expect he will *choose* to do it. Commitment on his part merely alters the game that is to be played, and therefore alters your expectation of what he will choose to do and, what is subtly tied to this, simultaneously alters *his* expectation of what *you* will choose to do.[8]

The factors we are invited to consider in this passage are described as various *present* conditions. It is not the past promise as such that constrains the agent, for it lies in a dead past and what remains is the entirely new deliberation about whether to make good of the promise. Promises, however, introduce a new element of pressure in the form of expectations and sanctions on the agent. In this way previous commitments, history and context are factored into their impact on the agents' present dispositions. In his subsequent analysis, Dasgupta's aim is to provide a description of 'the reputation for honesty' as a kind of modification of the opposite party's subjective assessment of probabilities. While 'reputation' in itself must be built up in a series of transactions over time, Dasgupta's focus is on its function as a facilitator of individual one-off transactions: on why a trader with a reputation for honesty will, in any one transaction, be more favourably placed than his competitors.[9]

To further explore this kind of privileging of the present, I propose now to return to the Prisoners' Dilemma, as described in Chapter 2. Despite the existence of a rudimentary cover story, the model is usually presumed to be intelligible and unambiguous even in the absence of details about *why* the players would rank one outcome higher than another. This is not an oversight but an important ingredient of the model's claim to universal validity. As Origgi has pointed out, one advantage (if you like) of game-theoretic approaches is that they claim to offer a kind of anti-ideological justification of cooperative relations.[10] Cooperation is neither good nor bad in itself; its value depends on payoffs, which are determined on the basis of the agent's ranking of them, not by any *specific* normative system. The centrality of game theory in various debates concerning rationality chiefly depends on its success in presenting itself not as the description of a historically specific situation (say, of strategic interaction in late capitalism), but as a blueprint for rational choice, located in a timeless present where researchers and readers are free to insert details of their choosing.[11]

However, the Prisoners' Dilemma is context-free only in the sense that the scenario is deliberately left vague. Consider: Who are the 'prisoners'? How did they end up there? Do they have reason to trust the promises of the 'police'? If the details are *not* filled in, I would maintain it is not clear at all what we should think of the rudimentary scenario. But once the details *are* there, it would be less tempting to generalize from it.

Suppose two strangers are picked from the street at random, then shipped off to Guantánamo Bay and accused of some heinous crime. All that each prisoner knows is that there is another prisoner somewhere and that their futures will depend on the degree of their collaboration with their captors; and we assume they are filled in on the rules of the Prisoners' Dilemma. Those prisoners could only see the 'police' as thugs and the whole business as *blackmail*. One of them, or both, might make a false confession, but they might also blame themselves afterwards for buying their freedom at the price of an injustice. On the other hand, suppose instead that the two prisoners really are partners in crime, and that they have agreed not to confess. If they stay firm without further deliberation, the optimal aggregate payoff is happily secured. But in this case the 'game' was not really played at all because the prisoners' decision was already made before they were taken into custody. It might be more appropriate, then, to think of their mutual promise and its fulfilment not as separate actions, but as two parts of the same temporally extended, shared action. On the other hand, the game is also not really played at all if a prisoner withdraws from his agreement for some reason *other* than maximizing the payoff – for instance, because he really is guilty and feels remorse. Thus the fact that the prisoners are forced into this situation does not necessarily imply that they enter it in the spirit of a game where the goal is to maximize payoff.

Bringing in these possibilities of variation may appear unfair, because the original point of the theoretical exercise was precisely to reduce empirical complexity by demonstrating an underlying 'pure' form of strategic reasoning. We are not meant to think of how the detainees ended up in this tight place or the reasons why they rank one outcome higher than another. The mere fact that they have preferences, *some* preferences, is enough to allow for a description of their thinking in terms of a distribution of payoffs – the idea being that the prisoners will *by definition* act on the basis of their subjective distributions of payoffs. We are asked not to think of that as an empirical claim, but as a thinking tool. The conventional description of the game equates the subjective payoffs with different lengths of prison sentences (the shorter the more desirable). However, game theorists will point out that the model allows for nonstandard distributions of payoffs. An 'altruistic' mindset might be represented by a revised distribution where having one's *fellow prisoner* released represents the highest payoff. Considerations such as 'I am innocent', 'We are friends', 'I am guilty and want to confess', or 'I want to nail that bugger who got me into this' could all be factored into the agent's set of preferences.[12] The game-theoretic approach simply accepts the agents' present distribution of subjective payoffs as given and takes it from there.

Such defence of game theory is, it seems to me, quite valid as far as it goes – which is: not very far. If one is determined, come what may, to treat an agent's choices as indications of her present distribution of payoffs, one is always free to do so given a sufficiently inclusive concept of 'present distribution of payoffs'. However, the act of abstraction also robs the model of any reasonable claim to be telling us something about trust or cooperation, or of any other specified human relationship or species of human motivation. Two points should be made here. First, at this level of abstraction

– where all we know is the basic setup of the game and the distribution of payoffs – we can say next to *nothing* about the thinking of the two 'prisoners'. The terminological choice to call one move 'cooperation' and the other 'defection' is arbitrary. Secondly, in a real case, our understanding of the situation would depend on a background that has so far not been offered: a genuine time dimension. We know from the model that the agents' choices will either differ or coincide. But we could only know that they are instances of cooperation or defection, not of random variation or cooperation in some *other* direction, if we had an independent idea of the relations between the prisoners before they were detained. For instance, by 'defection' we would normally mean more than the failure, in the absence of any possible agreement or communication, to do what an unknown other person probably wants. To speak of 'cooperation' and 'defection' here (and to mean the words to be more than arbitrary technical terms) is already to assume a background.[13] To pursue the Prisoners' Dilemma seriously as a model for trust or cooperation would take one beyond the rational choice scenario. As far as I can see, this point remains the same whether one considers one-off scenarios or iterated games.

Timelessness in non-formal treatments of trust

Also non-formal attempts to approach trust are often construed on the tacit assumption that the time dimension can be stuffed into a black box. This, I think, is further enhanced by the fact that most theorists see their ambition as normative or action guiding.[14] That will naturally direct their attention towards temporally restricted decision-making situations. In a typical scenario, an agent needs to arrive at decisions about whom to trust and how valuable goods to entrust to them, or where rationally to 'place'[15] one's trust.[16] In one of her papers, Trudy Govier invites us to consider under what circumstances we should accept the help of a stranger on a busy street. This particular problem, of course, would arise precisely because, for want of previous acquaintance, we have no obvious reason to think one way or other about the stranger.[17] Govier concludes that our degree of caution should on the whole be proportionate to the value of what is at risk. Thus '[t]o accept a man's help carrying packages across a busy street, a woman needs to trust him, but slight trust will be enough – unless the packages contain exceedingly valuable items'.[18]

I hasten to add that Govier discusses more complex cases too. Some of her examples concern trust between married couples and friends, where their shared history will obviously be the central source of their beliefs about each other. Govier's general view is that our judgement of a person's trustworthiness will be based on available information (if any) about his or her past actions and intentions.[19] Yet I would say this approach is still timeless, rather in the manner of the one I previously cited from Dasgupta. It is built on the paradigm of two strangers incidentally thrust together – the more complex cases being derived from it by throwing in detail. Govier is not an exception here. The nature of the normative inquiry itself easily forces a kind of timelessness onto it. The focus lies on the trustor and his or her attempt to make the best of the situation at hand. Some decision must be made *now*. The relevance of the past supposedly lies in its role as a source of information about the interests, beliefs and past performance of the possible recipients of trust, but the situation itself must be understood as a snapshot on its own present merits.[20] The aim of my objections is not to downplay the fact that we regularly trust strangers, nor to deny that we are required sometimes to make momentary, explicit decisions about whom to trust. But it will be helpful even in those cases to look for the background that confers on the situation the character of a meaningful choice.

Assessing probability

What is then wrong with the snapshot conception? I would say it distorts our understanding even of the reasoning that *does* go on within the limited time frame in question. This is especially seen in the ways in which considerations about the other person's trustworthiness are supposed to enter the agent's decision to trust. Consider Gambetta's functional definition of 'trust' as quoted in Chapter 2. Trust is based on the agent's assessment of the other's probability of cooperating, which motivates the decision either to cooperate or to withdraw. This is a possible scenario, even though it reads more like an idealized model than a messy real-life situation. But the central problem is obvious as soon as we ask the natural question: How do we then assess the probabilities? In Gambetta's model, the relation between assessment and trusting is supposedly *external*. In other words, there is some agreed-upon, putatively neutral way to arrive at a probability value. The problem here, as it seems to me, is that there is no context-free method to judge the implications of a person's earlier behaviour for what she is likely to do in the future. The relevance of the record of her past performance – the kind of use that we should make of her record – cannot be assessed separately from the question of whether we are prepared to trust her.

The fact that someone made a mistake last time may give me reason *either* for distrusting her *or* for thinking that she will be very conscientious this time precisely because of her earlier failure. As a different example, a friend's tone of voice might reveal to me that he is hiding something. What I am now thinking of is not acoustic qualities in the technical sense, but of all kinds of fine shades of behaviour and inflexion. They assume this kind of role in situations that already make suspicion appear natural in some other way. That is in turn dependent on my ideas of the kinds of thing the two of us should 'properly' not hide from each other, or what would constitute failure of openness in our relationship. I know my friend and if he is in trouble I would see it. Here the importance of a relationship extended in time comes in.

Consider a situation in Dostoevsky's *The Brothers Karamazov*. Mitya Karamazov is in custody, accused of killing and robbing his father. His brother Alyosha believes that Mitya, who hated his father and was in desperate need of funds, would certainly have it in him to do it. Yet he does not believe he committed the murder. He can tell it from the look on Mitya's face when he visits him at the police station.[21] Alyosha's statement is of course inadmissible as evidence at the murder trial, because it can be put down to Alyosha's natural partiality towards a family member. Nevertheless, we often do have this sort of ability to read off the truth from the faces of those close to us.

This connects with the fact that 'knowing' – as in 'knowing a friend' – is not simply 'to have knowledge'. It is true of course that if I know someone personally I am also likely to have much information about him. But, as İlham Dilman has pointed out, when I say I know *about* him the appropriate question would be, 'What do you know about him?' while, if I say I know *him* the question would be, 'How well do you know him?' My answer might be in some case, 'I know him only to say hullo to, but not well enough to ask him for a loan.'[22] In cases of that kind:

> [t]he dimensions of which our question seeks an illumination are the depth in which I know the other, the terms of our relationship, the circumstances of our contact, what part of ourselves we bring to it and what part we keep out or reserve.[23]

Thus the fact that we are often good at judging people whom we know personally is not simply the result of our many past opportunities to collect information about them. Our perception of the other is shaped by the ongoing relationship. Our tendency to construe the 'probabilities' in one way or other – or perhaps more frequently, simply not to think of probabilities at all – is already indicative of our trust or distrust. It is true that we could normally, if challenged, produce justifying 'reasons' or 'evidence' in support of trusting. We might say that we know our friend to be trustworthy. But while our judgement is sometimes literally a conclusion we draw from her earlier record of punctuality or honesty, we would not even be *looking* for those qualities in her unless we were basically open to the possibility (or fact) that she can be trusted. On the other hand, these sorts of questions and responses also imply a background. One must presuppose that someone has raised a question about our friend's trustworthiness. Some reasonable suspicion has been identified, but there is no general agreement either way. There is a paradox at work here: we are adducing evidence in support of trust or distrust, but trust and distrust are in turn used to interpret evidence. Trust is ineliminable from interpretation, and interpretation is ineliminable from our 'assessments of the trustworthiness of others'.[24]

At Mitya's trial in *The Brothers Karamazov*, the prosecutor presents a convincing case. Mitya is notoriously hot-headed and occasionally violent. He was seen outside his father's house, where he admits to having knocked down the butler with a heavy weapon. His hands and clothes were stained with blood, and he has suddenly got money. The only possible other culprit was Smerdyakov, a house servant, but he was seriously ill in bed. The defence attorney construes an equally plausible narrative where Smerdyakov is the murderer. He has feigned illness and set up Mitya. The money that was found on Mitya was his own after all. On the fateful night, Mitya had approached the house but then fled in panic, striking at the butler as he passed. After this incident, Smerdyakov killed and robbed his master.[25] The same facts that point to Mitya's guilt also point to the cunning of the other possible culprit. For instance, it was known that the missing money had been kept in an envelope which was found discarded on the bedroom floor. A plausible indication would be that the murder was committed by someone who did not live in the house – by Mitya, in other words – because Smerdyakov, who already knew there was money in the envelope, would have simply picked it up unopened. On the other hand, if Smerdyakov was the culprit he may have thought of this; he might have torn the envelope and left it on the floor precisely in order to indicate an outsider.[26]

For readers of *The Brothers Karamazov*, the conclusive evidence does surface. Smerdyakov makes a confession, shows the money to Mitya's brother and kills himself. But even in this case the confession is 'conclusive evidence' only relatively speaking. It closes the avenues for doubt within the conventions of the realistic novel but not by the standards of an Agatha Christie – subject to enough unread pages being left of the book! We might imagine Smerdyakov getting hold of money in some other way and making a false confession for reasons of his own. Generally speaking, evidence is called conclusive when it excludes further reasonable doubt, but there are different ideas about what is reasonable. The look of Mitya's face was conclusive enough for Alyosha.

Trust as an interpretative activity

The main point of the previous section was that our use of evidence in our assessments of the trustworthiness of others always implies interpretation, and the interpretation we give to the evidence will be dependent on our previous relations with people. But it is possible to think of an objection. Does this not signify bias on our part? It may be true, as a general observation, that our interpretations of facts are influenced by human relations. For instance, in many cases we believe our friends more easily than strangers. But if the question is whom we should *rationally* trust, philosophers might argue that we should look for neutral ways to assess the evidence. And if rational standards are followed, this evidence could in principle be passed on to others and used also by them as material for decision-making. In other words, one might argue that Alyosha's trust of his brother was either rational or biased; it was either based on the impartial assessment of evidence or it reflected prejudice on his part. Their family history could have been relevant in two ways: either because it gave him good opportunities to monitor and assess Mitya's performance or because it introduced a non-rational and potentially harmful cognitive bias.[27] But it seems to me that the problem with this way of presenting the alternatives lies in the apparent tacit assumption that our normal relation to facts presented as evidence is *not* dependent on relations of trust and distrust.

I would suggest by and large that by 'evidence', we mean facts and information that give us reason to believe in the existence of other facts bearing on an issue we are considering. The existence of evidence is not something given; evidence is not a 'natural kind' if you like, but the classification of a fact *as* evidence is tied up with its role in the reasoning process. The fact in question has this role, or it may be 'reasonably' recruited for such a role. But what is seen as reasonable is notoriously dependent on one's general outlook on things. For instance, if we believe that a witness is not telling the truth, we will not think of her testimony as constituting evidence in favour of the claims she is making. This would be compatible, however, with treating her testimony as evidence of something *else*, for instance of her desire to protect someone. For Alyosha, facts that tended to establish Mitya's guilt in the eyes of the jurors were not evidence against him: they were problematic facts calling for further investigation. In this way, identifying 'evidence' is in itself a form of judging.[28]

The connections of trust with these issues have been explored by Karen Jones in several papers.[29] While she has earlier described trust as an 'affective attitude', in her later work she has focused on its cognitive aspect as *interpretation*. This change of emphasis need not detain us here. Jones has consistently stressed the character of trust as a 'lens that changes how agents understand their situation and the reasons it affords'.[30] Trust guides our perception of the facts: it 'reveals itself in patterns in the agent's interpretations of reasons',[31] for example in the fact that we tend to interpret information as evidence in favour of a person we trust. This is an important point, because it suggests an idea of trust as something enmeshed in our cognitive pursuits, not something additional and separable from them.

As a case in point, Jones considers the way in which, in Shakespeare's play, Othello's perceptions of Desdemona, Iago and others are shaped by his tendency to interpret their actions in the light of trust and distrust.[32] The lesson is that trust and distrust are not separable attitudes tagged on to 'data', but they determine Othello's very understanding of what the relevant data consist of. Iago, Othello's trusted servant, manipulates Othello to believe that his wife has committed adultery. The chief candidate for evidence is Desdemona's handkerchief, planted by Iago in the bedroom of Cassio, the supposed lover. Othello is immediately prepared to think of it as a decisive proof. To make things worse, he overhears a conversation that he falsely understands to be Cassio's admission of his affair with Desdemona. Othello's interpretations of these and other facts are shaped by his trust of Iago[33] and, by the same token, his preparedness to distrust Desdemona. A vicious circle is created: Othello does not think of Iago's words as ensuing from ulterior motives because he trusts Iago; on the other hand, he trusts Iago *because* he interprets Iago's words as not ensuing from ulterior motives.[34] Jones's reading of the play seems right, but it leaves her with the question of why Othello was caught in this circle of trust and distrust to start with. Why would Othello, or anyone, rely on Iago instead of independently finding out about things?

Before any further analysis, perhaps we should consider whether one should see Othello as an abnormal figure. His eventual murder of Desdemona indicates pathological jealousy. On the other hand, the interplay of trust and suspicion leading up to the catastrophe is not depicted as obviously pathological. Jones certainly wants to use *Othello* as an example because she thinks it illustrates aspects of trust that also belong to ordinary cases. Similarly, one might guess Shakespeare wanted his main character to appear sufficiently normal to permit the audience to identify with his plight. But now, since Othello would probably have been better off not trusting Iago, we are naturally led to ask what lesson Jones would want to convey. Would she apply the lesson to all of us and claim that trust, by definition, *must* involve distortion?

This looks like a plausible reading of Jones's point. She writes: 'Othello's trust in Iago closes down potential lines of inquiry that would have seemed worth investigating by someone similarly situated who had a neutral attitude, and downright compelling to someone who distrusted [Iago].'[35] This suggests that Othello acted irrationally. Why, except for fear of facing the truth, would he willingly 'close down' lines of inquiry that seem 'worth investigating', especially in a question of such importance as the one he is facing? Such 'blinkered vision' is surely not to be recommended, as it 'opens one up to harm'.[36] A natural conclusion from Jones's argument is that we should not take our friends on trust. We should aim at a neutral attitude towards them and then judge whether they are likely to be telling us the truth. If Othello had been better off with a neutral attitude, wouldn't we all be?

One answer – mine – is: A person with a neutral attitude would simply not be 'someone similarly situated' as Othello. A dominant fact about Othello's predicament is his failure to connect with his wife or basically anyone outside a narrow circle of former comrades-in-arms. The Moor of Venice is a professional soldier, a self-made man, conspicuously an outsider to the Venetian aristocracy of his wife's family; at home with the male world of war and military administration, but not with the female or mixed world of domestic life and family politics. Iago, in contrast, is at his ease in both worlds, and for exactly that reason he appears indispensable to Othello in a milieu turned alien and hostile. Given Othello's situation as he then perceives it, it is not obviously irrational of him to trust Iago. One should then ask what 'a neutral attitude' would amount to in Othello's case. Judging by Iago's words, a neutral attitude is exactly what *he* recommends to Othello. He never levels direct accusations against Cassio and Desdemona. He explicitly asks Othello only to *look into* certain facts. But already looking at those facts as possible indications of adultery implies suspicion. Bias enters with the definition of the question itself, not with the answers. The lesson that Jones wants to draw is, roughly, that both trust and distrust may involve harmful cognitive distortions and that we should aim at a neutral view. This is fine as far as it goes, but the problem here is of course that it will not help us in a real situation. If we trust our source of information we *will* take him or her to be offering a neutral view. The application of Jones's implicit precept requires the assumption that we have already identified the desirable neutral perspective.

We, Shakespeare's audience, may in a sense be said to embody a neutral attitude because we can *see* Iago's manipulations happening. It is safe to say that Othello would not have acted as he did had he enjoyed the bird's-eye view afforded to us. But our neutral position really just results from the conventions of literary fiction. Suppose it was found out that the play deals with real events, in the manner of Shakespeare's historical plays. We would understand immediately that it is not a proper historical document and that it only lets us see the playwright's interpretation. The illusion of neutrality would vanish and we would think of Jones as hopelessly biased because of her indiscriminate trust in Shakespeare. Another significant difference between our position and Othello's is that *we* are not married to Desdemona. We are not required to find out the truth and we cannot be crushed when it dawns on us. The option of just keeping out of it is available to us but not to Othello.

In sum, it is not clear what is recommended if the suggestion is that Othello should or even might have taken a neutral view of his situation. As audience, we may certainly hold the opinion that he should have been more sceptical of Iago and instead developed a more open relationship with his wife. He might have profited from someone like us telling him this. But this recommendation would be, as it were, on a level with everything else that occurs in the play. If we had a chance to meet Othello in the flesh we would of course enter the play as its fellow characters. We would recommend him trust and distrust in *new* directions, not holding out a qualitatively new, neutral position somehow independent of the local interplay of human relations. What counts as 'adequate reasoning' must in other words be understood within the bounds of the limited perspective available to us: within the bounds of what it is like to be a mortal and emotional human being navigating with others similarly positioned. Here we might want to consider what kind of therapy philosophy could offer to Othello. Could philosophy break the hold of his dogmatic or fixed account of the situation? This was Socrates' general ambition of awakening people to the limitations they face when they delude themselves into thinking that they know something.[37] This possibility of enlightenment lies, as it were, immanent in the dialogical situation; it does not invoke a privileged perspective from the outside.

Now we can turn to the problem that Jones sees as the main dilemma connected with her account of trust. Trust, as an attitude expressed in the agent's interpretation of reasons, is never forced on us by the facts alone. We must trust at first, in order then to give facts the interpretations that we do. But then, Jones contends, there is a '"start-up" problem for trust': if trust is *based* on a certain interpretation (favourable to the trusted person) of facts, and if trust is what *makes* us interpret facts in one way rather than another, it looks like we have to trust in order to trust; how does trust ever get started?[38] I think this is a false dilemma and that it arises precisely because Jones does not consider her own relation to the events and attitudes that she describes, aiming instead at a bird's-eye view. We learn from her that trust is something embedded in our cognitive pursuits from the very start. But it seems that Jones still cannot help implicitly thinking of trust as something to which we can relate from the outside, apart from the ordinary run of life. At least tacitly, she presupposes the possibility of a neutral attitude, which we might maintain *before* sliding into the more problematic attitudes where trust and distrust are exhibited.

The point I have been making is, on the contrary, that there is no qualitative shift from neutral to trustful attitudes in our interpretations of facts.[39] In a sense, a fact not interpreted, not *taken* in one way or other, is a fact ignored; trust, as a background for interpretation, is with us from the start. In these and other cases, reasons may emerge which make it natural to speak of our attitudes as trustful. The fact that we speak of trust in those cases does not, however, indicate that a qualitatively new element has entered. The important point is that we, as human beings and fellow participants in social life, figure always already as elements of each other's worlds. We can decide what to do about it, but we cannot stay outside of it without bidding farewell to ordinary human life. This is a general background of 'normality' that we are not questioning.

Normality in ongoing interaction

The role of such normality was illustrated in Harold Garfinkel's ethnomethodological experiments, some of which will be further discussed in the next chapter. He asked his students to put various everyday attitudes to the test by engaging in unexpected behaviour and waiting for reactions. One experiment engaged students who were either married or lived with their families:

> [S]tudents were asked to spend from fifteen minutes to an hour in their homes imagining that they were boarders and acting out this assumption. They were instructed to conduct themselves in circumspect and polite fashion. They were to avoid getting personal, to use formal address, to speak only when spoken to.[40]

On the whole, the experience was quite unsettling to those concerned. Garfinkel reports that the students' family members did not find them polite at all but, on the contrary, arrogant or ironic; or they suspected they were ill or troubled in some way. One thing these experiments illustrate is that we cannot simply step back and decide to take up this or that attitude in a human relationship. This is not, as it were, a limitation of our mental agility. We can certainly behave with family members in ways that, in a sense, would be the 'same' as those that signify politeness in our relations with someone *else*. Politeness makes friendly communication possible across social distance. But when there is no distance to overcome, the attitudes that otherwise count as politeness may come across as attempts to *create* distance. In this way, the already ongoing relationship places constraints on what my behaviour can imply. This is not to say that humans are constantly engaged in intellectual acts of social construction and interpretation ('skilful' or otherwise), but simply that human behaviour acquires the meaning it has in the continuum of ongoing activity. Thus, what I mean by time dimension here is not just the fact that the past is a source of information for tackling the present, but a kind of presence of the past in the form of relationships whose character is defined by their history. You are your parents' son or daughter because you were born to them, welcomed (or not) into the world by them, and not because of a set of implied beliefs and preferences in the present.

The relevance of a time dimension is obvious in the cases of friendship, family relations and social networks, where we actually have memories of shared past engagement. But past events also inform our relations with strangers. Wars and crises, even those that we have not personally experienced, influence the collective memories of our 'imagined communities' – such as nations, social classes, assumed ethnic groups or age cohorts.[41] For instance, relations between locals and immigrants in North America and Europe are, in various ways, influenced (mainly negatively) by the formative experiences of 9/11, Abu Ghraib, the creation and subsequent dismantling of the welfare state and, further back in history, by the Cold War, by colonialism and the slave trade. These are ways in which even our encounters with strangers are coloured by a shared past.

Methodological timelessness and methodological individualism

Now it is possible to see how the idea of methodological timelessness is connected to the Hobbesian idea of methodological individualism, a question that was not explicitly raised in the first part of this chapter. Methodological individualism holds that the full analysis of social or cultural phenomena must be reducible to the properties and actions of individuals.[42]

My conclusion from the preceding argument is, in brief: social relations are the main form in which the past makes itself felt in the present. Our ongoing engagement with each other cannot be described in snapshots. Either the snapshot leaves us with the mere externals of two strangers trying to figure out what to make of each other, or else it is not a snapshot after all but could be called the frozen record of a more extended story. Wittgenstein, in his *Philosophical Investigations*, asked whether one could imagine someone feeling intense love or hope for a split second quite regardless of what happened before or after that moment.[43] His implied answer was no. The reason why we cannot imagine this is not the weakness of our imaginative powers, but the fact that the identity of a psychological state depends on its context. We cannot correctly and meaningfully attribute love, hope or grief[44] to a person unless that person's situation as a whole makes those descriptions applicable. This kind of context dependence is at variance with methodological individualism, understood as the thesis that a social situation should at least ideally be completely analysable in terms of the actions and states of individual agents. Conversely, it is possible that a strictly individualistic take on human action *must* work on the methodological assumption of timelessness. If rational choice is to be explained strictly in terms of the individual's preferences and beliefs, the questions of how the individual has acquired those preferences and beliefs, and how she has come to see the choice in the particular way she does, will be of secondary importance. What makes those questions even less appealing to methodological individualists is that addressing them requires attention to a background larger than the individual agent.

The suggestion presented in this chapter is that it is important to think of trust not mainly as the result of some one-off decision by which the agent places herself in the power of someone else, but as one of the characteristic aspects of our usually unchallenged background activities, contacts and commitments. At some point, an ongoing engagement may come to a point where it feels appropriate to speak of it as involving trust. The development of trust and the ceasing of trust involve changes of perspective that are not fully voluntary. But asking what is needed for a decision to trust to be *possible* would be slightly to misrepresent the issue. The question is not under what conditions certain kinds of mental act are possible, psychologically or otherwise, but what the right framework should be for certain descriptions of mental life. Furthermore, the question of exactly when we should describe someone as 'making a decision' is *also* context-dependent.

CHAPTER FIVE

'Trust' as an organizing tool

Descriptions are not innocent. In several places in the previous chapters there has been a call for reflexivity concerning our uses of 'trust' and related expressions. The question whether A should be said to trust B is often not so much a question about the mental life of A as an implicit question about the *speaker's* perspective on the people who figure in the description. What is the speaker's interest in the situation and how does it give rise to alternative descriptions? Similarly, it was pointed out that by identifying certain scenarios as *possible* – for instance, pointing to B as a potential source of harm – the utterer not only describes a situation but takes up a perspective of distrust towards B.

These issues are directly connected to the insights about language that underlie the methodology of Ludwig Wittgenstein's philosophy of psychology. In that work and in his later work in general, Wittgenstein consistently argues against the tendency to think that one single function somehow underlies all other uses of language, namely, that of giving factual descriptions. Connecting with this, he also objects to the idea that the most basic use of words is to refer to things, and that the meaning of a word is consequently to be investigated by trying to identify its reference. To cite just one of his various alternative metaphors, words can be treated as tools. In order to understand psychological concepts, we should look into how the relevant words are used in human interaction: they are something we use in organizing our lives. The analysis of the psychology of trust consequently needs to focus on the fact that some instances of human interaction are at times singled out and *described* as 'trust'. This highlights the fact that our *talk* of trust is just as much part of the web of human relations as are the states and dispositions to which the word 'trust' is applied.[1]

Is trust a psychological state?

Grammatically, trust is a state that an individual is in, a state somehow relating to another individual (as in 'A has trust in B' or 'A trusts B to ϕ because p'). However, this description so far does not specify what *kind* of a state trust is. By 'state' one may mean a person's current state of mind or body, but also dispositional states; with suitable rephrasing, even such 'states' as being out of work or having money in one's bank account. The point of speaking of a state in all these cases is that some lasting state of affairs pertaining to an individual is used as a point of reference when something about the individual's life is explained or judged.

Is trust a *psychological* state? For instance, when, if ever, can a feeling of trust be identified?[2] According to Baier, trust 'has a special "feel", most easily acknowledged when it is missed, say, when one moves from a friendly "safe" neighbourhood to a tense insecure one'.[3] An obvious problem with this description is that it does not specify a feeling of trust but one of distrust. This highlights a general difficulty about pinpointing feelings or thoughts that might constitute trust as a psychological state. Often trust is, on the contrary, characterized by the *absence of* certain feelings and thoughts – for instance, suspicion and fear. Also, when I trust someone it is not for the most part something I think about; rather the opposite, as we will see. Nor do I mostly trust a person because I have at some point in time formed the judgement that he or she is trustworthy. For instance, if I am short-changed at the supermarket, but only realize it afterwards, it will be correct to say I had trusted the shop assistant to hand me the correct change. However, perhaps I never actually addressed the question in my mind. And I need not have harboured specific feelings about the shop assistant.

In his *Philosophical Investigations,* Wittgenstein takes up an analogous question. He discusses the 'feeling of familiarity' that may strike us, for instance, when we enter the same old room after a long absence. He remarks that, outside such situations, familiar objects in our surroundings do not typically give us a feeling of familiarity. It is easier to get a feeling of strangeness at the sight of unfamiliar objects, even though we do not have that feeling every time we see something unfamiliar.[4] Feelings of familiarity do exist, but their presence is not the criterion of what is familiar to us. Wittgenstein makes a point of this kind again in a discussion of the concept of expectation. Roughly, we can distinguish between feelings and 'states' that do not involve a specific feeling:

> We say 'I am expecting him', when we believe that he will come, though his coming does not *occupy our thoughts*. (Here 'I am expecting him' would mean 'I should be surprised if he didn't come' and that will not be called the description of a state of mind.) But we also say 'I am expecting him' when it is supposed to mean: I am eagerly awaiting him. We could imagine a language in which different verbs were consistently used in these cases. And similarly more than one verb where we speak of 'believing', 'hoping' and so on. Perhaps the concepts of such a language would be more suitable for understanding psychology than the concepts of our language.[5]

'I am expecting him' perhaps just means I stay at home at the appointed time with nothing particular in my mind. Or it means that I am unable to think of anything else, constantly thinking of our future meeting, imagining him at the door, rehearsing the things I plan to say. These are, we might say, two ways of doing the same thing. 'Expecting someone' would designate activities of this general kind, ones that in some sense lead up to the expected event as their fulfilment. In another sense, the two cases involve quite different activities. 'Same or different?' is here mainly a question directed at the inquirer: what is the focus of the inquiry? My intensive state of expectation might be interrupted by the telephone ringing, but in another sense I would also be waiting for my visitor during the telephone conversation.

The difference between two senses of 'expecting' is an example of a more general theme addressed in *Zettel*. In that work, Wittgenstein distinguishes between cases of believing, feeling and thinking that involve 'genuine duration' and others that do not.[6] A psychological state has genuine duration if it makes sense to ask whether the state endures from one moment to the next. Also, if a state has genuine duration, we can imagine it being interrupted. Being in pain is a clear case of genuine duration. We can imagine asking 'Do you still feel the pain?' and a few minutes later, 'What about now?' On the other hand, suppose I ask you, 'Do you still vote Conservative?' and again, after five minutes of silence, 'What about now?' This could hardly be understood as anything but a joke unless, of course, you have received some quite extraordinary revelation in the meantime. Nor could we imagine someone being interrupted in being a Conservative. The state of being a Conservative does not have genuine duration according to this definition.[7]

Sleep, physical pain, intense thinking and intense expectation have genuine duration. Knowledge, ability, understanding and intention, on the other hand, do not.[8] They are not interrupted when a person is asleep or in a faint. One can be interrupted in thinking or planning, but not in intending.[9] Anything that can be measured with a stopwatch would be a clear case of genuine duration. This may not always be possible, though, contrary to what Wittgenstein suggests, because the beginning or end of the state may be diffuse.

In the quoted paragraph Wittgenstein wants to restrict the use of 'state of mind' to cases of genuine duration. His choice of terminology here is in some ways unfortunate.[10] Perhaps Wittgenstein went too far in accommodating a language use originating in a philosophical image to which he was deeply opposed. It was the Cartesian and Lockean view of the mind as a kind of place or container, a site for inner states. To describe someone's thoughts or feelings is, according to that view, to specify the states that occupy that person's mind (and possibly brain). Wittgenstein then correctly observed that most of the psychological phenomena that interest us do not fit that description because their role in our mental lives is not of *that* kind. For instance, if we wish to examine the psychological effects of familiarity and unfamiliarity on people, it will not be helpful to identify the *condition* of familiarity with the *feeling* of familiarity. On the other hand, 'states of mind' may be understood more inclusively. For the present investigation (and also for Wittgenstein) the main thing is to be clear about the distinction between cases that do and do not involve genuine duration.

An important connecting theme in the *Investigations* is Wittgenstein's emphasis on the fact that in many cases, the intelligibility of attributing a feeling or attitude to someone is dependent on that person's overall situation. Thus we can meaningfully attribute love or hope[11] or grief[12] to a person only because that person's situation as a whole makes these descriptions applicable.

We cannot correctly and intelligibly attribute feelings of grief to a person unless she has, for instance, recently lost a loved one, regardless of what else may be true about her states of mind at a given point in time. For instance, someone at a cinema may feel like crying at the death of the film's fictitious main character, but this will not qualify as genuine grief unless some very peculiar explanation is produced.[13]

Turning to trust in the light of these considerations, first of all it seems clear that the state of trusting typically does not have genuine duration. Trust is not for the most part manifested as a particular state that occupies one's mind. The presence of trust must be established by looking for an overall pattern in a person's thinking and acting – a pattern in the weave of life, to apply what Wittgenstein said about grief.[14] Someone's trust in another may show itself in her being relaxed in his company, as well as in things she does *not* do, such as not taking certain precautions. It may show in her thinking about the future: perhaps plans that include the person she trusts or rely on information from him; or perhaps in the complete absence of any plan where one might be expected. But it does not need to involve specific feelings towards him or explicit thoughts about him. Again I would not deny that, in the right circumstances, it may be natural to describe a person's state of mind as involving feelings of trust. But the presence or absence of the feeling does not settle the issue on its own.

Trust and suspicion are patterns in the weave of life. To call something a pattern is to see it under the aspect of meaning and purpose, not as a random combination of elements. I should then propose the question: what are we doing when we recognize such a pattern and point it out to others by our use of the word 'trust'?

The 'dys-appearance' of trust

My trust in a friend may consist in the fact that I do *nothing*. For example, I do not suspect my friend of wanting to steal from me. I would typically not even say I *trust* her in this respect, because the very idea of her doing so would be foreign to me. There would be no particular reason for me to say I 'trust' her in this particular regard in contrast with other completely unexpected things that I would equally obviously rule out. When I leave for the bathroom at a restaurant, I expect my bag to be safe with her until my return. Whatever uncertainty I might feel would be caused by the presence of other patrons, while my friend's presence would have a reassuring effect. We do not even have to suppose that I have *learned* to trust her at some earlier point, because things like this are more or less taken for granted also in relation to new acquaintances. Thus if my friend now actually seized the opportunity to take money from my bag, it would strike me for the first time that I have trusted her unquestioningly.

The conceptual relation between distrust and trust may be compared with that of disease and health. We would not be conscious of our physical health unless made aware of the possibility of disease. Accordingly, Drew Leder has described disease as the 'dys-appearance' of the body. My healthy body normally belongs to the unquestioned background of my everyday activities. It only catches my attention 'at times of dysfunction or problematic operation':[15]

> In order to understand the principle at play here, it is useful to refer back to Heidegger's discussion of the tool. Heidegger notes that the 'ready-to-hand' tool withdraws insofar as it functions unproblematically. We concern ourselves with the work and its goals, the 'towards-which' the tool is used. Only when the tool manifests a certain 'un-readiness-to-hand' by virtue of becoming unuseable, missing, or standing in the way, must we take explicit account of it. It stands forth as 'present-at-hand' because of a dysfunctional break in its employment.[16]

The body, like the tool, withdraws from our sight when it functions properly but it appears in the foreground or 'dys-appears' in the case of dysfunction, hunger or pain. This is similar to Wittgenstein's remark about familiarity: feelings of familiarity are not present in our normal dealings with the environment, but they may be triggered by the contrast with some unexpected element. Analogously, in human relations we would not think of our present attitudes as involving trust unless something happened to highlight the possibility of betrayal. Annette Baier has an idea of this complexity when she observes that trust is often 'posthumous'.[17] Trust would often pass quite unnoticed until, as Baier puts it, 'our vulnerability is brought home to us by actual wounds'.[18] Trust is the air we breathe, and 'we notice it as we notice air, only when it becomes scarce or polluted'.[19] In the words of J. M. Bernstein, 'trust tends to become visible only through breakdown'.[20] Conversely, it 'turns out to be most effective or most fully actual when it remains unnoticed: trust ideally occurs as the invisibility of trust'.[21]

This means first of all that we are not likely to *think about* the trust we harbour towards others except in connection with some suggestion of betrayal. But there is a further point that comparisons with tools, bodies and the air fail to capture. Those things exist in an obvious physical sense, whether or not we take notice of them. The 'existence' of trust does not seem in the same way independent of our attitudes towards 'it' or of our propensity to talk about 'it'. Admittedly, mental states exist and may at times be picked out by the word 'trust', but the word can latch on to any such state only when the appropriate context is in place. The comparison with grief highlights the need of context: a state of mind is identified as grief when a background of bereavement is present. Another comparison, good for this limited purpose, can be made with the concept of *having a reason*. Reasons are mainly something that may be invoked or dismissed. In a sense, reasons have no 'existence' of their own independently of thinking beings engaged in some form of deliberation. The condition for talk of reasons, roughly speaking, is that there should be a question in the air to which they may provide answers. At the same time, something else does 'exist' here regardless of whether it is invoked as a reason: namely, the facts that may or may not be mobilized for this role. Analogously, my attitude towards you may or may not be identified as an attitude of trust depending on the background.

The 'dys-appearance' of trust takes the form of a reaction, of giving a specific form to possible or actual disappointment. In the most central case, it comes in the form of moral criticism: when 'I trusted you' (and 'you trusted me', 'he trusted her', etc.) is a reaction to betrayal, trust makes itself felt as something unjustly 'broken'. In another kind of case, I am made aware of my trust in you because my eyes open to the hardships or temptations that you must face so as not to let me down. Now my trust in you 'dys-appears' in the form of gratitude and sympathy. In both cases, trust makes itself manifest in the experience of a morally significant relation, one that has either been violated or preserved in face of challenges.

The appearance of trust as 'dys-appearance' – including both the advantages and possible pitfalls of that insight – is brought into focus in Harold Garfinkel's celebrated 'breaching experiments', briefly discussed in the previous chapter.[22] Garfinkel asked his students to put various everyday attitudes to test by engaging in unexpected behaviour and waiting for reactions. His idea was to demonstrate the presence of trust in social interaction by deliberately introducing scepticism and distrust, highlighting the destructiveness of such breaches of the normal run of things. Students were, for instance, instructed systematically to engage others, mainly friends, roommates and family members, in conversation while imagining that the latter were trying systematically to mislead them.

> The attitude was difficult to sustain and carry through. Students reported acute awareness of being 'in an artificial game,' of being unable 'to live the part,' and of frequently being 'at a loss of what to do next' [...] One student spoke for several when she said she was unable to get any results because so much of her effort was devoted to maintaining an attitude of distrust that she was unable to follow the conversation [...] With many students the assumption that the other person was not what he appeared to be and was to be distrusted was the same as the attribution that the other person was angry with them and hated them.[23]

In another experiment, the students tape-recorded discussions and finally produced the recording device in front of their unsuspecting interlocutors.[24] The reactions of the latter, as would be expected, were ones of extreme annoyance. Garfinkel concluded that we normally enter interaction with a large number of unself-conscious expectations – for instance, expecting our words to be taken as meant and expecting the discussion not to be tape-recorded. As he put it, '[a] society's members encounter and know the moral order as perceivedly normal courses of action – familiar scenes of everyday affairs, the world of daily life known in common with others and with others taken for granted'.[25]

If we were to be exposed to the treatment given to Garfinkel's victims we would no doubt see it as a breach of trust. Indeed the unease felt by the students who carried out the procedures shows they saw themselves as betraying the trust of their interlocutors.

Garfinkel interpreted the result as implying that our everyday dealings with people are accompanied by constant feelings of trust, feelings that the experiments brought to light. That would open the door to a kind of metaphysics of feelings where constant and rather exotic expectations lie at the bottom of our mental lives. We are made aware of them in exceptional situations, just as the existence of kidneys in our bodies may be brought home to us in the event of kidney failure.

However, as Rod Watson points out in his discussion of Garfinkel, the latter used his breaching experiments 'mainly as teaching devices and abandoned them after a few weeks'.[26] This seems to be connected with Garfinkel's changing view of what he had achieved. He realized that the background expectations that the procedures made visible may more plausibly be seen as *artefacts* created by the experiments themselves. What happened was not so much the uncovering of a previously unacknowledged element of trust as the unexpected intrusion of a *new* complication. We have presumably never learned explicitly to assume that others do not tape-record our everyday discussions. One might rather say that a normal discussion between persons who trust each other is marked by the *absence* of expectations of this kind – as opposed to, say, what might be a real issue with telephone conversations between businessmen involved in complex lawsuits. Thus while Garfinkel's experiments can be correctly described as breaches of implicit trust, one may ask in what sense such trust was 'present' in the minds of the research subjects before the experiments were carried out.

As a general statement, it seems correct that we on the whole expect our friends not to tape-record our conversations and to give our words the best possible interpretation. This can be said, for instance, in order to contrast normal interaction with manifest breaches of trust. At the same time, it would be odd to say we have these expectations every time we engage in conversation. My claim is: we should not think that there is a 'factual' disagreement here. The question is instead: When does it make sense *to speak of us* as having a particular expectation? Similarly, there is the question of exactly when it can be meaningfully claimed that a given instance of social life involves trust. Talk of trust implies a perspective where something that might otherwise be perfectly natural reveals a problematic aspect.

First- and third-person perspectives

The characteristic way in which unproblematic trust withdraws from sight creates a kind of disparity between first- and third-person perspectives. To trust is *not to* expect betrayal and *not to* take precautions. Someone who observes me might nevertheless (rightly or wrongly) believe that I am running the risk of betrayal. Yet from my own point of view I am not *taking* a risk. You might respond: 'You think so from *your own* point of view; but the risk nevertheless exists and it can be seen by *others*.' However, as we saw in Chapter 3, assessments of risk are dependent on ideas of what is reasonable, which in turn depend on the perspectives we take. It would be misleading to ask quite generally which perspective is the *right* one. In any case, at present I am not concerned with the rightness of the possible perspectives but with the fact itself that my trust is expressed in the form of such incommensurability. It seems generally to hold that the more unquestioningly I trust my friend (as described from an observer's perspective), the less likely will I be to *say or think* that I trust her.

I ask for my friend's confidential advice without fearing that she will pass on embarrassing details about me to outsiders. Admittedly, the fact that I speak of myself as seeking 'confidential' advice already implies that I am to some degree aware of the exceptional character of the situation. Similarly, my description of certain information as 'embarrassing' indicates that I have considered the need to protect my privacy. But it is not necessary to assume that I am thinking of our tête-à-tête in those terms at all. Perhaps I seek my friend's advice as a matter of course. I am not likely to *describe* my attitude towards my friend as trustful unless reasons for not trusting have already been brought up by someone. Thus in a sense, trust is in the eye of the beholder: you can see my attitude as one of trust precisely because *I* am not thinking of it in those terms. To speak of trust is to imply the possibility of betrayal, but the person who trusts is not going to see betrayal as possible. The present section will flesh out this apparent paradox and then discuss reasons why it is not a paradox after all.

I do not suspect my friend of trying to steal from me. But there is a difference between what I would naturally say of my own case and what might be said by others, or what might be said at a general level. Suppose my friend is coming over for dinner. Do I also *trust* that she is not going to pocket the family silver? The reader might reply, 'Of course!' because I would probably refrain from inviting anyone whom I cannot trust on this score. Similarly, as a general description it seems fair to say that people who invite others to their homes do not suspect them of stealing. But if you were to ask me the question in a real situation I would probably not answer 'Of course!' but 'What do you mean?' In other words, what makes you ask this silly question? Are you trying to tell me something? Furthermore, the fact that the example probably strikes the reader as silly indicates that there is something not quite right about the claim that we trust our friends in normal circumstances not to steal the family silver. Almost no one would spontaneously make that claim in one's own case, even though one might agree with it as a general description of the difference between receiving a friend in one's home and receiving a complete stranger.

Let us change the example slightly. When my friend enters, I *tell* her, 'I trust you, of course, not to pinch the family silver.' One obvious oddity here is that if my utterance comes across as a serious expression of anything at all, it will reasonably be seen as an expression of distrust. But the oddity goes deeper. It is not just that it is strange that I should say this because my trust in my friend's honesty is too self-evident for me even to bring it up; after all, sometimes we also state self-evident things. It would not even be clear *what* it is I am saying. Is it a joke? A jibe at someone else I cannot trust? Is it a warning? It cannot be answered that the statement should simply be taken at face value, because in this situation it just does not have an obvious face value. In any case, it is not simply a description of my trustful frame of mind. My utterance could only be understood against the background of imaginable suspicions of some kind. Thus the statement, 'I trust you' appears, in this situation, to question the very relation I am assumed to be describing.

On the other hand, suppose I later find out that my friend really stole something from the house. If you now ask me why I did not take any precautions, my spontaneous answer would be, 'I of course trusted her'. At this later point, 'I trusted her' comes across as a true description of my attitude in the past situation. It explains and justifies my behaviour. Yet it does not follow that, at the earlier point in time, I could have meaningfully used the phrase 'I trust her not to steal' in the present tense. The applicability of my description to the past circumstances now seems to depend on the problematic situation that develops *afterwards*. But doesn't this imply that the facts in the past (my attitude to my friend at the time) have somehow changed because of a *later* event (the discovery of a theft)? That, on the other hand, looks inadmissible; surely if the description of my attitude at the past point in time is *true*, it must be so because of what took place *then* and not because of something that happened at a later point – and then it must have been possible for me also truthfully to say it at the earlier point? Thus a certain kind of 'realism' about mental descriptions would seem to require that the *right* description of my state at t_1 must be the same regardless of what happens at t_2. Yet it now seems that the meaningfulness of the description at t_1 depends on what happens at t_2.

One might perhaps want to respond that there is no paradox here. It might be suggested that the facts of the matter remained the same all along, but it was not *appropriate* of me at the time to bring them up. The first-person description, 'I trust(ed)', was in both cases a *true* description of my psychological state.[27] But that response would still concede that there would have been something inappropriate about bringing up the subject at the earlier point; it would have naturally indicated suspicion, while the same expression (allowing for the change from present to past tense) at the later point would be employed precisely to indicate that there was no suspicion. At any rate it would then be agreed that the implications of 'I trust(ed)' would *change* between the two situations, which still retains the paradox I have identified.

The sense of paradox is created by the 'realist' insistence that the phrase, 'I trust(ed) her' describes definite 'facts of the matter' – for instance, a mental state of trusting that either was or was not present in my consciousness. Given such a view, it does seem odd that I cannot describe my ongoing state of trust without apparently falsifying it. The paradox does not arise, however, if we think instead of my utterance as my way of *justifying* my past behaviour. Later developments do not change the facts of the past, but by changing the significance of those past facts they give a meaningful role to my utterance. On this reading, 'I trusted her' states the reason (the justification of) why I was not keeping an eye on my (ex) friend's movements. The analogy with the discourse of reasons is helpful once more. The apparent paradox is cleared up by moving talk of trust from the space of mental descriptions to the space of reasons.[28] Like when we appeal to reasons, we talk about trust as a response to specific challenges.

The need for challenge

Similar considerations made Wittgenstein, in his discussions with G. E. Moore and Norman Malcolm, and in the notes subsequently published as *On Certainty*, to question the meaningfulness of some of Moore's statements.[29] Moore insisted that he, looking at his hands, knew for certain that he had two hands. While pointing to a tree trunk standing a yard away in broad daylight, he knew it was a tree. The absurdity of it all lay not simply in the fact that these things were too obvious for anyone to state. There was nothing to contradict the assertion that Moore knew these things, but it was unclear what the assertions came down to. What was the certainty that Moore wanted to *defend*? Moore's utterances had no definite meaning – he had not really stated anything – as long as he had not identified an intelligible challenge to which they would constitute an answer.[30] Wittgenstein comments:

> I should like to say: Moore does not *know* what he asserts he knows, but it stands fast for him, as also for me; regarding it as absolutely solid is part of our *method* of doubt and enquiry.[31]

Wittgenstein's caveat, 'I should like to say…' indicates that he is not entirely happy with his formulation. He can still discern why someone might want to speak of the situation as a case of 'knowing', only it does not strike him as helpful. Perhaps we should say: the general certainty characteristic of getting about in one's familiar environment cannot be readily articulated in terms of 'knowing'.[32] Such talk would presuppose a running discourse where expressions of doubt and requests of evidence come into play. But barring some complication such as failure of eyesight, the idea of 'knowing that *that* is a tree' has no obvious role to play:[33]

> Someone says irrelevantly 'That's a tree'. He might say this sentence because he remembers having heard it in a similar

situation; or he was suddenly struck by the tree's beauty and the sentence was an exclamation; or he was pronouncing the sentence to himself as a grammatical example; etc., etc. And now I ask him 'How did you mean that?' and he replies 'It was a piece of information directed at you'. Shouldn't I be at liberty to assume that he doesn't know what he is saying, if he is insane enough to want to give me this information?[34]

On the other hand it might be said that there still was a sort of challenge to which Moore was responding. We can imagine Moore saying that he knows something is a tree in response to *someone else's* doubts about his eyesight. More to the point, Moore made his (purported) assertions about what he 'knows' in the general philosophical context created by sceptical questions about the external world. In such a context there may perhaps be a point in reminding us of the unreflective certainty characteristic of our dealings with familiar objects.[35] Moore's 'proof of an external world' may be seen as an (arguably misleading) attempt to formulate this familiarity in terms of 'knowing'.

You ask me whether I trust my friend not to steal from me. In most normal circumstances I would not understand your question any more than I would if I were asked in the park whether I know that what I see in front of me is a tree. Suppose then that, after thinking a while, I take your question seriously after all. That will be because I come to see some way in which you have formulated a realistic challenge. Perhaps you have told me about your own bad experience with a friend of yours. By introducing a complication, you have raised a *new* question to which I can now relate. Suppose I tell you I nevertheless trust my friend. By saying this, I vouch for her against your implicit suspicion. This is to bring the trustful relation to the foreground: I am no longer taking it as self-evident, but now I contrast it against your imaginable suspicion. This is, however, not to say I must now also be suspicious; only that I understand that others may, for good or bad reasons, harbour suspicions that are alien to *me*. Thus the philosophical claim here is not that I cannot say (or think) that I trust someone without engaging in performative contradiction.[36] The claim is instead that we say these things not as simple 'pieces of information' but as responses to challenges of some kind.[37] Similarly, meaningfully ascribing trust to a *third* person presupposes that one speaks within a certain context. David Cockburn presents an example:

> One relevant kind of context is of this form: while neither those spoken of, nor the person speaking of them, takes there to be a possibility of the one letting the other down, someone else – perhaps the one addressed – does take there to be such a possibility. For example, Mary is aghast at John's willingness to lend £100 to someone who approached him in the street. I explain: 'He trusts her. They are neighbours'.[38]

In this case, a meaningful context is in place for the attribution of trust because of the disparity between two perspectives. David understands Mary's question because he sees the discrepancy between her epistemic situation and that of John and of his own.

In sum, our uses of 'trust' show characteristic discrepancies depending on the perspective from which it is used. One way to put the point at issue is by saying that the formula, 'A trusts B', or 'A trusts B to ɸ', does not have a stable meaning (or sense) regardless of who 'A' and 'B' are. To take up just a few possibilities: If *you* are A, and *I* am B, I will perhaps take your remark ('I trust you') as a reminder of a promise I have made ('I trust you to write that letter'). If A and B are two of our mutual acquaintances, your remark may be a description of A's general attitude towards B. It may belong to your description of some undertaking in which A is implicitly relying on the help of B. It may imply criticism of B (for letting down A), or criticism of A (for unthinkingly taking the help of B for granted).[39] 'A trusted B' may be a way to absolve A of the blame of recklessness. The formula does not pin down a unitary kind of attribution, now applied to you and me, now to A and B. It makes a difference to whom you say it, and about whom you say it.

Conclusion

The main observation of this chapter was that it seems impossible to identify a specific mental state of trusting, and in any case the presence of such a state would not constitute the criterion of correctness for attributions of 'trust'. Trust is often unself-conscious and shows itself precisely in the fact that *I* am not thinking of my attitude as one of trust. For this reason, one typical form for the manifestation of trust is 'dys-appearance'. The full extent and character of the trustful relation is not revealed when things go as they should, but it appears in the face of some challenge. This connects to a second point: the conditions for attributing trust are dependent on a characteristic discrepancy between first-person and third-person perspectives. The two points of this chapter are connected in that they both question a certain kind of 'realism' of mental descriptions. Utterances about trust are not descriptive statements in the narrow sense, but they place facts into a reasoning context; and the context will change depending on who is speaking and what the current situation is.

I take it that these points capture central features of how talk of trust works in everyday interaction. However, one cannot legislate about these things – about what people may or may not say. As I already argued at the beginning of this book, we should not expect any single definition to capture, or put constraints on, all phenomena to which the word 'trust' may be meaningfully applied. What we can do is describe some crucial language games where 'trust' makes its appearance. The vocabulary of trusting figures, so to speak, as a set of organizing tools that both describe and modify our understanding of the human relations to which it is applied. Hence, it also modifies the very context in which those relations are embedded. The utterances people make in a situation are *also* part of it, even though it is not up to them alone to decide exactly how their words will be taken. The general lesson of this chapter is that what trust 'is' is best seen not by looking for the psychological and behavioural phenomena the relevant words stand for, but by looking at situations where 'trust' *is raised* as an issue. In important cases at least, to raise the issue of trust is to activate a moral perspective.

CHAPTER SIX

Communication, truthfulness, trust

The focus of this chapter lies in the implications of a contrast between two possible ways to think of language and communication. Linguistic behaviour might be understood roughly as the activity of making sounds, from which conclusions may be drawn concerning the utterer, his or her intentions and beliefs. But this does not really add up to a fully fledged conception of speech as communication. On an alternative conception, to think of speech as communication is to think of the utterer as having something to say – which, as I will argue, implies preparedness to *believe* what is said. The idea of an utterance having a meaning implies the idea that the utterance has face value; and my argument will be that *that* implies that *taking* the utterance at its face value is the default stance. To see utterances as belonging to language in the first place cannot be understood apart from what has been called a commitment to the norm of truthfulness.

However, 'truthfulness' should not here be defined merely as the conformity of the speaker's declarative sentences with his or her beliefs and intentions. Also our performances as listeners may be truthful or otherwise. Truthfulness in communication presupposes that we are prepared to *receive* the speaker as intended. The possibility of linguistic meaning builds on a kind of mutual dependence that, in some cases and for some purposes, may be described as trust. For which purposes? Addressing this question finally requires us to consider a way in which philosophical discourse is not a perspective-free enterprise. The meaningfulness of what is said in it depends on how far we are able to take seriously the perspective that it invokes. Thus the question of meaningfulness in philosophy is also a question about our own attitudes as philosophers.

Communication as manipulation and mind-reading

In his book *Trust: Self-interest and Common Good*, Marek Kohn writes:

> The conundrum of language is that an animal clever enough to speak seems too clever to be believed. [...] [N]o evolutionary innovation has done more to increase the potential for deception than language. [...] [T]he central problem for an evolutionist interested in animal signals is why they are reliable. Language poses this question in its most intriguing form. How could a signalling system that facilitates deception become established in an intelligent social species? As hominids began to speak, how did they find reason to believe each other?[1]

Kohn cites work by Richard Dawkins and John Krebs.[2] The very features of behaviour that make the transmission of information possible also make deception possible and sometimes advisable – and, it seems, in some cases next to inevitable. The ultimate function of communicative behaviour, as of any behaviour, is to enhance the animal's fitness – mainly, the transmission of the animal's genetic material to the next generation. This typically requires ensuring the animal's survival and chances of mating. If those goals are best served by deception, deception will be functional from an evolutionary point of view. On the other hand, it will not necessarily be functional for anyone *else* to believe the messages the animal sends out. This invites the question how a system of communication could be established at all in such circumstances. A classical Prisoners' Dilemma-type situation ensues. Short-term individual gains always seem to trump both long-term interests and the interests of the collective.

The scenario is built on a specific view on language and communication. Kohn sums up:

> An animal will often pursue its interests [...] by manipulating

objects in its environment. If the object is inanimate, the animal must apply physical force to make it move. If it is animate, the animal may be able to induce it to make the desired movements itself, by sending it signals. This form of manipulation is called communication. [...] Communication could be characterized, Dawkins and Krebs say, 'as a means by which one animal makes use of another animal's muscle power'. It can be said to occur 'when an animal, the actor, does something ... to influence the sense organs of another animal, the reactor, so that the reactor's behaviour changes to the advantage of the actor'.[3]

This view on communication is thoroughly Hobbesian. Just as the individual's relation to the inanimate environment consists in looking for benefit and avoiding harm, the point of communication is to steer the movements of *animate* objects in ways that serve one's interests. But the target individual – the 'reactor' in Krebs and Dawkins' terminology, sometimes also called 'the victim' – obviously thinks in the same way in return, which introduces an additional difficulty. Reactors will be disposed to act only if it seemingly lies in *their* fitness interest to perform the movements indicated to them. In a later essay Krebs and Dawkins develop this idea further by suggesting that communication has the twin aspects of manipulation and mind-reading.[4] Communication induces the reactor to perform movements, but it also serves as the basis for the reactor to draw conclusions about the actor's state of mind and future behaviour. The latter feature of course implies an additional need on the part of the actor to develop methods of obfuscation, since it may often lie in the actor's interest to protect its mind from being read. Thus we have a kind of arms race of increasingly sophisticated mind-reading techniques pitted against developing methods of manipulation and obfuscation.

These conclusions are radical enough, but the account just cited is still an understatement of the difficulties that must have been involved in the development of language if anything like the scenario just presented is assumed. The authors think that communicating animals at some point are faced with the question of whether the opposite party is to be *believed*. But the question is whether they could get as far as asking that question. The account of communication as manipulation raises the question of how the reactor could ever get past simply viewing the communicative act as a natural sign in the same sense as heavy clouds indicate impending rain, fever indicates illness, and a peacock's handsome tail is a natural sign of its physical fitness. Unless a qualitative leap of some kind is assumed, the reactor will perceive acts of communication as so many indications of facts about the *actor*. There seems to be no reason for the reactor to think of communicative behaviour as something to be believed, as opposed to something to use as evidence for drawing conclusions about the actor and its circumstances. Then, of course, communication cannot be *disbelieved* either and thus it in a certain sense cannot even count as communication. The idea of communication having content with face value comes across as strained: the sounds emitted by the actor are simply natural signs of *its* motives, including the possible motive to create confusion.

To put this in another way: insofar as a distinction can be made between successful and unsuccessful, good and bad communication, on this view it can only be made in terms of usefulness for prediction or manipulation. This of course flies in the face of the traditional idea of communication as transfer of information (an idea that certainly involves problems of its own, to be considered later on). As Dawkins and Krebs put it, 'If information is shared at all it is likely to be false information.'[5]

The authors view the conundrum sketched out in the first quoted paragraph as a practical problem, and they suggest it was gradually overcome in the animal world via the development of stable patterns of interaction. Lively research now exists on the role of deception in the animal world, a research area that for obvious reasons cannot be reviewed here. But the problem of deception not only concerns animals and the early stages of human prehistory during which language was presumably developed. Insofar as language is *essentially* seen as a matter of manipulation and mind-reading, the problems of the picture on offer are carried on to whatever communication takes place in present society. Alternatively, a qualitative leap must be imagined to occur somewhere on the way from animal to human. The introduction of language not only adds to available methods of deception but it creates a qualitatively new *type* of deception, differing from mere deceptive natural signs.

My diagnosis is this: The question of how truthful communication is evolutionarily possible is created at the theoretical level because the relations between language, sociality and rationality are seen as external ones. The individual is seen as the locus of ready-made motives largely identified as self-interest. Linguistic signs are mere vehicles for the pursuit of such ready-made motives, not contributing with anything qualitatively new – even though they admittedly increase the sophistication and complexity of the pursuit. A similar view is explicitly developed in the early chapters of Hobbes's *Leviathan*.[6]

But perhaps communication already in its animal stages needs to be conceptualized in some other, non-Hobbesian way. An alternatively imaginable original situation would be one where animals do a broad range of things together: fleeing predators, panicking, pursuing interesting smells, hunting, mating, fighting and playing. The notion of 'doing together' should in this case be understood as implying more than just coordinated individual performances. It indicates a sense in which togetherness appears 'primitive': we are to think of young animals as *first and foremost* joining their parents and peers in their activities and only then learning both the methods and merits of, say, picking worms or stalking a deer. In these pursuits a kind of mutual attunement develops – perhaps, as current neurobiological research suggests, enabled by the neuronal 'mirroring' of the animals' motor systems.[7] In these shared pursuits, cooperation and antagonism would be mixed from the very start and in many cases (e.g. in play) impossible to distinguish. The reasoning capacities of animals would develop along with the increasing variability of their shared activities; all this might be described under the collective heading of 'sociability' or 'mutual attunement'. On this alternative view the idea of rationally pursuing one's interests develops within sociability, not in opposition to it.

The qualitative difference between natural signs and language implies that the actor's linguistic behaviour is seen under the aspect of intentionality – in other words, as something essentially and not just accidentally related to meaningful content. The alternative view just sketched at least partly defuses the problem of how the qualitative shift was possible. If a kind of primitive sharing is assumed to lie at the bottom of communication, communication can be seen as just an extension of other shared pursuits which already imply shared intentions.[8] *This* is a solution to the evolutionary 'dilemma' about language.

Evolutionary biology is for evident reasons more behaviouristically oriented than most debate on human language. It cannot, for instance, countenance the suggestion that we should solve questions about animal intentions by asking animals what they are up to. Perhaps also for that reason, evolutionary approaches to language do not typically consider the distinction between linguistic and natural signs to be important. In contrast, the distinction is central in the current debate in the philosophy of language and epistemology on what is involved in *telling* things to others.

The testimony debate

Something of a minimal argument has been proposed for the idea that, if we are to understand language as having intentional content, the assumption of truthfulness is required as a necessary default stance. One version of this is the 'principle of charity' proposed by Donald Davidson. We can ascribe meaning to people's utterances only if we assume that the relation between their verbal behaviour and their beliefs is not completely random. We must presuppose correlation between the sounds people make and the conditions under which they would constitute true sentences.[9] For instance, we would then perhaps be able to establish a reliable connection between cold weather and people saying in their language, 'It's cold outside', just as we might observe a connection between the weather and seeing them bundled up against the cold.

However, it can be argued that the assumption of correlation would not yet introduce the difference between natural signs and language. It is a central feature of linguistic communication that we take utterances to be something to be believed (and occasionally disbelieved), not only evidence for drawing conclusions about the circumstances of the utterer. There is a difference between observing people from a window, drawing one's conclusions, and *being told by them* that it is cold outside. Richard Moran, in his paper 'Getting told and being believed', makes this point.[10] 'Being told' is something over and above merely confronting people's linguistic behaviour as a reliable indication of their beliefs.

Moran's paper is a contribution to the current lively philosophical debate on testimony, including work by C. A. J. Coady,

Richard Moran, Benjamin McMyler and others.[11] In this debate, 'testimony' means not mainly assertions made in courts of law and similar settings, but any statement that we take to be true *because* of the say-so of a person whom we trust. Testimonial knowledge is characterized by 'second-handedness', because the listener does not acquire knowledge by directly observing the facts. There are two interconnected main issues here. On what grounds can we justifiably say we know something *because* someone else has told us? Further, if knowledge by testimony is accepted as a species of knowledge, how does it compare epistemically with first-hand information based on experience?

Moran distinguishes between two possible views on the status of testimony, identified as the *Evidential View* and the *Assurance View*.[12] On the Evidential View, 'speech is seen as a kind of interpretable human behaviour like any other'.[13] Testimony is treated simply as evidence for deciding on the truth of what the speaker says. It is something from which we, as jurors, must draw conclusions for which we alone are responsible. Our claim to know cannot justifiably be based *simply* on the fact that someone has told us.

The popularity of the Evidential View may no doubt be traced to the fact that it connects seamlessly to the Empiricist theory of knowledge. As Moran points out, the rationale for it was formulated by that Empiricist philosopher par excellence, John Locke, and further argued for by David Hume.[14] If all our knowledge stems from sense perception, being told something is simply one more way for our senses to provide us with material to be processed by our rational faculties. The evidential model holds out the promise to assimilate testimony to a unitary conception of the justification of knowledge claims. I would indeed agree that, on one level of description, the Empiricist view must be said to be self-evidently true as soon as the idea of innate knowledge is disposed of. But it would be so on a very trivial level, namely in the sense that to hear anything at all *is*, if you like, to receive data from sense perception. However, Empiricism ignores the complexity of all the things that might be described as 'data from sense perception'.

A complexity particularly important in the present context is the way in which our *relation* to 'data' is mediated by our relations with other subjects. This was already discussed in Chapter 4. The Evidential View suggests in effect that our epistemic dependence on others is more or less a sort of *noise* that prevents us from getting an unbiased view of how things stand. Consider the fact that the individual witness wants to be believed; in other words, she intends to influence her listeners' beliefs. On the Evidential View, this very feature of testimony would tend to undermine its value as evidence, just as when 'evidence' is purposely planted by someone on a crime scene. Unintentional statements and signs – slips of tongue, blushing and so on – would provide us with less biased evidence about the speaker's real thoughts precisely because of their unintentional character.[15]

Benjamin McMyler distinguishes an additional variety of the Evidential View which he calls *the inheritance model*. On that model the justification of beliefs is 'inheritable'. The witness is treated as a 'believer' who apparently has good grounds for what she is claiming to be true.[16] Perhaps she has been around during the event now being discussed. Similarly, persons interviewed as expert witnesses can be assumed to have respectable reasons for their views. Nevertheless the final responsibility for assessing their statements remains with us, the audience. McMyler argues that this way of understanding testimonial knowledge still fails to consider what is distinctive about it, namely the fact that we justify our belief in testimony by deferring to the *authority* of the witness.

All varieties of the Evidential View ignore what Moran and McMyler would describe as the main distinguishing trait of our relation to testimony. When we relate to someone's words under the aspect of testimony, we do not take it simply to be human behaviour open to interpretation. We see it as an 'invitation to trust' by a witness 'assuming responsibility'.[17] Our relation to a witness, as McMyler puts it, involves 'epistemic right of deferral'.[18] Crucially, testimonial knowledge depends on 'relations of authority and responsibility existing between the addresser and the addressee'.[19] When we assert something and say it is true because we have heard it from someone, we are 'entitled to defer challenges to this content [of the testimonial statement] to the original speaker'.[20]

In sum, testimonial knowledge is *sui generis*. Its existence is accepted as a brute fact about our epistemic practices, somewhat similar to our ability to trust our senses.[21] Giving testimony is also in a certain way similar to making a promise. In both cases the original speaker assumes blame in case of falsity.[22] There is also a similarity between taking the witness at his or her words and obeying a command. In both cases, McMyler argues, we at least ostensibly do something for the only reason that *the other person says something*. 'It appears to be a reason that would not exist but for the authority the speaker assumes in addressing the reason to the audience.'[23] On the other hand, while the parallel is illuminating, it is arguably misleading in the sense that if we believe a person without further ado we do not *do* anything specific (we simply *do not* question her) and we do not offer reasons for believing, precisely because the truth of what is said is accepted at once.

Before considering this discussion further, it is worth noting that the Assurance View seems to work best with cases of normal *undisturbed* communication. One situation where we literally speak of witnesses giving testimony is a court case. But in that situation it is hardly correct to say the jurors accept testimony *simply* on the authority of the witness. *They* bear the final responsibility for their verdict. Jurors are expected to be sceptical of witnesses and to form their own opinion, even though it would not be quite right to say that testimonies have no authority at all apart from their status as possible evidence. In some cases – for instance, when children are interviewed as witnesses – a delicate balance may have to be struck between various ways of relating to testimony.[24] Thus we may, in communication, exhibit different degrees of 'evidentialist' attitudes towards our interlocutors while still accepting that the latter make justifiable claims to be speaking the truth. Also the concept of authority seems to be more at home in contexts in which someone's epistemic claims are disputed. When my friend tells me he has just come home from a visit to his aunt, it would usually sound strained to say I accept his 'testimony' about his journey on his 'authority'. The idea of invoking an *authority* presupposes a debate where the truth of what is said has been challenged or where it is otherwise natural to expect disagreement. I must return to this general line of objections in the end of the present chapter. But the objections notwithstanding, the Assurance View undoubtedly captures an important feature of our epistemic practices.

McMyler offers a helpful overview of the debate.[25] But he might be criticized for understating his case. He constantly contrasts reliance on testimony with other cases described as ones involving 'epistemic autonomy'. Those are supposedly cases where the agent comes to his or her 'own conclusions about things' somewhat along the lines of the Empiricist view. The implication is that 'autonomy' in the pure Empiricist sense does *not* involve believing the words of others. But it should be noted that the intelligibility even of the cases described as ones of the agent coming to independent conclusions is dependent on assuming the background of undisturbed communication. To think of epistemic autonomy and trust as two exclusive and rival approaches to knowledge would lead to absurd conclusions. For instance, it might then be possible to argue that learning to read tends to restrict one's epistemic autonomy, because it encourages one to read books instead of finding out about things for oneself. The more realistic view is surely that we enhance our epistemic autonomy precisely by relying on others.

McMyler presents the Evidential View and the Assurance View as descriptions of alternative but equal and mutually independent ways of collecting information from speech.[26] But as far as I can see, their relation is not symmetrical. At a very basic level, the idea of *attributing meaning* to a communicative act must be seen as internally related to preparedness in principle to accept knowledge by testimony. The speaker's words could not be intelligibly used as evidence at all – as a case of someone truly *or* falsely claiming something – unless we were prepared to consider speakers as possible sources of truth. In other words, our relation to speech involves *a form of* 'Assurance View' as a matter of course. We accept that it is possible for a listener to relate to the utterance as an assurance; once *that* is in place there is room also for rejecting it, as well as perhaps for further 'evidentialist' considerations about it. The intelligibility of other people is dependent on the default position of believing that their beliefs converge at the truth and that they generally tell us what they believe.[27] The starting point cannot be that people in general are *just as likely as not* to tell us the truth; that would not count as a neutral position but as general distrust of the possibility of communication.

The norm of truthfulness

In his essay 'Nature and convention', Peter Winch proposes what has subsequently become known as the 'life-form argument for truthfulness'.[28] He argues that 'the notion of a society in which there is a language but in which truth-telling is not regarded as the norm is a self-contradictory one'.²⁹ Even if we can tell someone a lie in an individual case, what we cannot imagine is a functioning language where the norm of truthfulness is not generally presupposed. Thus, 'adherence to the norm of truthfulness *goes along with* the distinction between true and false statements; without the one there could not be the other'.³⁰ The possibility of using communication deceptively, as in a game of cards between mutually distrustful card-sharpers, presupposes a background of practices where non-deception is the norm.³¹ Winch cites the case of Senator McCarthy, 'that arch-manipulator of reactions', who, it is reported, did not himself harbour any strong convictions beyond his personal pursuit of power:

> McCarthy's operations presupposed the existence of men who *were* true fanatics, who *could* experience true outrage and indignation, and so on. Similarly McCarthy's use of the 'paraphernalia of rationality' – stuffed brief-case, footnotes, etc. – in order to impress people presupposed the existence of the real thing: something that could not be accounted for in terms of its usefulness in getting people to do and believe certain desired things, but which implies that certain values are respected for their own sakes.³²

There are of course predecessors to Winch's argument, the most famous being Kant's thesis that by telling a lie, 'so far as in me lies I cause that declarations in general find no credit'.³³ Deception could not be made into a generally accepted practice, for that would annul the possibility of promising altogether. One potentially misleading way to frame Kant's point would be to say that if we wish to be believed, we cannot at the same time wish that telling lies should be generally acceptable. That statement in itself is true; but the formulation would be misleading because it would suggest the initial existence of something – the *wish* to be believed – and a subsequent conclusion concerning the right way to attain the pre-existent end, as if humankind had one day decided to institute a norm of truthfulness *because* they wished their statements to be believed. Such readings of Kant's argument are rendered implausible already because of Kant's well-known dismissal of means-to-ends reasoning in questions of morality. To think I must have a particular reason for telling you the truth is already to consider me a liar. But most of all, that rendering of Kant's argument would miss a more fundamental point. Without the norm of truthfulness there just would be no statements to start with. Truthfulness and communication come in a package: the wish to communicate *is* the wish on the whole to communicate truthfully. We cannot wish to speak *untruthfully* until truthfulness is established as the norm.[34]

How, then, is Winch's argument different from Kant's? I suggest one way of putting it: for Winch, the 'package' is larger than for Kant. It includes an entire way of life: when we think of rational discourse we must in the end think of people who address each other and who take each other to task for what they say and do. The very idea of a difference between true and false, which is constitutive of rational thinking, is tied up with a social life where we can be taken at our words. What we must now consider are the conditions for there *being such a thing* as taking someone at their words. We must presuppose a social life where people stand responsible before each other. In a life of that kind, saying something is to stand for it or to take the blame or ridicule if one cannot. To be rational is to be someone who can commit oneself to one's words and, via them, with those with whom one is speaking. Rationality, truthfulness and morality are connected; rationality exists *between* agents in the form of shared social practices.

This also implies, as far as I can see, that what is known as the obligation to honour one's promises is not a separate norm that might have been introduced at some time *after* meaningful communicative relations were established in the human population. Communication is already something akin to a promise. The rule that I bind myself to something by what I say is, on this view, not operative only when someone consciously invokes it, for instance in the context of speech acts that include versions of the phrase 'I promise'.[35] Words have meaning in the first place only 'in a society where people are so related that for one person to say something is for him to commit himself with others'.[36]

One more thing: truthfulness should not be equated with one-to-one correspondence between one's statements and reality. The commitment to truthfulness appears not to require some *particular* relation always to hold between one's words and facts about how things are. Truthfulness is not only required of declarative sentences about purported facts. Jokes and stories do not constitute exceptions to the norm of truthfulness but they are further developments of it. Truthfulness is not so much a commitment to the truth of one's *words* as a commitment to the truth of *one's relation to the interlocutor*. Wit and laughter and the responses to them are also expected to be 'truthful' as opposed to duplicitous or manipulative.[37] Think of the difference between harmless jokes and joking as a form of bullying. Humour is not always benign, but we could not imagine jokes to have developed as a practice unless the absence of all malice is generally taken to be the norm in joke telling.[38]

An objection to 'the life form argument' was raised by R. F. Holland.[39] While the life form argument shows that communication presupposes general adherence to truthfulness, it does not explain the weight that truthfulness may have in an individual's ethical outlook. This is a point that Winch subsequently recognized as justified,[40] but as far as I can see it does not affect his general argument. In fact it rather deflects from it, because it was hardly Winch's intention to come up with any kind of justification or explanation of the norm of truthfulness. It was not a concern of his at this juncture to discuss specific considerations that might guide a person's ethical commitments in an existing society. He wanted to express an idea of the whole package of society as a moral community, not to extract one part of it for separate treatment. Winch's discussion of Wittgenstein's *On Certainty* elsewhere makes his aims more obvious.[41]

'Nature and convention' is not written as a sustained critique of Hobbes, but it clearly was part of Winch's larger project of working out an alternative to the Hobbesian conception of the relation between social life and rationality. While Hobbes saw society as a collection of individuals whose cooperation must be established by appealing to their rational interests, Winch saw social life as a spontaneous creation whose origin is necessarily connected with the very development of rationality. This was not to say that society is rational or that the origins of society can be derived from rationality. Quite on the contrary, Winch thought that the kinds of ethical relation and relations of dependence that characterize social life are an *aspect* of our rationality. Practical reason is not to be seen simply as the faculty that enables us to reason from ends to means and vice versa. It comprises the entire web of practices and modes of thinking that together constitute *Homo sapiens* as a thinking being.

Thinking was then, for Winch, an essentially social activity, and sociality itself an aspect of thinking. The unity of human society is 'a unity essentially involving *concepts*'.[42] By sharing a 'grammar' in terms of which we make our world intelligible – by living in a shared intelligible world – we also stand in relation to one another. This is one illustration of Winch's claim that 'the social relations between men and the ideas which men's actions embody are really the same thing considered from different points of view'.[43] Such spontaneous unity of social life contrasts starkly with Hobbes's belief that a society can only be united by being subjected to the absolute power of the Sovereign. And it also contrasts with post-Hobbesian social theorizing insofar as such theorizing aims at solving the Hobbesian dilemma without questioning its starting points. In his description of the ethical relation that creates the communicative context, Winch also uses the word 'trust'.[44]

Løgstrup: Trust in conversation

In his work on the ethics of trust, the theologian K. E. Løgstrup highlights these issues. He starts from the observation that spontaneous trust is normally characteristic of human encounters. Generally speaking, we never assume from the very beginning that the person we meet is a liar; we do so only when we have already once caught him or her lying. We believe the other as it were in advance, even if he or she might be a complete stranger sitting next to us on a train.[45] These observations of course presuppose an assumption of normality, the idea being that the conditions that motivate scepticism should be treated as complications imposed on a simpler situation, a situation that logically counts as the norm. Løgstrup's idea of basic trust has also relevance to the question of what commitment to truthfulness may mean. He writes about our responsiveness to a tone of voice:

> Trust in an elementary sense belongs to every conversation. In the mere conversation the speakers expose themselves, which shows itself in the fact that in the mere act of addressing the

other a certain demand is directed to the other [...] [I]n the address as such – regardless of whether the content is of importance –, a certain tone is struck, in which the speaker, so to say, goes outside himself or herself, so as now to exist in the relation of the address to the addressee [...] Not listening to the tone that the speaker has struck or refusing to hear it is therefore to ignore the speaker's self, insofar as the speaker himself or herself has ventured forward in it. The fact that all speech is embedded in such elementary trust is also shown by the fact that even a completely trivial remark will ring false if the speaker does not believe it will be received in the spirit in which it is meant.[46]

Løgstrup also speaks of us as 'delivering' more or less of our lives 'into the hands' of the other.[47] This perhaps involves unnecessary dramatization, in some situations at least. As he points out, this relation may come down to something as little as spoiling one's mood for the moment, but it may also be something so terribly important that one's entire life hangs in the balance.[48] Løgstrup's emphasis on 'striking a certain tone' in the communicative situation and receiving it from others in the right way highlights an important but usually neglected aspect of truthfulness. *Saying something* is not to be seen as the one-sided but possibly reciprocated act of a speaker laying his cards on the table. The speaker's utterance gets its meaning in being taken up by the addressee; it is not complete in itself. Thus 'truthfulness' in communication is itself dependent not only on its content and the relation of the content to the truth, but on the communicative relation between speakers. I am painfully reminded of this when I hope to offer an apology but forgiveness is refused. I might then say without dramatizing that the other holds my life in her hands. Other examples of my tone of voice being refused would be: intending to tell a joke and being met with a blank face; bringing up a grievance and being told to stop whining. This sort of giving and taking and feeling one's way about is something very typical of communication as a whole. Inch by inch we venture out on the thin ice between us and see how far it will carry us. Our relations deepen or stagnate as we subtly encourage or reject such closeness. This sort of venturing out to meet the other involves trust, Løgstrup says, regardless of whether the content of what is said is of any inherent importance.

Løgstrup's last sentence in the quoted paragraph – about one's remark 'ring[ing] false' – is not an empirical thesis about how the speaker's voice *sounds*. If it were so it would be a mistaken empirical claim, for it is obviously possible for a good actor falsely to use a tone of voice that sounds convincing. Løgstrup is making a point about the nature of the relation between the speaker and the addressee. The suspicion that my utterance will not be received as intended brings into it a sense of loss of immediacy. My voice sounds awkward because the *situation* is awkward.[49] Thus there is a demand of trust directed both to the speaker and to the addressee: to the speaker that she should venture forward with what she really thinks, and to the addressee that he should meet the speaker with interest and openness.[50]

Cockburn remarks in his discussion of Løgstrup that conversation for him is '*a form of contact* between human beings'.[51] To consider a contrast: overhearing a remark is also a way in which we may find out about things by listening to people's speech, but it would not be a form of contact with them.[52] And, as in Boye's novel, confessions may be wrought out of people. But these situations would not involve an ethical demand of mutual truthfulness. In communication as contact, the speaker addresses the listener and may be held accountable by him. Correspondingly, the justified expectation is created that the addressee should give the speaker's words the best possible construction. Cockburn points out that these requirements and this kind of trust are the natural context for this kind of contact, not means to some further end; for instance, they are not in place 'in order' for communication to be possible.[53] This way of looking at communication also redirects our focus away from mere questions of the factual accuracy of the communicated content, to the wider sense in which the relation itself embodies 'truthfulness' or lack thereof. To see communication merely as the transfer of information is to ignore its more fundamental role as a relationship between the speakers who, to a greater or lesser degree, show openness and commitment towards each other. Cockburn writes, developing Løgstrup's view:

> Conversation is a form of contact between people; and in so far as I have no interest in the *person*[54] – in so far as my interest in what she says, in what she *means* by her words, relates purely to my need of information or my ability to predict or control

her future behaviour – there is a sense in which I am not talking with (talking *with*) her at all.[55]

'Image' vs real presence

For Løgstrup, truthfulness is established in the communicative relationship when the speaker's words are really meant and are taken up as meant. He points out, however, that communication is often marred by what he calls 'images'[56] of the other. Instead of seeing others for what they are, we talk to the images we make for ourselves of 'the kinds of' person we are presumably facing. As communication proceeds and deepens, the physical presence of the other typically makes the 'image' collapse as reality takes its place.[57] On the other hand, Løgstrup also discusses a case where 'image' wins over real presence.[58] In this example from E. M. Forster's *Howards End*, a meeting takes place between the chief protagonists, Leonard Bast and the Schlegel sisters. Their relations are disturbed from the start because of their preconceived ideas about the sort of person the other clearly is. They rely on stereotypes supported by visual cues such as dress, furniture and general demeanour, signals of social status in a highly class-conscious society. Thus even the bodily presence of the other, considered in this wide sense, can keep us from finding each other because each of us is really just attending to the paraphernalia with which we always surround ourselves.

Prince Myshkin, the hero of *The Idiot* by Dostoevsky, illustrates both the hold of the 'image' over us and the emancipatory power of trust. Gloria Origgi briefly discusses Myshkin in her concise and readable book on the philosophy of trust. The novel has many ambiguities but Origgi, probably in agreement with most readers, would describe its hero as trustful and innocent. Myshkin's attitude towards Nastasia Filippovna is of particular interest, a relationship to which the book owes its main dynamic tension. In St Petersburg society, Nastasia is seen as a woman of doubtful reputation. In contrast with everyone else, Myshkin believes in her immediately; she in return describes him as 'the first human being that [she has] seen in [her] life'.[59] Origgi describes Myshkin's attitude as an expression of his innocence. She writes:

Myshkin [...] arrives in St Petersburg, to a sensual, cruel and corrupt society, with an outlook full of naïveté and goodness [...] Myshkin's trust in others, in everyone, is a sentiment not motivated by self-interest, but based on his ignorance of human nature, on his pure and naïve outlook on the world. And yet his trust has the wonder-working quality of transforming the people he meets, of making them alive to a dimension of their selves that had previously been beyond their reach.[60]

Origgi is right to emphasize the transformative powers of Myshkin's trust. It is an example of how the truthfulness of one speaker begets truthfulness in the other. But I do not think the description of Myshkin as innocent and naïve captures his most crucial features. The book itself leaves this point remarkably open; the other characters of the novel are constantly of different minds about him. The narrative includes several instances of Myshkin seeing through the schemes of others, even though he sometimes knowingly goes along with them nevertheless. Thus he does not generally come across as more naïve than those who try to fool him. While different readings of the novel are possible, it seems to me that interpretations of Myshkin as simply ignorant of the ways of the world have the drawback of diminishing his relevance, even though I am sure Origgi would not want to do that. We may admire the innocence of a child but we cannot emulate it, and it does not directly challenge our self-understanding as adults. If Myshkin's trust in Nastasia is described as an outcome of his naïveté, the net result is to dismiss a more serious suggestion: that Nastasia is *not* a malicious forlorn creature, that Myshkin was right about her while others were blinded by prejudice.

The dismissal of Myshkin's challenge to social convention serves to prop up the culture of self-congratulation typical of the society of which Dostoevsky offers us a glimpse. Dostoevsky often plays with the contrast between convention and reality by letting his narrative voice adopt the polished tone of this *soi-disant* high society. The narrator describes its leading members in a language of the very kind in which they would presumably have liked to present themselves. The wealthy Afanasy Ivanovich Totsky is characterized as:

> a man of fine appearance and dignified character, tall, rather stout, a little bald and turning grey. He had soft, pendulous,

rosy cheeks and false teeth. He wore his clothes loose and well cut, and his linen was always exquisite. His plump white hands were pleasant to look at. On the first finger of his right hand he wore a costly diamond ring.[61]

Totsky is 'of artistic temperament and extraordinary refinement'.[62] But as the plot unfolds the reader is left in no doubt that this 'great admirer of feminine beauty' is completely unscrupulous with women.

Nastasia's redoubtable past consists entirely of the fact that Totsky, her then legal guardian, has sexually abused her from age sixteen, 'calmly and happily in tasteful surroundings'.[63] At twenty-four, she is no longer living with Totsky. She is now proving an embarrassment to him – although 'he could at once have got rid of the annoyance by some trifling and quite pardonable [!] piece of villainy'.[64] Totsky would like somehow to stuff her away; and now conveniently Ganya, a minor official, is willing to marry her for money. Ganya's employer, General Epanchin, apparently has further plans to induce him later to 'selling [his] wife' to him.[65] While everyone agrees privately that Nastasia's life is now impeccable – she is 'a woman of virtuous life'[66] – the stain of lost female virtue [sic] can never be removed.

Myshkin is the only one fully to see through this charade. He perceives Nastasia as a woman grievously wronged. His refusal to condemn her is an expression of his ability to look past the socially defined persona. In this way, he is an exponent of the capacity that Simone Weil describes as *attention*: the readiness to receive what the other has to say without reading one's own ideas into it. Weil remarks in her essay 'Human personality' that this kind of attention is compatible with saying to someone, '*your person* does not interest me' but not, '*You* do not interest me'.[67] This is a consistent trait in Myshkin's actions; he does not adjust his talk to differences of class, gender or even age group. In an early chapter, Myshkin is detained in talk with a footman while waiting to be received in General Epanchin's house:

> The prince's conversation seemed simple enough, yet its very simplicity only made it more inappropriate in the present case, and the experienced attendant could not but feel that what was perfectly suitable from man to man was utterly unsuitable from a visitor to a manservant.[68]

In a word, this attitude is one of *Sachlichkeit*, of letting people's utterances and actions count for what they are, not as moves in a social game. Myshkin is a realist in a more real sense than the men of the world crowding in on him and Nastasia. He listens to *them* and not to images they make of themselves; and he *listens* to them instead of shoehorning their words into his plans and ideas.

The place of 'trust' in different ideas of language

The three main arguments about communication that I have viewed with sympathy – those of Moran and McMyler, Winch as well as Løgstrup and Cockburn – all tell us in some way that communication implies a kind of 'moral' relation between speaker and addressee. The speaker is accountable for her words and the addressee takes her on trust. There was a reason, however, for my use of scare quotes around 'moral' in the sentence above. In each of these cases, basically the same objection may be raised against the picture offered. I have hinted at different forms of it in my discussions of the individual cases. To put the worry in general terms: What is the *force* of claiming that our reliance on the speaker's words involves authority (as with Moran and McMyler), moral commitment (as with Winch) or trust (as with Løgstrup and Cockburn)? Each of these big words represents a concept that might be naturally invoked when something is *at stake*. But what kind of a role do they have in descriptions of unproblematic cases?

I will not be telling you, 'Tom told me about his holiday plans yesterday, and *I took him on trust*', except when hinting than Tom is up to some mischief. However, suppose there is nothing doubtful in the case and Tom went to see his aunt exactly as he told me. We would nevertheless not refer to my conversation with Tom as an example of his *truthfulness*, any more than a normal movement of my arm would typically count as a case of me 'trying' to move my arm and 'succeeding'. Such talk is meaningful when the normal course of life is disrupted. The concept of truthfulness is mobilized for instance when, as Holland puts it, '*not to falsify*' becomes 'a spiritual demeanour'.[69] I perhaps speak of Tom as someone committed to truthfulness when he refuses to tell lies despite strong external pressures. But by the same token, that is precisely a situation where the presence of undisturbed moral relations is *not* taken for granted.[70] In this way, it is difficult to see exactly what role one should give to the statement that communication involves a moral relationship. In the absence of *specific* contrasts between truthfulness and falsity, what would give life to the claim that my discussion with Tom involves truthfulness and trust?

On the other hand, one function of these philosophical statements is to contrast communication that proceeds as it should with illegitimate, manipulative instances. Somehow the latter are described as less 'real' instances of communication. But this also causes problems, for those manipulative actions *also* involve talking. How is it that these cases are less 'real'? The description of communication as involving commitment to truthfulness or trust thus might appear as either irrelevant (in routine undisturbed communication) or contingent (when something real is at stake).

The idea that gives mileage to this kind of talk must be that some sort of contrast is invoked; in normal or ideal communication, there is no distrust *despite* the fact that distrust *might* somehow be imagined plausibly to exist. My question of what might be meant by saying that 'all' communication implies a moral relationship is meant to be a real one, not my roundabout way of dismissing that description. The description is not – at least not in any simple way – a factual claim because deceitful communication does exist. Rather, it presents a perspective. The question to ask is what can be accomplished by making the claim; what the contrasting possibility is that the claim excludes.

Cockburn, who acknowledges this difficulty,[71] points out in response that the claim *does* have one natural place; namely, the philosophical debate, which itself creates a certain context. Our philosophical culture tends to treat doubt – concerning both people and the natural world – as the default position. In such an environment there is room for meaningfully claiming that trust is involved in all conversation.[72] The claim indicates refusal to accept the idea that the most fundamental aspects of our lives as social and thinking beings must be in doubt until external justifications are produced. This is then the context, or at least a part of it: the discourse of philosophical scepticism and Hobbesianism. The authors I have cited of course have partly different agendas. Moran and McMyler seem explicitly to want to rise to the sceptical challenge, while Winch wants to show the incoherence of the assumptions – in this case Empiricist and Hobbesian – that underlie scepticism about communication. Løgstrup in his turn tries to develop an understanding of the command to love one's neighbour.

However, while philosophical scepticism is an important part of the background picture, I do not think it is the whole of it. The idea of trust as inherent in normal communication is not only a corrective to confusion in an internal philosophical debate. The way in which it is more than *that* is related to the way in which Wittgenstein's *On Certainty* is not only, or even mainly, an attempt to refute scepticism. In that work Wittgenstein, on the one hand, describes the ordinary absence of doubt characteristic of our various pursuits, demonstrating that we as a matter of fact do not take scepticism seriously. On the other hand, by focusing on our everyday practices *generally* as something that involves 'certainty', 'trust', 'taking things for granted' or 'absence of doubt', he implicitly invokes a reflective perspective from outside those practices, a perspective from which normality appears as something remarkable and worthy of wonder. This *general* certainty is something different from the specific certainty that may characterize someone's actions. For instance, the work of an accomplished surgeon may be described as involving a degree of certainty as opposed to that of an apprentice. In *that* case, we wonder at a specific performance. Speaking of the general certainty now under consideration, however, the contrast is not one between more and less accomplished action but one between a natural and a reflective stance.[73]

The philosopher Christopher Robinson distinguishes between two kinds of perspective relevant for philosophical activity: the 'street-level view' of ordinary life and the mountaintop view of the 'observing theorist' looking at the layout of the city of language from above.[74] He speaks specifically of Wittgenstein's work, but the distinction seems more widely applicable – not only to philosophy but to our thinking activities as a whole, at least when they take on a philosophical aspect. By taking up a perspective from outside the practice immediately at hand – though not necessarily a view 'from nowhere' – we get a view of some feature of it that perhaps *ought* to strike us as puzzling. But this kind of 'ought' is conditional on the interest that we have in the matter; there is nothing to prove that this kind of reflective attitude is the universally correct one.

For instance, it is not a 'fact' that communication always implies trust, because that description could be easily defeated by citing examples of communication characterized by distrust. To say that *real* communication implies trust is, however, not to try to legislate about the right use of the word 'communication'. It is to highlight the fact that our concept of communication requires the distinction between genuine and corrupt cases as a general framework.

At a general level of this kind, the idea that communication implies trust is a defining feature of communication in the same sense in which the existence of the true-and-false dichotomy is a condition of logical thought. Real communication presupposes subjects committed to each other as sources of truth. The bottom line is this: Any understanding of what takes place in a communicative situation is conditional on how it relates to distrust and the absence of distrust. The possibility of distrust in communication is only possible against the background where trust is the default stance.

CHAPTER SEVEN

Basic trust

The notion of *basic* trust plays an important role in the philosophical trust debate. The idea is, in brief, that some form of generalized trust is necessary for human life and even sanity to prevail. We need to believe in the essential continuity of the social life around us, and we must act on the assumption that people generally are not hostile or out to deceive us. The idea of basic trust also implies that this attitude is essentially groundless; basic trust must be innate or primordial. Initially, we encounter the world with a self-evident sense of trust, a natural substratum for the subsequent growth of more reflexive approaches to the world of human and physical relations. This basic attitude is a 'protective cocoon' that shields us against the realization of our utter helplessness in the face of the world.[1] The cocoon bursts on some occasions, such as in the case of violent abuse, each time leaving the victim with profound doubts concerning the world and his or her own worth.

The different concerns that motivate talk about basic trust mostly appear together in the discussion, but for analytical reasons it is helpful to treat them separately. First of all, basic trust has been introduced as a local remedy to internal problems in rationalist-cum-individualist pictures of agency. It is recognized that their main assumptions about individual rationality leave in doubt whether reasoning of any kind could produce the sort of trust that normal social life seems to entail. Reason appears to stand on the side of scepticism. It appears that something is needed as a counterweight. The idea that the foundations of trust have a non-rational origin suggests a way out of this dilemma. While the authors who advance this view occasionally make use of research in developmental psychology, it must be stressed that the argument is independent of empirical results. Basic trust as a pre-rational condition of human agency is seen as an assumption forced on us *given the generally rationalist approach to social agency* otherwise typical of much of the debate.

The idea of basic trust may also be advanced as a way to question such rationalist understanding of agency instead of trying to patch it up. On this alternative view, interpersonal dependence and human reason come together. Taking others on trust is not merely a psychological precondition for rationality but is itself an aspect of human reason. For instance, in On Certainty Wittgenstein explores the fact that our thinking is *self-evidently* embedded in social contexts. The question *what* we can believe entails the question *whom* we can believe. Taking a critical or sceptical stance, while possible and often commendable in specific cases, cannot intelligibly take the form of wholesale scepticism because it always implies trust in some other direction.

Thirdly, the idea of basic trust has emotional plausibility, mainly as a way of describing cases where it is violated or absent. The traumatized condition of survivors of violent crime may be described as a generalized loss of trust in the world.[2] This kind of concern obviously points in a direction different from the questions about rationality just mentioned. The concept of basic trust becomes topical, not as a response to scepticism about rational agency, but as a vehicle for voicing the ethical dimension of human psychology. To say that someone's basic trust has been shaken is to say that he or she has been grievously harmed, without necessarily committing oneself to any particular theory about the psychological emergence of trust. It would, for instance, be a good way to describe Nastasia Filippovna of *The Idiot*. Speaking of certain kinds of harm as destructive of the subject's basic trust does not necessarily imply that the everyday experiences of those *not* thus harmed are characterized by constant feelings of trust. Thus it seems to me that at least some of the interest in the psychology of trauma shown in the philosophical debate owes its origin to concerns that call for an ethical language of trust. The ethical theme is pronounced in the work of writers such as K. E. Løgstrup and Simone Weil.

Trust as a response to scepticism

Trudy Govier, citing Laurence Thomas, describes 'basic trust':

> Basic trust, or basic social trust, is an expectation that others whom we do not know are not deliberately setting out to harm us – by lying, wounding, or killing [...] Without such basic trust, Thomas says, life would be 'unbearable' [...] Mundane activities such as sending children to school, driving, eating in restaurants, using subways, and shopping involve such vulnerability – whether we realize it or not.[3]

Examples from the philosophical literature might easily be multiplied. For instance, Niklas Luhmann claims, '[o]ne who goes unarmed among his fellow men puts trust in them'; 'a complete absence of trust would prevent him from even getting up in the morning'.[4] Without such background trust, Lorraine Code sums up, society would 'simply fall apart'.[5] For the most part the idea that life in society is inherently risky is taken for granted. In a thought-provoking essay on basic trust, J. M. Bernstein also develops this view on the all-pervading necessity of trust. He emphasizes that we need trust, but he also brings up what looks like an inescapable problem: the condition identified as 'the deliberative paradox of trust'. According to Bernstein, 'we would only rarely if ever, prospectively or retrospectively, be in possession of sufficient reason to adopt the stance of trust'.[6] Prospectively, in planning, trusting can only come out as an insecure option. Retrospectively, trust is most easily discerned where it has turned out to be misplaced. Bernstein writes:

> From the point of view of reason the only question could be: Can I take a trusting attitude toward this other? But once the question is put in this way, the requirement of reason is that in order to trust I must decide whether or not I have sufficient reason to take an affirmative attitude toward her. The question of reason must be a question of endorsing an attitude toward the other because once I place the other into question then I have taken a distance from her; I can only overcome that distance through coming to a judgment or decision in the affirmative. Nothing less will suffice.[7]

If I start to look for reasons for trusting, the game is already over. I am already looking at the other with suspicion, perhaps in the same way as I would already consider her a liar if I thought reasons are needed for believing that she tells me the truth. The starting point of the inquiry itself assures that my attitude can at most amount to reliance – that is, unless it is subsequently turned into genuine trust through a rationally unaccountable 'leap of trust'.[8] Thus what Bernstein identifies as 'the point of view of reason' cannot give rise to a general stance of trust. The argument is rather straightforward.[9]

On the whole Bernstein accepts Baier's entrusting theory of trust: trust means that we entrust others with some aspect of our well-being. Our acts of entrusting are rationally justified if they can be shown to contribute to our well-being. However, he believes that we could only rarely, if ever, put that theory into practice. Trust is not based on the rational assessment of available data because trust itself is a distorting unconscious 'filter' on the data. '[B]locking and distorting countervailing evidence', Bernstein argues, trust is 'blinkered in its interpretive outlook', implying 'partial insensitivity to deliberative scrutiny'.[10] Moreover, Bernstein believes that reason is not sufficient even for the more circumscribed task of motivating *reliance*. Strategic reasons for reliance could hardly prove rationally compelling. Any kind of reliance would by definition land us in a condition of vulnerability. There is no logically safe route from rationality to trust of any description. This reasoning leaves Bernstein with the question, 'how is trust possible?'.[11] In order to meet the other with trust I simply must already be predisposed to trust and do so independently of reasons:

> Trust functions by obviating the question [of why I should trust the other], by relating us to potential interaction prior to and independently of the question of affirmation. Trust can do this only by operating as a baseline or primary attitude that does not require antecedent justification; on the contrary, as a primary orientation, trust is best conceived of as a primitive and original relation to the other, how others first appear to us, and hence part of the original physiognomy of social interaction.[12]

The deliberative paradox can be avoided only by assuming that a primitive trusting stance is part of our lives 'prior' to argument of any kind. This is a form of priority, both logically and temporally. Logically, the positions of trust and distrust are not symmetrical. Trust must be assumed as the default stance and distrust as a subsequent challenge to it. Speaking temporally, the personal development of the individual proceeds from the initial stance of unconditional trust towards greater distrust and discernment. Bernstein concludes that '[t]rust carries into the adult world a remnant of the infant's unreflective, spontaneous acceptance of his primary others'.[13]

This is a line of argument that has, among others, been briefly presented by Baier.[14] Bernstein's paper as a whole is to an extent an exploration of certain ideas floated but not fully developed in Baier's essay. Like Bernstein, Baier believes that the existence of trust in human life can only be explained by assuming our trustful disposition to be innate. We must assume that some kind of 'ur-confidence'[15] is present in the human child; otherwise 'it would appear a miracle that trust ever occurs'. This initial attitude is, however, extremely vulnerable: trust 'is much easier to maintain than it is to get started and is never hard to destroy'.[16]

In *Modernity and Self-Identity*, Anthony Giddens makes rather similar points but he makes the need of trust an even more radical issue. 'Basic trust', he says, is the origin of 'the feelings of *ontological security* characteristic of large segments of human activity in all cultures'.[17] Such security pertains not only to social relations but also to our ideas of the identity of objects, other persons, and the self: the coherence and intelligibility of everyday life. Trust not only enables us to ignore potential threats but it is fundamental for seeing reality as intelligible in the first place. Our sense of ontological security is shown in the taken-for-granted character of much of what we do. However:

> On the other side of what might appear to be quite trivial aspects of day-to-day action and discourse, chaos lurks. And this chaos is not just disorganisation, but the loss of a sense of the very reality of things and other persons.[18]

Giddens speaks here also of 'a flooding in of anxiety which the ordinary conventions of day-to-day life usually *keep successfully at bay*'.[19] The antithesis of trust is not simply disbelief but 'existential *angst* or *dread*'.[20] This condition is, according to

Giddens, analogous to what happens in philosophy when sceptical questions are brought up. The groundlessness of our believing is exposed. The metaphor of anxiety 'flooding in' suggests the idea of a constant but usually suppressed feature of our existence suddenly revealing itself. We seldom stop to think about risks 'implied in the very business of living'; this, according to Giddens, is an expression of, or derives from, our sense of basic trust.[21]

What these approaches to basic trust have in common is a strong sense of the inherent vulnerability of the human condition, together with a conception of basic trust as a cognitive shield against the full implications of that insight.

A self-deception theory of basic trust

While helpful in some ways, this general approach has disquieting features. Accounts of basic trust along the lines just described endorse trust as ethically and psychologically valuable, but the endorsement comes with the *dismissal* of basic trust as rationally untenable. The implication seems to be that basic trust is either due to an intellectual deficiency of some kind or else it is a form of self-deception. If we were fully rational thinkers we could only conclude by giving up the stance of trust; the only reason why we keep it is that doing otherwise would be *psychologically* unbearable. Bernstein's account in particular makes it difficult to see how trust can be honestly sustained at all once we reach intellectual maturity because, for him, the very act of trying to think of good reasons for trusting tends almost inevitably to *undermine* it.

Basic trust must now be described as an epistemic shortcoming – implying 'the rational suppression, overlooking, forgetting, or fortunate ignorance of each individual's utter dependence on surrounding others, and hence each's categorical helplessness'.[22] The extent to which our everyday existence rests on an illusion is brought home to us in cases of sexual or physical assault. In this account, the difference between the traumatized and non-traumatized person is described in epistemic terms: the traumatized person *knows* something that the other either does not know or fails to acknowledge. Bernstein writes:

In each of these cases [war, torture, rape, violent assault, child abuse, domestic abuse] the experience is one of revealing underlying and intractable dimensions of vulnerability, dependence, and potential helplessness that are normally hidden from consciousness, a hiddenness that, in turn, enables a trusting and confident relation to an individual's personal, social, and material environments.[23]

Taking this down to a personal level, Bernstein's description implies that my generally good relationship with my parents was due to a kind of 'hiddenness' – in other words, my ignorance or suppression of the facts about my complete dependence on them and my vulnerability to them. But I cannot see how that can be true. On the whole, it is hard to imagine *any* child growing up ignorant of the dependence characteristic of the parent–child relation. Moreover, Bernstein has not explained why dependence as such would need to be a source of anxiety. He seems quite unquestioningly to think that dependence must at least *prima facie* be a bad thing.

The definition of 'personal dependence' must admittedly involve the notion of something being outside the agent's own control. Thus as soon as we describe a person as dependent on another we tacitly acknowledge the possibility of the relationship having some outcome that the person cannot control. But it does not follow that the outcome would have to be unwanted. Knowing that someone who *loves* me is more resourceful than me, knowing that she can influence the course of my life and that she provides for me in various ways should not undermine my trust in her; it should make my trust stronger. Dependence in itself should not constitute a problem for me unless I harbour the pathological belief that I can only ever be safe in the company of people whom I can fully control. In other words, dependence emerges as a problem in the condition of distrust.

A possible answer to this might be: 'You were lucky to have loving parents. But they *might* have been child molesters. You loved them without reservation because you were ignorant of that possibility.' This of course brings us back to my earlier question of what it means genuinely to invoke a possibility.[24] I might reply that there never *was* that possibility in my case. However the objection I am now imagining would perhaps not address my situation personally, but it would be a way of saying in a general way that 'anyone' might be a child molester. But these questions are still made from *some* perspective; they cannot be fully understood if the personal aspect is entirely dropped. Imagining one variety of the situation, someone whose world has been shattered by abuse might find it simply impossible not to think of all adults of his parents' age as possible child molesters. In this way his statement directs my attention to him, not to *my* parents. Distrust in his case is natural but also destructive and incapacitating. What can I do in order to restore him to some of his basic trust? This would be an example of a meaningful and specific statement of the form, 'anybody might be a child molester'. A police officer who investigates allegations of child abuse might also have use for this sentence. Finally, 'anyone might be a child molester' could be presented simply as a corollary to the general statement that 'anyone' might in principle (By *which* principle? Never mind ...) be just *anything*. As long as we do not know, anyone might be an impostor, a new Mother Teresa, an Oriental prince in disguise, or yet something else. But if we are caught at this completely abstract level there is very little that can be made of such statements.

Bernstein's conception of social life as inherently risky owes a great deal to the *Leviathan*. He refers to Hobbes, pointing out that 'in principle any man can kill any other'; 'terrible risks'[25] are never far beneath the surface. Trust is supposedly needed as an antidote to the pervasive consciousness of risk that would otherwise have an incapacitating effect on us. In much of the debate even generally, the idea of basic trust is spelled out by contrasting it with largely Hobbesian scenarios. It is true that social life as a whole is connected to vulnerability at a simple conceptual level. By definition, the idea of organized social life implies the concept of cooperation. That concept in turn implies the intelligibility of speaking of defection and non-defection. In this minimal and theoretical sense social life always implies a kind of tension between vulnerability and safety. But are these logical connections sufficient to establish the thesis that universal angst and suspicion would be the adequate responses of any clear-headed observer who thinks of human relations?

Here is one way to formulate my general response. In the debate, the normal attitude of the individual in society is characterized as trustful. It is contrasted with an allegedly *objective* general perspective – the perspective from which the social world appears to be a very dangerous place. My question here is: how do we establish the superiority of the one perspective over the other?

Connecting with this: what is it that we *do* when we endorse the one over the other? My diagnosis here is that Bernstein, in spite of his misgivings about rationalism, conserves some of its basic tenets. Like the view he criticizes, he treats rational argument and rational justification as context-free enterprises. This also has the consequence of assimilating the world-shattering experience of the victim of abuse to the merely theoretical scepticism of rationalist political philosophy.

Paranoia and scepticism

Contrast the person who carries on a normal social life against someone who constantly thinks that people in her vicinity might be out to physically harm her. We may imagine that the two persons have equal access to facts. Both might, for instance, agree in a general kind of way that it would be 'physically possible' for certain disastrous scenarios to occur. They might also agree that the likelihood is usually very low; yet one of them would shake off the whole thing easily while the other would react with anxiety. We might say the first one moves on with life while the second is prey to paralysing fears. But we might also think that only the latter has fully faced reality. How do we choose between these descriptions?

I have already quoted Govier's claim that mundane activities such as 'eating in restaurants' involve 'vulnerability – whether we realize it or not'. In crime fiction, it may be a good idea to keep in mind that cooks have the opportunity to poison the food at a restaurant. In *Good and Evil: An Absolute Conception* Raimond Gaita similarly discusses someone who brings up this possibility. However, unlike Govier, he cites it not as an obvious factual point but as an example of paranoia:

> If someone insanely believes that their food is poisoned, you cannot prove otherwise to them because anything that would, for us, count as a proof is vulnerable to their paranoid ingenuity. Something is a proof only within the ranks of the sane and the sober: those, who, as the colloquial expression has it, 'are in tune with reality' – that belongs to the concept of a proof [...] [W]e do not believe that it is *extremely improbable* that the

cooks will try to poison us. If it should occur to us that they might, then we will quite rightly fear for our sanity and we will not be consoled by the thought that that is very unlikely.[26]

The contrast described here is in some ways parallel to Bernstein's contrast between basic trust and 'the standpoint of reason'. Gaita, however, does not describe the paranoid perspective as one of *reason*. The latter would not be vindicated by invoking anything like the objective physical possibility of poison, for the intelligibility of invoking that possibility in the first place depends on accepting its *relevance*. 'Relevance' does not now mean 'likelihood'; as Gaita remarks, we would usually have no idea of the probabilities anyway. For Gaita – presuming that there is no particular reason for suspicion in the case he is describing – the crucial difference 'lies in the fact that someone who is sane "rules it out of consideration" while someone who is mad does not'.[27] In sum, Gaita is critical of the idealization of scepticism and suspicion. It is not the mark of a 'fearless thinker' to be prepared to give every (theoretically) possible position serious consideration.

Gaita's question is what reasoning can do in the situation. He emphasizes that the paranoiac cannot in any straightforward way be taken out of his or her delusion by means of argument. This is why Gaita is prompted to describe the paranoiac as 'mad', citing Chesterton's dictum that 'the madman' is someone who has lost everything *except* his reason. Here one might think that Gaita goes along with the idea that universal suspicion *is* the perspective of reason, or at least compatible with reason. His general point is, however, different. 'Reason' does not stand on its own; it is not, for instance, to be identified with the abstract ability to perform the standard operations of the logical canon. The employment of reason means that we *take* certain data[28] to be reasons for conclusions, and 'reason' understood as a mere abstract faculty stands in need of sound judgement. In the present case, reason in a full sense would presumably include judgement concerning the relations in which we stand to others; for instance, whether we have reason to expect enmity from anyone in particular.

One might want to describe the non-paranoid perspective here as a perspective of *trust*. Assuming the idea of basic trust, the point would be precisely that basic trust, by shielding the subject from the endless possibilities of suspicion, *enables* her to keep mentally sane. But we should note that, thinking of a realistic case like the one Gaita has described, we would typically not characterize the sane person as trustful. The question of whether the food can be trusted would simply not be an issue, because the risk of poison could not be invoked in any serious way. The contrast is not one between 'trustful' and 'suspicious' but one between 'sane' and 'paranoid'.

On the other hand, the attitude that usually counts as simply sane will naturally stand out as 'trustful' if we change the example slightly. Imagine that my friend is an oppositional journalist working on the ramifications of a political murder case, for instance the Litvinenko poisoning. I might want to warn him against being too trustful when he eats out. My views on what constitutes reasonable suspicion would be different here, although it does not follow that I must also fear for my *own* life. Another kind of contrast is created if my friend has been seriously traumatized in the past, so that he simply cannot bring himself to feel safe even in a completely normal environment. His lack of basic trust could now be contrasted with my trustful attitude. What in these latter cases invites the description of the non-suspicious attitude as one of trust is the fact that a specific contrast has been evoked against some realistic challenge to the normal attitude.

The overall result of this section is to question the dichotomy between 'reason' and 'trust' that was taken for granted in Bernstein's discussion of basic trust. A wider understanding of the concept of reason acknowledges that at its core lies an idea of *reasonable* questions, arguments and suggestions. These are ideas embedded in our lives with people. Whether it is reasonable of me to expect those in my vicinity to try to harm me is something I will have to address *in situ*, not *in vitro*.[29]

I am not offering these remarks as direct refutations of Bernstein's general view. They rather raise the question of *under what circumstances* the idea of basic trust as implicit in normal social life could be accepted as relevant. When would it be relevant to claim that our everyday lives are constantly accompanied by an underlying trust? The question of whether the non-paranoid patron 'trusts' the cooks and waiters is not a factual question in any simple way, because what needs to be specified is the meaning of the question to whoever is asking it. Supposing we on the whole agree on the general situation (someone eating lunch in a more-or-less normal way in a more-or-less normal restaurant), what is *our* message in describing her behaviour as 'trustful'? If it is simply a response to general-level scepticism, its meaningfulness is dependent on whether we can take that kind of scepticism seriously.

'The substratum of all my enquiring and asserting'

The connection between reason and social context is something of a leitmotif in Wittgenstein's *On Certainty*.[30] That work starts off with a discussion of G. E. Moore's attempted refutations of scepticism.[31] Moore had wanted to prove the existence of an external world by citing the irrefutable existence of his two hands. He also cited other examples of propositions that he could not doubt, for instance that he was a human being and that the world had existed for a long time before his birth.

One traditional reaction to sceptical challenges is to look for statements that for logical reasons either cannot be doubted in the first place or should not be doubted on pain of incoherence. They would count as fundamental and as first steps towards a general vindication of our knowledge claims. However, Wittgenstein's and Moore's examples do not qualify as logical truths in a conventional sense. Also, most of them are not of a type that could be imagined as logical foundations of knowledge. For instance, nothing of universal importance hangs on the fact that *Moore* has two hands. For the rest of us, 'Moore has two hands' is an ordinary empirical statement.

Moore's proof of the external world can obviously be challenged by just pointing out that the sceptical reasoning that applies to the existence of the world as a whole also applies to his two hands. Moore was of course aware of this. The underlying more interesting point was that regardless of any argument he, i.e. Moore, could not bring himself to doubt the truth of his statement. Moreover, statements of this general kind are ones that no sane person would doubt in his or her own case. Thus Moore did not attack scepticism directly but in an oblique way, highlighting the remarkable *fact* that certain statements about the world and our own lives in it are not doubted. On the other hand, Moore still retained the philosophical framework where he felt obliged to rise to sceptical challenges by citing these facts as something he certainly knew.

Wittgenstein takes the discussion one step further by asking whether it is meaningful at all to cite Moore's statements as something he 'knows'.[32] By bringing in the question of knowledge, Moore has inadvertently also bought into the framework where it appears reasonable to ask for evidence for what he claims to know. But as Moore, too, points out, in cases of this kind I could not point to specific evidence that has settled the question for me.[33] It is not that doubt has been explicitly shown to be impossible, but only that, assuming a normal case – thus excluding the failure of my senses and various other disaster scenarios – I would not see what 'doubt' might possibly amount to in the situation. On the other hand, supposing I made an effort to make sense of doubt here, I could not do so by simply questioning the existence of two specific objects – my hands – but it would have to be part of some kind of wholesale challenge to my mental faculties.

It is not that the specific statement that I have two hands is *too obvious* for me to doubt. Rather, in normal circumstances, my having two hands does not confront me as a 'statement' at all. It has come to me as a natural background when I learned to do things with my hands. Acting with two hands is my normal method of coping with a material environment. According to Wittgenstein, my convictions form 'a system, a structure' which 'is not so much the point of departure, as the element in which arguments have their life'.[34] I do not explicitly learn such convictions – and in this sense the word 'conviction' may be misleading[35] – but I can later recognize that they are implicit in what I do learn, 'like the axis around which a body rotates'. Like the axis of a globe floating in space, it does not support the body but instead 'the movement around it determines its immobility'.[36] *What* stands fast for me is shown by what kinds of ideas and questions are shown to be rotating around it, not because what stands fast is 'intrinsically obvious or convincing'.[37] Certain questions and suggestions are taken seriously and discussed, while others are dismissed as absurd. As Wittgenstein notes, 'I have a world-picture. Is it true or false? Above all it is the substratum of all my enquiring and asserting.'[38]

At this juncture it is worthwhile to point out a certain ambiguity in the interpretative debate. It is customary, with reference to an expression that Wittgenstein used, to speak of certain statements discussed in *On Certainty* as 'hinge propositions'. He compares 'some propositions [...] exempt from doubt' with 'hinges' on which questions and doubts turn.[39] This image is different from that of the rotating planet, because the hinges of a door physically support it and guide the movement. The hinge metaphor seems to me unfortunate, because it looks like retrogression to traditional foundationalist responses to scepticism. The main thrust of Wittgenstein's argument is, however, not that certain statements as such must be exempt from doubt but only that some *are*. In any *given* human pursuit, it will be possible to identify propositions that would not be treated as questionable.[40]

The statement that the world has existed for more than two hundred years is, for instance, not discussed at all by historians. It is different from geological statements about the exact age of the earth, and also from historical statements about the age of some particular structure. 'The belief that the world is more than two hundred years old' is not a historical belief in a normal sense, because it is not something that anyone might try to prove by historical methods. I could not cite a letter by Napoleon for evidence, for I can take the letter to be authentic only if I already accept that the world existed at the time. At the same time, the 'belief' at issue is tacitly included in historical research in a way it is not, for instance, implicit in discussions about medicine. The proposition is not basic for history in the sense that any interesting historical propositions are derived from it, but in the sense that questioning it would only be possible in the form of introducing pervasive uncertainty and confusion. Wherever there are historical inquiries or talk about history it will be taken for granted that many things of this general kind are not doubted.[41]

This is not to say that no one could ever doubt, for instance, scientific facts that reasonable people with a normal Western education take to be beyond conceivable doubt. What we cannot doubt today perhaps some future generation will.[42] But insofar as such a thing as scientific inquiry will exist, some ideas of this general kind will be commonly treated as unquestionable.

Insofar as the debate on basic trust is concerned, the central insight in *On Certainty* is that our idea of what constitutes 'reasonable' thinking is the collective product of a culture. A world picture is not formed by one individual but it takes shape in a discourse. Our intellectual life as a whole is characterized by what one may call an epistemological division of labour. Our ability to distinguish between serious and spurious disagreement is something we acquire by being brought up in a culture. For instance, we generally take as true what we read in books, but otherwise we consult *other* sources. Our preparedness to identify and use them as 'sources' and not, for instance, as fiction is part of what it means to be at home in this culture of learning.[43] Thus 'I learned an enormous amount and accepted it on human authority, and then I found some things confirmed or disconfirmed by my own experience'; in the learning process '[d]oubt comes *after* belief'.[44] Here the word 'after' does not necessarily imply temporal succession, but it marks one element as a condition of the other. For instance, to dismiss everything said by one's teacher is simply to refuse the teaching situation, which should include the starting point that the teacher has something true and worthwhile to communicate. While trust may involve intellectual distortion in some cases, the general fact that we have faith in the judgement and testimonies of others is *'part of judging'*.[45] Wittgenstein sums up his idea here: 'I really want to say that a language-game is only possible if one trusts something (I did not say "can trust something").'[46] The final clause, it seems to me, makes the point that the question of whether one *can* trust (i.e. whether the rationally right conditions for trusting are in place) will only be possible to state *'after* belief'.

There is an important asymmetry here between the place of trust and distrust in human growth. No critical faculties will develop unless the child starts by not doubting. Analogously, there is an asymmetry between pretence and genuine communication. Wittgenstein points out that a child must learn a great deal before it can pretend, presumably including the use of the corresponding genuine expression.[47] However, trust in the testimony and sound judgement of others is not only characteristic of children. On the contrary, as we grow older we learn to make *more* use of the information and expertise available around us.

Some of Wittgenstein's descriptions come across as indicative of fairly authoritarian ideas of teaching methods. He insists that the child 'learns by believing the adult' and imagines the teacher telling it off: 'Stop interrupting me and do as I tell you.'[48] Elsewhere in his work, he frequently offers mechanical training as a model for teaching language or specific rule-following activities – admittedly always in stylized illustrations of specific activities and not as a general model for learning.[49]

In a realistic scenario one should not think just in terms of one-way communication. Unlike what Wittgenstein's discussion suggests, children do not begin intellectual life by simply 'believing the adult'. There is the corresponding element of the child expressing *its* beliefs and the adult taking them seriously. The child also learns where and when there is leeway to opposing the parents or ignoring them. In a learning environment characterized by trust, they can do so without fear of rejection. Indeed situations of that kind may also be expressions of the child's trust in its parents. Moreover, adult reactions shape both the child's and the adult's understanding of the issue in question; e.g. of what is negotiable in the situation. 'Believing the adult' may perhaps be said to start in the fully fledged sense only when there is also room for disbelieving, ignoring and opposing.

Just as it may be misleading to say that children immediately 'believe' their parents, we should perhaps not say that babies trust their parents from the very start but only that they *do not distrust* them. Both descriptions, however, might be right depending on the context. Saying that a child trusts its parents is, for instance, one way to criticize fathers and mothers who ignore its needs or talk ironically to it. The present point is that normal human lives will, from the very start, involve relations of mutual dependence that are not questioned. In the small child, the opposite of trust is typically not called doubt, distrust or suspicion but, perhaps, fear. An infant who did not start life with a basically trustful attitude towards those around him (that is, an infant whose attitude is an overwhelmingly *fearful* one) would be considered abnormal. It is doubtful whether one could coherently describe such an infant as *distrustful*.

Rather than questioning Wittgenstein's main insights about the social nature of thinking, these remarks serve to deepen and highlight them. On the whole, *On Certainty*, like *Philosophical Investigations*, shows Wittgenstein as a 'social' thinker.[50] He describes meaningful thought as an activity bound up with human interaction and interdependence. We learn from him that there is no *one* 'standpoint of reason' given to us independently of our relations with people.

Meeting the other in trust: Weil and Løgstrup

The references to trust in *On Certainty* connect, however obliquely, to the epistemological concerns voiced in the basic trust debate. But the overall appeal of the idea of basic trust owes much to the ethical strand also present in the debate.[51] I now turn to that issue. What are we to make of the idea that basic trust must be understood as 'the ethical foundation of everyday living', as Bernstein puts it?[52] It was already indicated that this idea cannot be made sense of by merely invoking Hobbesian horror scenarios. Yet there is something to be said for the idea that human relations gain their moral significance from the fact that we are irrevocably left in the hands of each other. To think of human interaction as immersed in a milieu of basic trust is, in this case, to take up a perspective where the other, merely by virtue of meeting us as a fellow human being, is already included in our world as someone with a claim to our attention.

A valuable exploration of this theme is found in the work of Simone Weil, a thinker whose ethical thought revolves around the idea of the vulnerability of the other; if I may put it thus, her work is characterized by attempts to find sense in suffering without reducing away its senselessness. In much of her work on human power relations Weil dwelled on what she saw as our natural tendency towards oppressive attitudes. Whenever someone wields unchallenged power over another, the other is almost inevitably turned into an object, a thing. Weil describes this vividly in her depiction of Achilles in the *Iliad*. King Priam, now completely defeated, is brought to Achilles. For a moment, Achilles is moved by the old man pleading for mercy; then he impatiently pushes him aside as if a dead object, a mere obstacle.[53] But according to Weil, 'it happens, although extremely rarely, that a man will forbear out of pure generosity to command where he has the power to do so'.[54] Weil calls this impulse supernatural, as it conflicts with a natural human tendency to view the world solely from one's own point of view, reducing other people to opportunities and obstacles.[55]

However, as Peter Winch points out in his book on Weil, Priam is *not* turned to a thing.[56] At least, if I may put it thus, he will not be a thing in the same way as a *thing* is a thing. 'Turning someone to a thing' is only an intelligible description because it describes a response to a fellow human or living being. It is, for instance, significant that Priam is in a sense defiled, which cannot be said of a rock removed from a piece of waste ground.[57] There is something in our relations towards other humans that takes them beyond the mere physical balance of power. According to Weil:

> The human beings around us exert just by their presence a power which belongs only to themselves to stop, to diminish, to modify, each movement which our bodies design. A person who crosses our path does not turn aside our steps in the same manner as a street sign, no one stands up, or moves about, or sits down again in quite the same fashion when he is alone in the room as when he has a visitor.[58]

Weil adds that 'this undefinable influence' is absent in the case of those who wield absolute power over others, such as Achilles of the *Iliad*. Perhaps another type of indifference is possible too. Weil speaks of a 'visitor' and not of a family member; the magic of human presence sometimes seems at least less tangible when the other person belongs to the same household. But on the whole Weil's remark about the power of people to influence us seems to be meant as a description of a normal or characteristic trait of human interaction. The remark appears not to be empirical but it perhaps belongs to the same order as Winch's point about the impossibility of treating people as things. Regardless of the precise 'ways' in which I step aside for the human being or the street sign, the difference between them is shown in the fact that a different set of questions comes into play in each of the cases if my behaviour is to be described. My movements in front of someone standing on the street may convey friendliness, embarrassment or hostility – while the very same movements in front of the street sign would not 'convey' anything because *it* is not a being to which anything would be conveyed. And unlike the case with meeting physical obstacles, descriptions of my behaviour towards people would also take account of the other person's reactions. Indeed supposing there is no reaction at all, precisely *that* might become a central element of the description if a human being is standing in front of me. The character of my behaviour as friendly or unfriendly may be both a more apposite and a more easily accessible feature of it than might be conveyed by any physical account of my movements.

This sense of human presence is reciprocal. For Weil, however, those reduced to slaves or things – 'a compromise between a man and a corpse' – also for their part lose the sense that their presence can make a difference to others. 'Before these men others behave as if they were not there; and they in turn, finding themselves in danger of being in an instant reduced to nothing, imitate nothingness.'[59] Weil recognizes the contradiction in saying that a human being has become a thing, but 'when the impossible has become a reality, that contradiction is a rent in the soul'.[60]

By contrasting human beings and objects in this way, Weil indicates that a person can be a limit to my will in a way conceptually different from how objects figure as limits. In the normal case, that is: when the person is not reduced to a thing, there are certain actions I 'cannot' commit against her even if nothing physically restrains me. Conversely, her relation to *me* is coloured by the self-evident sense of making a difference, of being present for me, of being there as an irreducible part of the world in which I move. In her essay on 'Human personality' Weil locates a sense of human 'sacredness' in this tacit expectation of making a difference to others:

> At the bottom of the heart of every human being, from earliest infancy until the tomb, there is something that goes on indomitably expecting, in the teeth of all experience of crimes committed, suffered, and witnessed, that good and not evil will be done to him. It is this above all that is sacred in every human being.[61]

Weil offers this as a description of what holds us back from harming the other; in her graphical image, it is what keeps Weil from tearing out the eyes of a man she sees on the street, even though she were to fancy it and might do it with impunity. Significantly, what stays her hand is not identified as a motive in *her*, it is not contingent on something *she* wants, but it consists of the expectation that the potential victim directs at her. By *recognizing* that the other expects goodness and not evil she acknowledges the wrongness of violating him.

The passage might invite the question of how it is that Weil *knows* what she says she knows about the expectations deep down in the human heart. Has she *asked* people about this? Does everyone expect goodness from everyone else? And is the prohibition against violence waived if and when exceptions to this rule are discovered? Once more Weil is making use of a general description that looks empirical; but again, she is clearly not making an empirical point. Weil is painfully aware that the cry of the unhappy is 'silent', and hence hearing the cry of the unhappy cannot be a matter of empirical observation. Moreover, their cry is, according to Weil, 'impersonal'; it is not specific to the person who might utter it. The expectation of goodness hidden in every human heart can only be perceived through a kind of attention which is love. Something of what Weil is getting at might be expressed in this way: To understand a human being fully is to understand what lies at the bottom of her heart; but this, Weil wants to say, is not something personal and specific to that particular man or woman. It is an orientation towards the good, something that remains the same for you, for me and for everyone. To understand a human being fully *is* to be receptive to the expectation of goodness that she directs at us.

Weil's description must be seen as a model, a point of comparison the value of which depends on the extent to which it can help us organize our understanding of existing situations. This must of course mean *ethical* understanding. Weil directs a question to us – the question of whether we are, in our lives, able to follow the vision that guides us past the empirical person to the sacred core of every human being. In an actual situation, Weil's description means that I have to scrutinize my own attitudes. Am I, for instance, prepared to listen to persons who by conventional standards may not be regarded as worth talking to? How do I relate to the very young and the very old, or to people who strike me as irritating or else as being of no consequence? I am also called to think of my reactions when those I feel ought to meet me with gratitude give a hostile response. Somewhere in all these men, women and children, I am invited to discern what nevertheless exists in them as a tacit demand for goodness. While Weil stresses the difficulty of fully following the ideal she indicates, it is also important for her conception that the ideal in some imperfect kind of way is already embedded in our everyday dealings with people – for instance, in the instinctive magic of presence that influences our behaviour whenever other people are around. This connects to Weil's insistence on the *sui generis*, primordial character of our reactions to human beings. These are natural responses, seeds from which ethical concepts (such as that of 'being a neighbour to someone') subsequently develop.[62]

K. E. Løgstrup presents a somewhat similar understanding of human natural responses, although his account is not focused on suffering to the same extent as Weil's. Unlike Weil, he explicitly uses the concept of trust to frame his description. For him, trust is the natural medium in which human interaction takes place. We figure always already as elements of each other's worlds. On the whole, we do not treat our relations with others as something that requires us to pass judgement about their trustworthiness. Where such judgements are called for, we think of the alternatives against a general background of 'normality', implying openness and trust. While we can choose to withdraw from some trustful relations and dismiss invitations to trust, on the whole we have not *chosen* a life where we trust others and are trusted by them in turn. Løgstrup contrasts this observation with what he describes as the mistaken idea 'that the world where the other leads her life is something to which we really do not belong'; in other words, that we do not really influence the other except when one of us accidentally or deliberately impinges on the other's world and *takes* contact. However, 'in reality [...] it is quite different: we are each other's world and each other's fate'.[63] Trust is inescapable:

> If trust and the openness that is part of it were just something to be arbitrarily chosen by us, we could do without it and not lose anything; in our lives with others, no other demands would exist except those that it might occur to one person to make on another, let them be conventional, sentimental or based on illusory ideas of power. But it is not so. Trust is not up to us. It is given. Our lives simply are, not by any design of our own, shaped in such a way that they can only be lived so that the other is offered up to us in showing trust or asking for trust, delivering more or less of her life into our hands.[64]

As with Weil, one should not see this account as a psychological theory of the human consciousness; Løgstrup's idea of basic trust must be kept apart from the idea that our lives are accompanied by constant unself-conscious feelings of trust. Løgstrup, like Weil, offers a consciously idealized depiction of ordinary life. Here it is important that we should keep hold of both parts of this characteristic. The description is *idealized* because it is held up as a measuring rod against experience; we are to compare our experience with it. But it is a description of *ordinary* life because it takes hold of attitudes and reactions that naturally and instinctively characterize human encounters. Løgstrup urges the reader to see life in a certain kind of light where ethics describes the form that human life self-evidently takes. If I see myself as holding the other person's life in my hands, I perceive her demand of being received by me in trust. As soon as I perceive the demand, I cannot turn it down without doing violence to both myself and to the other. The demand is normally not uttered by this fellow human being of mine, and she may be quite unaware of it; she perhaps disowns any such demands. Thus the demand of goodness is tacit. It exists, but I cannot be made aware of it regardless of the perspective that I take on it:

> The demand that lies in each human encounter is never given a voice but it is tacit and remains so. The individual to whom it is directed must himself judge in each relationship what the demand is about. This is not to say that the individual can arbitrarily, capriciously, give it whatever content he feels like. In that case it would not be a demand. But it is still there and, because given in the very fact that the individual is part of the world where the other lives her life, and hence holds some of her life in his hand, it is a demand to care for that life.[65]

How do we then discover the existence of a tacit expectation of goodness in human encounters? Not empirically, for empirical discoveries would not be helpful here anyway. Expectations of goodness might also exist alongside contrary expectations; having discovered them we would still have to decide which of them, if any, we should meet. Throughout this book, I have emphasized that the presence of trust is not a psychological fact accessible to us regardless of our own attitude to it. Instead, recognizing trust and recognizing an obligation to respond to trust are two sides of a coin. They are perceived in the same act of spontaneous openness towards the other.

Ideas of basic trust in context

The notion of basic trust is a nodal point of mixed research interests, all largely addressing the relationship between human reason and ethics. Whether basic trust proves a useful conceptual tool must be deemed from the context. The suggestion that our tendency to trust must be innate is often offered as a necessary corrective to a view on human agency that otherwise retains features of rationalism. Trust is needed as a counterweight to the sceptical dictates of reason. Such views on the function of trust are based on an understanding of reasoning that presents the latter as a curiously abstract activity. From an alternative view, our ideas of the reasonable, of things being possible and impossible, belong to a life that is always already social. 'Trust' figures here as an element of the forms of life, or forms of thinking, that can already be described as so many ways of using one's reason.

Whether basic trust *exists* is not an empirical issue, although it might look like one. It is an ethical issue, and the question boils down to asking how we should conceptualize essential features of human encounters. I used Weil's and Løgstrup's works as demonstrations of how something like a concept of basic trust may be employed in attempts to describe the human ethical condition. These attempts are not uncontroversial, and some of us may have doubts about discussing anything as general as '*the* human ethical condition' in the first place. In any case, Weil and Løgstrup – and in another way, Wittgenstein – point to ways of making sense of the idea of basic trust outside the discursive framework defined by scepticism. They build on the neglected truth that philosophy begins with wonder but not with suspicion.

CHAPTER EIGHT

Conclusions

This last brief chapter highlights some common themes that run through my previous discussion. It is not a full summary but an invitation to reflection.

I have tried above all to think of the vocabulary of 'trust' as part of interaction; a central question in this book is how this vocabulary enters human relationships and shapes them. The question is not whether a particular instance of language use involves a correct use of 'trust' but simply what kind of a use it is. What are we doing when the vocabulary of trust is brought to bear on a given case? A short answer would be: it depends, and we cannot legislate on it. However, it is of interest to point out certain uses of 'trust' as characteristic or telling. I have emphasized that the word 'trust' can in certain cases be fully understood only as part of an ethical way of speaking; trust is contrasted with betrayal. In such cases, to single out a human relationship as one of trust is to treat it in a light where it makes sense to speak of moral responsibility. To go along with the description that someone trusts us is at the same time to recognize that an ethical demand is directed at us. We hold the other's life in our hands and we cannot let her down without committing an injustice. However, while I have emphasized trust as a moral notion, I have not put forward a normative theory of trust; for instance, I have not suggested any way of judging exactly when we ought to look at our relation with the other in this way.

In moral philosophy, theories of trust are typically expected to explain what trust is and, on the basis of that description, to explain why trust is a good thing, rationally justified, or the like. The theory is further expected to provide guidelines for where one should place one's trust. Theories of trust run the distinct risk of ending up either dogmatic or chatty (or both): dogmatic, when they nail down one example as the paradigm and shoehorn other cases into it; chatty, when they pile example upon example to make sure nothing is missed. Neither of the approaches can be successful at length, because how we should define 'trust' must depend on the particular interest we have in the question. Theories of trust (if we want any) must, in other words, be context-bound. The previous point about the vocabulary of trust being part of human interaction also applies to philosophical treatments of trust. They are put forward as responses to particular problems and need to be assessed as contributions to the relevant debates.

A survey of the most influential contributions to the English-speaking philosophical debate on trust nevertheless shows a degree of unity. What the overview reveals is the tacit guiding metaphor of *shopping* – a rather sad comment if philosophy is assumed to reflect central concerns of the culture in which it is produced. The dominating assumption is that the agent enters a social scene and looks for profitable objects on which to place her trust. If I trust a person, I first and foremost believe she is likely to do my bidding. This view in turn creates the natural demand for a justifying theory of trust, because trust carries with it the risk of disappointment. It also gives rise to the problems of rationality central in the literature.

Once the dominant metaphor is formulated in this way it will be easy to find problems about it, even though this is not to say that nothing worthwhile can ever be done with it. A large part of the research explicitly concerns market behaviour, which sometimes justifies the shopping theme. My criticism is that the metaphor offers an impoverished view when applied to life as a whole, just as a life that only involves shopping would be impoverished. To begin with, the question of rational justification is singularly misplaced in the phenomenology of personal trusting relationships. In important cases, trust is expressed in the fact that I do not seek justification where I otherwise might. Trust is thus more properly seen as a *framework* for my further justificatory and truth-seeking activities. If the philosophical description of trust, then, starts off with the issue of justification, it has already let go of a main distinguishing feature of trust.

One might perhaps want to suggest that 'rationality' and 'reason' should not be important issues at all when we discuss trust, a notion so closely associated with friendship and love. Friendship and love are not outcomes of rational choice in any obvious way. This is a valid point, but I think we should not go along with simplified ideas of reason as a mere calculus from ends to means and back again. 'Rationality' and 'reason' can also be understood as words that stand for thoughtful action, including ways in which we judge various suggestions as being, for instance, reasonable, plausible, probable or impossible. A more general point may be made here – and this point seems to me absolutely crucial to our understanding of human rationality. To assess human actions justly you need to think of what would appear reasonable from the agent's point of view. Considerations about trust show in a tangible way that 'reason' is a perspectival thing. An action, a belief, is 'rational' or 'reasonable' to someone, for something, together with someone, because of someone.

This point surfaces when we consider the notion of possibility – a theme that recurs in many chapters of this book. The received problem of rational trust is largely based on the idea that trust blinds the agent to possibilities that would be visible from a disengaged perspective. Also the frequent insistence on the 'fragility' of trust emphasizes the ever-present risks that supposedly escape the trustful agent's attention. However, a crucial feature of the situation is precisely that from the agent's point of view there is no risk. From her own point of view she is *less* vulnerable than when she trusts no one. This disparity of perspectives is not necessarily due to deficit of information on anyone's part (neither hers nor ours), for it may prevail even if we have the same information. But then, if the agent does not perceive a risk, why should *we* insist that she 'rationally' ought to prepare for possibilities that in her view just do not exist? In response, we cannot simply take recourse to some idea of *objective* possibilities and claim that the agent's assessment of the situation must necessarily be wrong. In conclusion, the presumed rationality deficit of trust is the outcome of a difference of perspectives between the agent and those who view the situation from a perspective of distrust. The taken-for-granted character typical of much of our interaction with others is neither irrational nor naïve, but expressive of a kind of first-personal rationality that is indeed constitutive of the rationality of social beings.

Returning to the 'shopping' metaphor, another characteristic feature of the metaphor is the empty shopping cart; the agent enters the scene with a completely open mind in order then to decide on whom to bestow her trust. I hardly need to emphasize that this is not a realistic depiction of the growth of trust in personal relationships. A massive background of shared life must be in place before we can even start thinking of individual instances of social action in terms of strategic choice. As soon as we are born we are caught in a net of mutual dependence. On the whole we do not trust people around us because we have one day decided to do so; rather, perhaps, one day it strikes us that an already ongoing relationship has this character. In the phenomenology of trust, what calls for attention is the development through which unquestioned aspects of our relations with others are singled out and brought to our consciousness as trust. This is connected with my previous point about the role of 'trust' as a way to organize our understanding of interaction. We do not discover trust empirically as a psychological state, but by having our attention turned to certain aspects of a situation.

One more feature of the shopping metaphor is the assumption of a ready-made shopping list. The agent shopping for trust looks for someone who satisfies specific requirements; if the trustee fails to meet her expectations it always counts as defection. Once more, this is a bad way to describe trust, at least when it comes to trust in friendship and family life. When I turn to a friend for advice I do not (or at least should not) expect him merely to say a specific thing I *want* him to; instead I trust *him* to come with a fresh point of view. I am not judging him on the basis of my desires but instead I accept that he may be the judge of my situation. In this way, trust, unlike mere reliance or entrusting, allows for a flexible and open-ended outcome. This has further implications to questions about rationality. Rationality is without doubt connected to the satisfaction of desires, but not only as a means to an end. Our ideas of the desirable are themselves formed in human relations, by the kind of rationality embodied in our lives with other human beings.

The general idea that I hope to convey is that trust, ethics and human reason are internally related. 'Reason' as we understand it is informed by our ongoing relations with other people. In this shared life we are committed to each other and stand responsible towards each other. Both trust and distrust must be seen against the background of such ongoing engagement.

NOTES

Trust and our worries with it

1. David Hume, 'Enquiry Concerning Human Understanding', in David Hume, *Enquiries Concerning Human Understanding and Concerning the Principles of Morals* (Oxford: Clarendon Press, 1902), Section VIII, Pt I, § 69.

2. I also recommend the overviews by Hartmann, Origgi, E. Simpson and T. Simpson; see Martin Hartmann, 'Einleitung', in Martin Hartmann and Claus Offe (Hg.), *Vertrauen: Die Grundlage des sozialen Zusammenhalts* (Frankfurt/New York: Campus Verlag, 2001, pp. 7–34); Gloria Origgi, *Qu'est-ce que la confiance?* (Paris: Vrin, 2008); Evan Simpson, 'Reasonable Trust', *European Journal of Philosophy* 21 (2011), pp. 402–23; Thomas W. Simpson, 'Computing and the Search for trust', in Richard H. R. Harper (ed.), *Trust, Computing, and Society* (Cambridge: Cambridge University Press, 2014, pp. 95–119).

3. John Hardwig, 'The Role of Trust in Knowledge', *The Journal of Philosophy* 88 (1991), pp. 693–708, at p. 693.

4. For a recent overview of the debate on trust and rationality, see Jeremy Wanderer and Leo Townsend, 'Is it Rational to Trust?', *Philosophy Compass* 8 (2013), pp. 1–14.

5. Martin Hollis, *Trust Within Reason* (Cambridge: Cambridge University Press, 1998).

6. Chapter 2 below.

7. See Chapter 6 below; see Benjamin McMyler, *Testimony, Trust, and Authority* (New York: Oxford University Press, 2011), pp. 10–44.

8. Immanuel Kant, 'An Answer to the Question: What is Enlightenment?', in M. J. Gregor (trans. and ed.) *The Cambridge Edition of the Works of Immanuel Kant: Practical Philosophy* (Cambridge: Cambridge University Press, 1996, pp. 11–22). See further Esther Oluffa Pedersen, 'A Kantian Conception of Trust', *Sats* 13 (2012), pp. 147–69.

9 Kant, 'What is Enlightenment?', p. 17.

10 As Esther Oluffa Pedersen points out, for Kant '[t]he capacity to reflect and judge privately stems from the *sensus communis* as a "faculty for judging that in its reflection takes account (*a priori*) of everyone else's way of representing in thought, in order *as it were* to hold its judgment to human reason as a whole"'. Pedersen, 'A Kantian Conception of Trust', p. 148 (fn 2); Immanuel Kant: *Critique of the Power of Judgment* (Cambridge: Cambridge University Press, 2000), p. 173 [293].

11 For instance, see C. B. MacPherson, *The Political Theory of Possessive Individualism* (Oxford: Oxford University Press, 1962).

12 Elizabeth Wolgast, *The Grammar of Justice* (Ithaca: Cornell University Press, 1987), p. 3.

13 See further in Chapter 6 below.

14 See Chapter 2 below.

15 As Jonas Ahlskog has recently pointed out with regard to testimony, the strong focus on justification characteristic of contemporary debates is surprising given that most philosophers writing on the topic want their accounts to stay close to ordinary practices. However, '[o]nly when doubt has already entered does one ask for justification, so if the first thing a philosopher of testimony asks for is "justification", it means that he has transcended ordinary practice from the get-go'. Jonas Ahlskog, '[Review of] Benjamin McMyler, *Testimony, Trust and Authority*'. *Philosophical Investigations* 36 (2013), pp. 98–102, at p. 101.

16 Russell Hardin is one prominent example. See Russell Hardin, *Trust and Trustworthiness* (New York: Russell Sage Foundation, 2002).

17 This is the most frequent of the three positions. See Annette Baier, *Moral Prejudices: Essays on Ethics* (Cambridge, MA: Harvard University Press, 1994); Annette Baier, 'Trust and Antitrust', *Ethics* 96 (1986), pp. 231–60 (reprinted in Baier, *Moral Prejudices*, pp. 95–129); Karen Jones, 'Trust as an Affective Attitude', *Ethics* 107 (1996), pp. 4–25; Diego Gambetta (ed.), *Trust: Making and Breaking Cooperative Relations* (Oxford: Blackwell, 1990).

18 See Lars Hertzberg, 'On the Attitude of Trust', in Lars Hertzberg, *The Limits of Experience* (Helsinki: Acta Philosophica Fennica, vol. 56, 1994, pp. 111–30; first published in *Inquiry* 31 [1988], pp. 307–22); Lars Hertzberg, 'On Being Trusted', in Arne Grøn and Claudia Welz (eds), *Trust, Sociality, Selfhood* (Tübingen: Mohr Siebeck, 2010, pp. 193–204); Olli Lagerspetz and Lars Hertzberg, 'Trust in Wittgenstein', in Pekka Mäkelä and Cynthia Townley (eds),

Trust: Analytic and Applied Perspectives (Amsterdam: Rodopi, 2013, pp. 31–51).

19 C. A. J. Coady, *Testimony: A Philosophical Study* (Oxford: Clarendon Press, 1992), p. 7.
20 Ludwig Wittgenstein, *On Certainty* (New York: Harper & Row, 1972), § 298.
21 See Chapter 6.
22 Christopher Robinson, email, 23 June 2014.
23 Hartmann, 'Einleitung', p. 24. Hartmann points out with some justice that also my own contribution to the volume ends up with a kind of definition 'ex negativo'. (Olli Lagerspetz, 'Vertrauen als geistiges Phänomen', in Hartmann and Offe, *Vertrauen*, pp. 85–113.)
24 Hartmann, 'Einleitung', p. 8.
25 Hartmann, 'Einleitung', p. 24. Hartmann refers specifically to the sociologist Piotr Sztompka who, despite his resistance to game-theoretic treatments of trust, puts forward a definition of trust as a 'bet' concerning the other's future contingent actions. See Piotr Sztompka, *Trust. A Sociological Theory* (Cambridge: Cambridge University Press, 1999), p. 25; cf. Hartmann, 'Einleitung', pp. 18–19.
26 Paul Faulkner, *Knowledge on Trust* (Oxford: Oxford University Press, 2011), p. 150.
27 Baier, *Moral Prejudices*, p. 159.
28 The example involves another complication too: if the husband did become violent through a sudden onset of brain disease, she probably would not consider that a betrayal of her trust.
29 One more example is Russell Hardin's discussion of the case of Alberich, in Wagner's *The Rhinegold*. Alberich, so the libretto tells us, forswears love forever in exchange for magical powers. Hardin asks whether one could 'reasonably trust his commitment'. It seems to me that, before the question can be fruitfully addressed, one would need to know who is trusting or distrusting Alberich on this matter, and in what way it would be important for that person that Alberich should hold on to his commitment. Russell Hardin, 'Trustworthiness'. *Ethics* 107 (1996), pp. 26–42, at p. 26.
30 However, the situation is a clear case of me making a factual assertion only because the general context is obvious to you or can be safely extrapolated. For instance, what I am prepared to call 'hunger' and what I will accept as a café to go to will be dependent

on circumstances that go beyond any merely neutral account of physiological and geographical facts. Charles Travis discusses some more outlandish cases of assertions where the context of the sentence is not obvious to both speakers from the start. What the sentence 'itself' says is indeterminate without context. Thus our ability to make factual assertions in a situation is subordinate to our general ability to find our feet in it (and the ability of our listeners to do so). Charles Travis, 'Pragmatics', in Bob Hale and Crispin Wright (eds), *Companion to the Philosophy of Language* (Oxford: Blackwell Publishers, 1997), pp. 87–107.

31 Also see Linus Johnsson, *Trust in Biobank Research: Meaning and Moral Significance* (Uppsala: Acta Universitatis Upsaliensis, 2013), p. 103; Katherine Hawley, 'Trust, Distrust and Commitment', *Noûs* 48 (2014), pp. 1–20.
32 Hartmann, 'Einleitung', p. 8.
33 Thomas Hobbes, *Leviathan* (London: Penguin, 1981).
34 Gambetta (ed.), *Trust*.
35 Hollis, *Trust Within Reason*, p. 29.
36 E.g., Francis Fukuyama, *Trust: The Social Virtue and the Creation of Prosperity* (New York: Free Press, 1995); Piotr Sztompka, *Trust*; Robert D. Putnam, *Bowling Alone: The Collapse and Revival of American Community* (New York: Simon & Schuster, 2000); also see the collection by Mark E. Warren (ed.), *Democracy and Trust* (Cambridge: Cambridge University Press, 1999).
37 Annette Baier, 'Trust and Antitrust'; see also e.g. Peter Johnson, *Frames of Deceit* (Cambridge: Cambridge University Press, 1993).
38 Hartmann, 'Einleitung', p. 25.
39 For further discussion see Chapter 4 below.
40 Hertzberg, 'On the Attitude of Trust'; Hertzberg, 'On Being Trusted'.
41 Hartmann, 'Einleitung', p. 14.
42 On the internet, see Richard H. R. Harper (ed.), *Trust, Computing, and Society* (New York: Cambridge University Press, 2014); on public health services, see Jennifer Jackson, *Truth, Trust and Medicine* (London: Routledge, 2001), Helge Skirbekk, *The Patient's Trust – Theoretical Analyses of Trust and a Qualitative Study in General Practice Consultations* (Oslo: Faculty of Medicine, University of Oslo, 2008), Linus Johnsson, *Trust in Biobank Research*; on terrorism, see Onora O'Neill, *A Question of Trust*. Reith Lectures 2002 (BBC Radio 4. http://www.bbc.co.uk/radio4/reith2002/lecture2.shtm [accessed 18 August 2012]).

43 However, Hertzberg points out in a later paper that, after making the initial distinction between trust and reliance, Baier devotes much of her essay to implicitly minimizing it. Hertzberg, 'On Being Trusted', p. 201. Luhmann has introduced an analogous distinction between 'confidence' and 'trust' where 'trust' involves a reasoned decision, i.e. roughly what is here described as 'reliance'. Niklas Luhmann, 'Familiarity, Confidence, Trust: Problems and Alternatives', in Diego Gambetta (ed.), *Trust: Making and Breaking Cooperative Relations* (Oxford: Basil Blackwell, 1990), pp. 94–107, at p. 95.

44 Baier, 'Trust and Antitrust', pp. 234–5.

45 Hertzberg, 'On the Attitude of Trust', p. 119.

46 Onora O'Neill, *A Question of Trust*, Lecture 2.

47 Hartmann, 'Einleitung', p. 28.

48 Simpson distinguishes between strategic and emotional trust, a contrast that largely coincides with the one just made between reliance and trust. Rational choice might explain 'strategic trust' but not the emotional aspects of trust, which in turn are strongly connected to moral judgements. Emotional trust involves negative reactions towards betrayal, together with the *normative* judgement of the reaction as reasonable and morally justified. Simpson, 'Reasonable Trust'.

49 Cf. Hertzberg, 'On Being Trusted': 'By characterizing a relation as one of trust, I commit myself to the view that certain ways of acting or failing to act will open up the person who is an object of trust to a charge of betrayal. Where nothing will count as betrayal, nothing will count as trust' (p. 200); 'if we call something a betrayal, we are not indifferent towards it' (p. 195 note 2).

50 See especially Chapters 3 and 7.

51 Annette Baier, 'Reply to Olli Lagerspetz', in Lilli Alanen, Sara Heinämaa and Thomas Wallgren (eds), *Commonality and Particularity in Ethics* (Basingstoke: Macmillan, 1997), pp. 118–22, at p. 121; Trudy Govier, 'Trust and Testimony: Nine Arguments on Testimonial Knowledge', *International Journal of Moral and Social Studies* 8 (1993), pp. 21–39, at pp. 24–5, 32–3; Hardin, *Trust and Trustworthiness*, pp. 77–8. Hardin also believes Hertzberg has been 'misled' about Wittgenstein 'by the English translation he uses' (p. 77). Incidentally, Hertzberg is the translator of several works by Wittgenstein (including *Über Gewißheit*) into Swedish.

52 Baier, 'Trust and Antitrust', p. 253. Emphasis added.

53 Russell Hardin, 'Do we Need Trust in Government?', in Mark

E. Warren (ed.), *Democracy and Trust* (Cambridge: Cambridge University Press, 1999), pp. 22–41, at p. 24.
54 Hertzberg, 'On Being Trusted', pp. 195–6.
55 Johnsson, *Trust in Biobank Research*, p. 100. For the argument he is addressing, see Baier, 'Trust and Antitrust', p. 235.
56 Johnsson, *Trust in Biobank Research*, p. 103.

Trust and Hobbesian reason

1 Hobbes, *Leviathan*, Part I Chapter 6, p. [23]. References to this work will include Part, Chapter and the page number of the 1651 edition, indicated in brackets in the 1981 edition.
2 Hobbes, *Leviathan*, Pt I Ch 6 p. [28].
3 Peter Winch, 'Seminars on Authority, The University of Illinois at Urbana-Champaign, Spring Term 1991' (lecture notes by Olli Lagerspetz, MS on file with the author).
4 Ann Cudd points out, however, that Hobbes is less unequivocal here than his Empiricist successors. On the one hand the words 'Good, Evill, and Contemptible' are defined simply in terms of what the subject desires or avoids. On the other hand Hobbes assumes that the subject's appetites and aversions are determined physiologically in accordance with their survival value. A rational subject will define as 'good' the things that are conducive to his or her survival. Ann Cudd, 'Game Theory and the History of Ideas about Rationality'. *Economics and Philosophy* 9 (1993), pp. 101–33, at p. 104.
5 Hobbes, *Leviathan*, Pt I Ch. 13, p. [62].
6 Hobbes, *Leviathan*, Pt I Ch 13, p. [63].
7 Hobbes, *Leviathan*, Pt I Ch. 7, p. [31].
8 Thomas Hobbes, 'Human Nature', in *The English Works of Thomas Hobbes of Malmesbury*, vol. IV (London: John Bohn, 1840), pp. 1–76, at p. 44.
9 Hobbes, *Leviathan*, Pt I Ch 14, p. [68].
10 Hobbes, *Leviathan*, Pt I Ch 15, p. [64].
11 Hobbes, *Leviathan*, Pt I Ch 15, pp. [71], [74].
12 Hobbes, *Leviathan*, Pt I Ch 15, p. [71].
13 Hobbes, *Leviathan*, Pt I Ch 15, pp. [71–2].

14 Peter Winch, 'How is Political Authority Possible?' in D. Z. Phillips (ed.), *Philosophical Investigations* 25 (2002), pp. 20–32, at p. 27.

15 Winch, 'How is Political Authority Possible?', p. 29. Also see Peter Winch, 'Certainty and authority'. *Philosophy* (supplement) (1990), pp. 223–37, at p. 227. Republished in A. Phillips Griffiths (ed.), *Wittgenstein Centenary Essays* (Cambridge: Cambridge University Press, 1991), pp. 223–38.

16 For instance, Philip Pettit points out that Hobbes stresses the foolishness of departing from the laws of nature (see Hobbes, *Leviathan*, Pt I Ch 15, pp. [72–3]). See Philip Pettit, *Made with Words. Hobbes on Language, Mind, and Politics* (Princeton: Princeton University Press 2008), p. 112. This is also pointed out in Simpson, 'Reasonable Trust', note 2, p. 420.

17 This was not a full summary of Hobbes's view on society, even less a refutation of it. Other interpreters have emphasized the aspects of Hobbes's work that relate it to contemporary ideological debates. See Quentin Skinner, *Reason and Rhetoric in the Philosophy of Hobbes* (Cambridge: Cambridge University Press, 1996); Quentin Skinner, *Visions of Politics: Volume III: Hobbes and Civil Science* (Cambridge: Cambridge University Press, 2002); MacPherson, *The Political Theory of Possessive Individualism*, pp. 18, 22.

18 Diego Gambetta, 'Can we Trust Trust?' in Diego Gambetta (ed.), *Trust: Making and Breaking Cooperative Relations* (Oxford: Blackwell, 1990), pp. 213–45, at pp. 218–19.

19 Niklas Luhmann, *Trust and Power* (Chichester: Wiley, 1979), pp. 78–9; Gambetta, 'Can we Trust Trust?', p. 233; Geoffrey Hawthorn, 'Three Ironies in Trust', in Diego Gambetta (ed.), *Trust: Making and Breaking Cooperative Relations* (Oxford: Basil Blackwell, 1990), pp. 111–26, at pp. 112, 114.

20 Luhmann, *Trust and Power*, p. 14.

21 Guido Möllering, 'Rational, Institutional and Active Trust: Just Do It?', in Katinka Bijsma-Frankena and Rosalinde Klein Woolthuis (eds), *Trust Under Pressure: Empirical Investigations of Trust and Trust Building in Uncertain Circumstances* (Cheltenham, Glos.: Edward Elgar Publishing, 2005), pp. 17–36, at p. 18.

22 Gambetta (ed.), *Trust*.

23 Gambetta, 'Can we Trust Trust?', p. 217. Similar positions are endorsed in several contributions to the volume, including David Good, 'Individuals, Interpersonal Relations, and Trust', in Gambetta (ed.), *Trust*, pp. 31–48, at p. 33; Bernard Williams, 'Formal Structures and Social Reality', in Gambetta (ed.), *Trust*, pp. 1–13, at

p. 8; Partha Dasgupta, 'Trust as a Commodity', in Gambetta (ed.), *Trust*, pp. 49–72, at pp. 55–6. Recent work expressing this view includes Bruce Schneier, *Liars and Outliers: Enabling the Trust That Society Needs to Thrive* (Indianapolis: John Wiley & Sons, 2012), p. 5; Mariarosaria Taddeo, 'Modelling Trust in Artificial Agents, a First Step toward the Analysis of e-Trust', *Minds and Machines* 20 (2010), pp. 243–57; Mariarosaria Taddeo, 'The Role of e-Trust in Distributed Artificial Systems', in Charles Ess and May Thorseth (eds), *Trust and Virtual Worlds: Contemporary Perspectives* (New York: Peter Lang, 2011), pp. 75–88. For a critique of Taddeo, see Thomas W. Simpson, 'Computing and the Search for Trust'.

24 Gambetta, 'Can we Trust Trust?', p. 218.

25 James Coleman, *Foundations of Social Theory* (Cambridge, MA: Belknap Press, 1990), p. 99. For a criticism of Coleman and this approach generally, see Simpson, 'Computing and the Search for Trust', pp. 100, 102.

26 Jonathan L. Adler, 'Testimony, Trust, Knowledge', *Journal of Philosophy* 91 (1994), pp. 264–75, at p. 274; Judith Baker, 'Trust and Rationality', *Pacific Philosophical Quarterly* 68 (1987), pp. 1–13, at p. 10; Trudy Govier, 'An Epistemology of Trust', *International Journal of Moral and Social Studies* 8 (1993), pp. 153–74, at p. 169; Gambetta, 'Can we Trust Trust?', p. 235; Antony Pagden, 'Trust in Eighteenth-century Naples', in Gambetta (ed.), *Trust*, pp. 126–41, at p. 129; Coleman, *Foundations of Social Theory*, p. 99.

27 Blaise Pascal, *Pensées de Blaise Pascal, Texte de Léon Brunschvicg* (Samizdat, 2010), Pt III § 233, pp. 55–9, http://www.samizdat.qc.ca/arts/lit/Pascal/Pensees_brunschvicg.pdf [accessed 29 December 2014].

28 Formally expressed, it is rational of A to trust B if $p/(1 - p) > y/v$, where p is the probability of cooperation by B, y is the potential loss for A due to defection by B, and v is the potential gain for A due to cooperation by B. See Möllering, 'Rational, Institutional and Active Trust', p. 19.

29 A full description is found in any standard work on game theory. See also, for instance, Hollis, *Trust Within Reason*, pp. 68–9; Schneier, *Liars and Outliers*, pp. 51–3; Williams, 'Formal Structures and Social Reality', p. 3; Gambetta, 'Can we Trust Trust?', p. 216. For a critique, see R. G. Grant, 'The Politics of Equilibrium', *Inquiry* 35 (1993), pp. 423–46, at pp. 425–30.

30 Using payoffs as given by Origgi, *Qu'est-ce que la confiance?*, p. 21.

31 Möllering, 'Rational, Institutional and Active Trust', p. 19.
32 Robert Axelrod, *The Evolution of Cooperation* (New York: Basic Books, 1984).
33 Expressions like 'egoism', 'altruism', 'reward' and 'punishment' must be used in scare quotes here because the formal model as such does not imply commitments about either the psychology of the player or the nature of the payoff that he, she or it strives to maximize.
34 Gambetta, 'Can we Trust Trust?', p. 228, italics in the original.
35 Marek Kohn, *Trust: Self-interest and Common Good* (Oxford: Oxford University Press, 2009), p. 38.
36 Origgi, *Qu'est-ce que la confiance?*, p. 23.
37 Another form of questioning involves internal critique. One version of the latter is known as backward induction (see Hollis, *Trust Within Reason*, p. 59). If the iterated Prisoners' Dilemma is played a finite number of times there will be a last round. In that last round the preferable strategy for both A and B is to defect, supposing they know it will be the last round. (In a war context, this is often shown in the fighters' last-ditch efforts to improve their positions once the date for a truce has been set.) Assuming mutual knowledge of this, they will predict that the opposite player will defect in the last round regardless of what happens in the penultimate round. Since it will in any case be irrational to play cooperatively in the last round they also have no reason not to defect in the penultimate round. But then the same reasoning that applied to the last round will be carried over to the last but one, then to the last but two, and so on through the entire number of remaining rounds. So it seems that Axelrod's conclusion about iterated Prisoners' Dilemma only holds if the number of remaining rounds is either endless or unknown to both players. However, Möllering defends Axelrod's model against this objection (Möllering, 'Rational, Institutional and Active Trust', p. 21).
38 Alasdair MacIntyre, *After Virtue* (Notre Dame, Indiana: Notre Dame University Press, 1981), pp. 92–4.
39 Kohn, *Trust*, p. 34, referring to Tony Ashworth, *Trench Warfare 1914–1918: The Live and Let Live System* (London: Pan, 2000), p. 144.
40 Pascal himself said explicitly that his wager was only useful for removing intellectual obstacles to faith but it would not induce genuine belief. That would have to come later via the believer's engagement in a religious life.
41 Hardin, *Trust and Trustworthiness*, pp. 1–3.

42 Fyodor Dostoevsky, *The Brothers Karamazov* (New York: W. W. Norton, 1976), p. 101, Book 3 Chapter IV.
43 Also see Origgi, *Qu'est-ce que la confiance?*, p. 19, for a description of Hardin's model.
44 Hertzberg, 'On Being Trusted', p. 196.
45 An expression of Möllering, in his 'Rational, Institutional and Active Trust'.
46 E.g. Möllering, 'Rational, Institutional and Active Trust'; Wanderer and Townsend, 'Is it Rational to Trust?'; Hollis, *Trust Within Reason*; Baier, 'Trust and Antitrust'.
47 Hollis, *Trust Within Reason*, pp. 126–7. See further on p. 54: 'Trust apparently involves relying on others sometimes to act contrary to the balance of their expected utility, with trustworthiness as a matter of willingness so to act. The model of rational action appears to make that impossible for rational agents. The difficulty is inherent in the concept of utility and not by-passed by smooth talk of preferences.'
48 Hollis, *Trust Within Reason*, pp. 142–63.
49 Hollis, *Trust Within Reason*, p. 154.
50 Hollis (*Trust Within Reason*, p. 146) discusses reasons for donating blood: 'unless the respondents were simply stupid, the reply that "I might need blood myself one day" was a cover for a non-economic motive which they did not care to voice.'
51 This is the main conclusion of Hollis, *Trust Within Reason*.
52 As Lars Hertzberg puts it: 'I regard it as acceptable (or making sense, or the like) to act on [the desire]. So I must already have learnt to take part in discussions about actions being or not being acceptable, making or failing to make sense, if I am to make an utterance that can be understood in this way. And this is, of course, different from simply having learnt to give expression to my desires' – Hertzberg, 'On the Attitude of Trust', p. 117. See also Hertzberg, 'On Being Trusted', p. 203.
53 Peter Winch made this point forcefully in his lectures on moral philosophy at Urbana-Champaign, Illinois, in the autumn of 1990. The following discussion owes much to those lectures. See Peter Winch, 'Lectures on Ethics and Value Theory at the University of Illinois, Urbana-Champaign, 1990' (notes by Olli Lagerspetz, 72 pp., MS on file with the present author).
54 Plato, *Gorgias* (London: Penguin Books, 1971), pp. 491–2. References to Plato's work will follow the standard (Stephanus) pagination.

55 Plato, *Gorgias*, pp. 494–5, 499.
56 Commenting on the use of game theory in the study of market behaviour, Robert Grant concludes: 'The reason why such comparatively abstract, cut-and-dried disciplines are applicable to the activities they study is that such activities already are, and are understood by those who engage in them to be, equivalent abstractions from human behaviour in general. The legitimate study of certain aspects of human life, and of the principles that govern them, strays beyond its competence when it offers to pronounce upon life as a whole' – Grant, 'The Politics of Equilibrium', p. 431.

Vulnerability and entrusting

1 By 'rationalism' I will mean, in this connection, the general approach to behaviour that either takes relations between people to be outcomes of the agent's conscious analyses of risks and benefits, or assumes that they are best understood by treating them *as if* they were motivated by such analyses. In this sense, the theories of Rawls (in *A Theory of Justice*) and Gauthier (in *Morals by Agreement*) would be examples of rationalist approaches in moral philosophy. No close relation is implied with the tradition exemplified by Descartes, Spinoza and Leibniz. See John Rawls, *A Theory of Justice* (Cambridge, MA: Harvard University Press, 1971); David Gauthier, *Morals by Agreement* (New York: Oxford University Press, 1986).

2 For similar positions, see e.g. Govier, 'An Epistemology of Trust', p. 156, identifying the question as 'when, why, and to what extent trust – or distrust – was reasonable or right'. According to Jones (in 'Trust as an Affective Attitude', p. 4), philosophical accounts of trust should '[set] constraints on what can be said about justification conditions of trust'. Hollis (in *Trust Within Reason*, p. 124) suggests that the important question is 'not why people do trust one another but whether and why it is rational for them to do so'; i.e. the 'Enlightenment question of who merits trust' (p. 105).

3 Origgi, *Que-est-ce que la confiance?*, p. 102.
4 Baier, 'Trust and Antitrust', p. 247.
5 Baier, 'Trust and Antitrust', pp. 248–9, 252.
6 '[E]ven when one does become aware of trust and intentionally continues a particular case of it, one need not intend to achieve any particular benefit from it – one need not trust a person in order to

receive some gain, even when in fact one does gain' – Baier, 'Trust and Antitrust', p. 235; also see p. 240.

7   Baier, 'Trust and Antitrust', pp. 252–3.

8   J. M. Bernstein writes: 'Baier's essays strike me as being as important to an understanding of the shape and meaning of morality as, say, Kant's *Groundwork*, with the obvious [!] proviso that Baier's account is true and Kant's false.' In J. M. Bernstein, 'Trust: On the Real, but Almost Always Unnoticed, Ever-changing Foundation of Ethical Life', *Metaphilosophy*, vol. 42 (2011), pp. 395–416, at p. 396.

9   McMyler, *Testimony, Trust, and Authority*, p. 114, footnote 3; Hertzberg, 'On Being Trusted', p. 201. McMyler's focus on the distinction between cognitivism and non-cognitivism perhaps mostly owes to the fact that this distinction is currently important in the philosophy of emotions. Arguably, in the philosophy of trust there are at least equally important differences *within* these broad categories.

10 Interview with Helge Skirbekk, published in Norwegian translation as Helge Skirbekk, 'Et praktisk syn på tillit til velferdsstater. Intervju med Onora O'Neill', in Helge Skirbekk and Harald Grimen (eds), *Tillit i Norge* (Oslo: Res Publica, 2012), pp. 316–33, at p. 319. O'Neill states: 'I think that the idea that [trust] is an immediate personal response to another person is often based upon assuming that the paradigm about trust is intimacy, and in particular, say, mother-child relations, you know, all that literature on the affective relationship between the mother and the infant. Of course, it is not wrong. So, you do have the phenomenon of blind trust – poor little baby, what else can it do but give blind trust. But that is not really a good model for thinking about trust in a complex social world [...] So, I think that that view, although it might be quite true about the phenomenology of intimate relationships of trust, is just not adequate for practical purposes, or for the world we now live in. I am thinking about people like Annette Baier among the philosophers, or Karen Jones, but many, many other people who write on virtue ethics tend to think of trust as immediate, and unmediated, relationships between people who share a lot.' I am grateful to Dr Skirbekk for a transcript of the original quote.

11 Baier, 'Trust and Antitrust', p. 257: '[S]uch explicitness is not only rare in trust relationships, but many of them must begin inexplicitly and nonvoluntarily.'

12 See, e.g. Baier, 'Trust and Antitrust', p. 236.

13 See Baier, 'Trust and Antitrust', pp. 236, 259, and passim.

14 Baier, 'Trust and Antitrust', pp. 236–7, 240.
15 Annette Baier, 'Doing Things with Others: The Mental Commons', in Lilli Alanen, Sara Heinämaa and Thomas Wallgren (eds), *Commonality and Particularity in Ethics* (Basingstoke: Macmillan, 1997) pp. 15–44.
16 Baier, 'Trust and Antitrust', p. 240.
17 Baier, 'Trust and Antitrust', pp. 244–5; also see p. 242.
18 Baier, 'Trust and Antitrust', pp. 235–6.
19 Baier, 'Trust and Antitrust', pp. 255–6.
20 Baier, 'Trust and Antitrust', pp. 258–9.
21 Annette Baier, 'Reply to Olli Lagerspetz', p. 119.
22 The suggestion does seem to lead to an infinite regress. It would imply that the trustful relationship between A and B consists in A entrusting B with the trustful relationship C between A and B, which consists in A entrusting B with the trustful relationship C' between A and B, which consists in A entrusting B with the trustful relationship C" between A and B ... and so on *ad infinitum*.
23 Baier, 'Trust and Antitrust', p. 236: 'Accepting such an analysis, taking trust to be a three-place predicate (A trusts B with valued thing C) will involve some distortion and regimentation of some cases, where we may have to strain to discern any definite candidate for C, but I think it will prove more of a help than a hindrance.'
24 Baier, 'Reply to Olli Lagerspetz', p. 119.
25 An additional question here is how one is to specify the crucial action described as betrayal. 'She lied to him' is already prima facie a description of a breach of trust. So the model of trust as entrusting seems to presuppose that we must be able to point further to a specific harm that was caused by this instance of deception, and further to claim that the trustful relation was 'about' avoiding that specific harm.
26 I.e. trust as a three-place relation between two persons and a thing, as opposed to a simple two-place relation between persons. Baier, 'Trust and Antitrust', p. 259.
27 Baier, 'Trust and Antitrust', pp. 257–9. Baier sees the difference between herself and 'contractualists' in the fact that the latter would assume self-interest as a motive whereas she has left the questions of motives open (p. 257). However, it must be kept in mind that also most game theorists would say their theory is neutral with regard to the specific content of the players' preferences.
28 Hertzberg ('On Being Trusted', pp. 201–2) points out that Baier's

two formulations of the grounds for reasonable trust prescribe rather different attitudes. The first formulation suggests we should be on our guard until provided with reasons for trusting, while the second only requires the absence of grounds for suspicion.

29 Baier, 'Trust and Antitrust', p. 235. Among others, similar views are expressed in Trudy Govier, 1997. *Social Trust and Human Communities* (Montreal and Kingston: McGill-Queen's University Press, 1997), p. 4 and O'Neill, *A Question of Trust*. Möllering, in 'Rational, Institutional and Active Trust' (p. 18) writes: 'I concur with Rousseau et al. [...] that fairly broad consent could be obtained for their definition of trust as "a psychological state comprising the intention to accept vulnerability based upon positive expectations of the intentions or behavior of another".' Möllering is citing D. M. Rousseau, G. B. Sitkin, R. S. Burt and C. Camerer, 'Not So Different After All: A Cross-Discipline View of Trust', *Academy of Management Review* 23 (1998), pp. 393–404, at p. 395.
30 Johnsson, *Trust in Biobank Research*, p. 87.
31 Cf. Wanderer and Townsend, 'Is it Rational to Trust?', p. 3: '[W]e take for granted that there is a basic difference between reliance and trust, where the hallmark of the latter is a propensity to feel resentment towards the one trusted when let down.'
32 Johnsson, *Trust in Biobank Research*, pp. 83–4.
33 Baier goes as far as to state that a relation where both parties 'suspect each other of willingness to harm the other' may qualify as a case – albeit a morally dubious one – of 'sensible trust'. Baier, 'Trust and Antitrust', p. 255.
34 Hertzberg, 'On the Attitude of Trust', p. 115.
35 Baier, 'Trust and Antitrust', p. 235.
36 For a discussion of the notion of what can be imagined, see Lars Hertzberg, 'Imagination and the Sense of Identity', in his *The Limits of Experience* (Helsinki: Acta Philosophica Fennica, 1994), pp. 96–112.
37 Karin Boye, *Kallocain* (Madison: University of Wisconsin Press, 1966), trans. Gustaf Lannestock. Original title: Karin Boye, *Kallocain. Roman från 2000-talet.*
38 Boye, *Kallocain*, p. 85.
39 Boye, *Kallocain*, pp. 10–11.
40 Boye, *Kallocain*, p. 10.
41 Boye, *Kallocain*, p. 10.
42 Boye, *Kallocain*, p. 9.

43 Boye, *Kallocain*, p. 11.
44 Boye, *Kallocain*, p. 153.
45 Boye, *Kallocain*, p. 155.
46 Boye, *Kallocain*, p. 156.
47 Boye, *Kallocain*, pp. 190, 191.
48 Knud Ejler Løgstrup, *Den etiske fordring* (København: Gyldendal, 1962), First published 1957. Published in English as *The Ethical Demand* (Notre Dame, Indiana: Notre Dame University Press, 1997).
49 Given the definition of 'trust' in opposition to betrayal rather than 'trust' as another word for risk management.
50 Baier, *Moral Prejudices*, p. 159.
51 Boye, *Kallocain*, pp. 149–50.
52 '... jene unsichtbare Mauer von Affekten, die sich gegenwärtig zwischen Körper und Körper der Menschen, zurückdrängend und trennend, zu erheben scheint, der Wall der heute oft bereits bei der bloßen Annäherung an etwas spürbar ist, das mit Mund oder Händen eines anderen in Berührung gekommen ist, und der als Peinlichkeitsgefühl bei dem bloßen *Anblick* vieler körperlicher Verrichtungen eines anderen in Erscheinung tritt, oft auch nur bei deren bloßen *Erwähnung*, oder als Schamgefühl, wenn eigene Verrichtungen dem Anblick anderer ausgesetzt sind, und gewiß nicht nur dann.' Norbert Elias: *Über den Prozess der Zivilisation. Soziogenetische und psychogenetische Untersuchungen. Erster Band: Wandlungen des Verhaltens in den weltlichen Oberschichten des Abendlandes* (Frankfurt a.M.: Suhrkamp, 1981), pp. 88–9. My translation.
53 Joel Backström, *The Fear of Openness. An Essay on Friendship and the Roots of Morality* (Åbo: Åbo Akademi University Press, 2007), p. 36.

The time dimension

1 Baier ('Trust and Antitrust', p. 244) speaks of 'conscious trust the truster has chosen to endorse and cultivate'. Hardin argues on the contrary that trust, being a species of belief and not an action, quite obviously cannot be subject to decision any more than beliefs generally are: 'All of this is wrong', he states. 'I just do or do not trust to some degree, depending on the evidence I have' (Hardin,

Trust and Trustworthiness, p. 59; also see p. 119. See also Hardin, 'Do we Need Trust in Government?', pp. 23–4). Luhmann, on the other hand, distinguishing between 'confidence' and 'trust' (in Luhmann, 'Familiarity, Confidence, Trust'), specifies the difference so that trust, unlike confidence, is by definition something subject to decision. As we have seen in Chapter 2, game theorists have based their entire treatment of trust on the premise that we more or less constantly make decisions in some sense to trust or distrust.

2   See Frederick Stoutland, 'In Defence of a Non-psychologistic Account of Reasons for Action', in Christoffer Gefwert and Olli Lagerspetz (eds), *Wittgenstein and Philosophical Psychology. Essays in Honour of Lars Hertzberg* (Uppsala: Uppsala Philosophical Studies Vol. 55, 2009), pp. 193–212.

3   This point is a very fundamental part of Hobbes's conception of human agency (Hobbes, *Leviathan*: Pt I Ch 6). See Winch, 'How is Political Authority Possible?'.

4   See Georg Henrik von Wright, *Explanation and Understanding* (New York: Cornell University Press, 1971), pp. 26–7; G. E. M. Anscombe, *Intention* (Oxford: Basil Blackwell, 1957), § 33. Anscombe herself clearly thinks of her suggestion as a perspective on action – as a way of making it intelligible by ascribing a way of reasoning to the agent – not as a psychological explanation of the action.

5   Explorations of this perspective are, for instance, a central theme of R. G. Collingwood's philosophy of history. See Robin George Collingwood, *The Idea of History* (Oxford: Oxford University Press, 1946), p. 214.

6   The snapshot conception would not be implied if the syllogism is not interpreted as a progression of psychological states but as a *justification*, a spelling-out of what would make the action appear reasonable in the circumstances. See Stoutland, 'In defence of a non-psychologistic account of reasons for action'.

7   See von Wright, *Explanation and Understanding*, pp. 132–3; Collingwood, *The Idea of History*.

8   Partha Dasgupta, 'Trust as a Commodity', in Gambetta (ed.), *Trust*, pp. 55–6.

9   Dasgupta argues that 'for trust to be developed between individuals, they must have repeated encounters, and they must have some memory of previous encounters' ('Trust as a Commodity', p. 59). This looks like an acknowledgement of the time dimension that I have stressed. However, the point of his analysis is to describe the

reputation for honesty in a way that allows it to figure as a factor in one-off transactions.

10 Origgi, *Qu'est-ce que la confiance?*, p. 17. Also see Russell Hardin, *Trust and Trustworthiness*, pp. 74–8.

11 For example, Jon Elster writes: 'To act rationally is to do as well for oneself as one can [...] In fact, once one has come to appreciate [game theory] fully, it appears not to be a theory in the ordinary sense, but the natural, indispensable framework for understanding human interaction.' Jon Elster, *Nuts and Bolts for the Social Sciences* (Cambridge: Cambridge University Press, 1989), p. 28.

12 Also the agent's honesty can be factored into an economy of payoffs assigned to each individual transaction conducted. In Dasgupta's model; for instance, the agent's honesty is operationalized in terms of payoffs from honest vs dishonest transactions (Dasgupta, 'Trust as a Commodity', p. 61). An honest salesman is defined as one whose payoffs for selling a good item are superior to payoffs for selling a defective item, while the opposite is true of the dishonest salesman. This of course implies that 'payoff' is not the same as economic gain, but an expression of the agent's overall ranking of the possible outcomes of each transaction. Also see Hollis, who presents an analysis of how the agents' preferences are altered by introducing normative considerations, in Hollis, *Trust Within Reason*.

13 See Grant, 'The Politics of Equilibrium', p. 429.

14 E.g. Annette Baier, in 'Trust and Antitrust' (p. 232), identifying the question as, 'Whom should I trust in what way, and why', and Trudy Govier, in 'An Epistemology of Trust' (p. 156), identifying the question as, 'When, why, and to what extent trust – or distrust – was reasonable or right'. According to Karen Jones, in 'Trust as an Affective Attitude' (p. 4), philosophical accounts of trust should '[set] constraints on what can be said about justification conditions of trust'. Hollis, in *Trust Within Reason* (p. 124), suggests that the important question is 'not why people do trust one another but whether and why it is rational for them to do so'; i.e. the 'Enlightenment question of who merits trust' (p. 105).

15 Onora O'Neill, *A Question of Trust*, Lecture One; Coleman, *Foundations of Social Theory*, p. 99.

16 E.g. Govier, 'An Epistemology of Trust'; Williams, 'Formal Structures and Social Reality', p. 7; Good, 'Individuals, Interpersonal Relations, and Trust', p. 33; Gambetta, 'Can we Trust Trust?', p. 222.

17 This assumption of course already presupposes that we have narrowed down the target group considerably. In a real case we

would have definite ideas about whom not to approach – not someone who is obviously busy, not a child or a drunk, and we rely on a variety of more indefinite cues from looks and behaviour in judging who is not to be trusted. In those cases, we would not even consider whether to ask for their help.

18 Govier, 'An Epistemology of Trust', p. 167. Cf. Jones, 'Trust as an Affective Attitude' (p. 21): 'Domain and consequences interact to determine which default stance [with regard to trust versus distrust] is justified and how much evidence we need to move from that default stance.'

19 Govier, 'An Epistemology of Trust', p. 169.

20 Hertzberg describes the view in question (addressing specifically the work of Baier): 'On [this] view, I may decide to trust or not to trust someone, to take note of the other's trust or to ignore it at my own discretion. Rather than trust being embedded in relations that are already in place, the individual seeks out objects of trust by trying to identify properties on which to base the expectation that the person in question will be disposed to act, or can be made to act, in accordance with her wishes' – Hertzberg, 'On Being Trusted', p. 202.

21 Dostoevsky, *The Brothers Karamazov*, pp. 559, 565–6, 642–3 (Book 11, Ch. IV; Book 12, Ch. IV).

22 İlham Dilman, *Love and Human Separateness* (Oxford: Blackwell, 1987), p. 127.

23 İlham Dilman, *Love and Human Separateness*, p. 127.

24 Christopher Robinson, email, 23 June 2014.

25 Dostoevsky, *The Brothers Karamazov*, pp. 698–9, 702–3 (Book 12, Ch. XII).

26 See Dostoevsky, *The Brothers Karamazov*, pp. 597; 678; 691; 702–3 (Book 11, Ch. VIII; Book 12, Ch. VIII, Ch. X, Ch. XII).

27 The same dichotomy is in evidence in recent discussion of the concept of testimony, to be considered in Chapter 6. The two main positions here imply that testimonial knowledge is treated either as *data* for the agent's independent reasoning, or as something accepted on authority and thus qualitatively distinct from the agent's independent reasoning. The first alternative implies reductionism of a kind, as it seems to blur the difference between knowledge by experience and knowledge by testimony. The second position assumedly raises the question of how we can be *justified* in accepting testimony on the authority of the person who gives it. See McMyler,

Testimony, Trust, and Authority; see also Jonas Ahlskog, '[Review of] *Testimony, Trust, and Authority*'.

28 Linus Johnsson, Gert Helgesson, Mats G. Hansson and Stefan Eriksson, 'Adequate Trust Avails, Mistaken Trust Matters: On the Moral Responsibility of Doctors as Proxies for Patients' Trust in Biobank Research', *Bioethics* 27 (2013), pp. 485–92, at p. 487. See also McMyler's comment: 'I will deny the claim [implied by noncognitivist accounts of trust] that trust occurs in the absence of or is not fully responsive to evidential considerations. I think philosophical accounts of trust are led to deny this only in virtue of employing an overly restrictive conception of evidence' (McMyler, *Testimony, Trust and Authority*, p. 114, fn 3).

29 Jones, 'Trust as an Affective Attitude'; Karen Jones, 'Trust: Philosophical Aspects', in Neil Smelser and Paul Bates (eds), *International Encyclopedia of the Social and Behavioral Sciences* (Elsevier Science, Amsterdam 2002), pp. 15917–22); Karen Jones, 'Trusting Interpretations', in Pekka Mäkelä and Cynthia Townley (eds), *Trust: Analytic and Applied Perspectives* (Amsterdam: Rodopi, 2013), pp. 15–29.

30 Jones, 'Trusting Interpretations', p. 15.

31 Jones, 'Trusting Interpretations', p. 16.

32 See William Shakespeare, 'Othello, the Moor of Venice', in *The Complete Works of William Shakespeare* (Chatham River Publishers, New York 1987, pp. 1113–50).

33 Jones, 'Trusting Interpretations', pp. 18–19, 26.

34 Jones, 'Trusting Interpretations', p. 26.

35 Jones, 'Trusting Interpretations', p. 18.

36 Jones, 'Trust as an Affective Attitude', p. 12. In 'Trust as an Affective Attitude', Jones describes trust as an attitude of optimism about the goodwill and competence of the other (p. 7 and *passim*). The actions of the other are 'viewed through the affective lens of trust' (p. 12). Thus she stresses also in that paper that our judgements of 'evidence' about the other are not independent of our existing relations with them. However, Jones presents this as a source of *distortion*, implying that there is (or could be) a context-free way to determine what degree of optimism is the rational one.

37 Thanks to Christopher Robinson for raising these questions (email, 23 June 2014).

38 Jones, 'Trusting Interpretations', p. 27.

39 I hope the reader understands that nothing I am now saying is

meant to indicate that there is no difference between neutral and biased opinion, or to claim that any opinion is just as subjective as any other. What I do believe is that the need to avoid bias may take very different forms. It is not obvious, for instance, that engagement coincides with bias and disengagement coincides with objectivity. The contrast must be sought in another dimension. In general, perhaps, by 'achieving an objective view', we mean arriving at a point where an inquiry may reasonably come to a halt. There will of course be disagreements about where exactly that point should be.

40 Harold Garfinkel, *Studies in Ethnomethodology* (Cambridge: Polity Press, 1996; first published in 1967), p. 47.
41 See Benedict Anderson, *Imagined Communities* (London: Verso, 1983).
42 There are some versions of individualism that we should hardly quarrel with; thus it goes without saying that there will be no society without individual members. It also seems obvious that we should not claim the presence of any social or cultural trait in a society, a collective consciousness or a general will, unless we can show its presence in how individuals think and act.
43 Ludwig Wittgenstein, *Philosophical Investigations* (Oxford: Basil Blackwell, 1953), I: § 583.
44 Wittgenstein, *Philosophical Investigations*, II: p. 174.

'Trust' as an organizing tool

1 Much of the argument in the present chapter has been presented in a different form in my joint paper with Lars Hertzberg; see Lagerspetz and Hertzberg, 'Trust in Wittgenstein'. For a partly similar argument see also Olli Lagerspetz, *Trust: The Tacit Demand* (Dordrecht: Kluwer, 1998), pp. 14–27.
2 Those who speak of trust as a feeling include Anthony Giddens, *Modernity and Self-Identity* (Cambridge: Polity Press, 1991), p. 36; Govier, 'An Epistemology of Trust', pp. 155–74, at p. 156.
3 Baier, *Moral Prejudices*, p. 132.
4 Wittgenstein, *Philosophical Investigations*, I: § 596.
5 Wittgenstein, *Philosophical Investigations*, I: § 577. Italics in the original. See also Ludwig Wittgenstein, *The Blue Book*, in Ludwig Wittgenstein, *The Blue and Brown Books* (New York: Harper & Row, 1965), pp. 20–1.

6   Ludwig Wittgenstein, *Zettel* (Berkeley: University of California Press, 1967), §§ 45, 78, 81. Also see §§ 46–7, 50, 76–7, 82–3, 85.
7   For a discussion of genuine duration, see Malcolm's contribution to D. M. Armstrong and Norman Malcolm, *Consciousness and Causality* (Oxford: Basil Blackwell, 1984), pp. 1–101); esp. pp. 79–81.
8   Wittgenstein, *Zettel*, §§ 82, 45, 50.
9   Wittgenstein, *Zettel*, § 50.
10 David Cockburn drew my attention to this. It was also rightfully pointed out in Annette Baier's 'Reply to Olli Lagerspetz'.
11 Wittgenstein, *Philosophical Investigations* I: § 583.
12 Wittgenstein, *Philosophical Investigations*, II: p. 174.
13 The foregoing remark is not an attempt to exclude unexpected cases by setting up ordinary language as a norm for language use. It is a reminder of the fact that intelligible uses of the word 'grief' presuppose *some* plausible background in the person's situation over and above the feeling itself. I appeal to the reader's ability to imagine herself confused if someone were to utter certain words in the circumstances described. This does not entail that her confusion would have to be irremediable. In his treatment of the inner-outer distinction Wittgenstein, as Chantal Bax helpfully puts it, may be said to situate the inner 'in the interspace between the subject and his or her fellow men' ... 'it is only in the context of a recurring social pattern that a person's doings and sayings make for, and can be taken as, instances of a particular psychological phenomenon'. Chantal Bax, *Subjectivity after Wittgenstein. The Post-Cartesian Subject and the 'Death of Man'* (London: Bloomsbury, 2012), p. 63.
14 Wittgenstein, *Philosophical Investigations*, II: p. 174.
15 Drew Leder, *The Absent Body* (Chicago: Chicago University Press, 1990), p. 85.
16 Leder, *The Absent Body*, p. 83.
17 Baier, 'Trust and Antitrust', p. 234.
18 Baier, 'Trust and Antitrust', p. 234.
19 Baier, 'Trust and Antitrust', p. 234.
20 Bernstein, 'Trust', p. 403.
21 Bernstein, 'Trust', p. 395.
22 Garfinkel, *Studies in Ethnomethodology*; Harold Garfinkel, 'A Conception of, and Experiments with, "Trust" as a Condition

of Stable Concentrated Actions', in O. J. Harvey (ed.), *Motivation and Social Interaction* (New York: Roland Press, 1963), pp. 187–238.

23 Garfinkel, *Studies in Ethnomethodology*, p. 51.
24 Garfinkel, *Studies in Ethnomethodology*, p. 75.
25 Garfinkel, *Studies in Ethnomethodology*, p. 35.
26 Rod Watson, 'Trust in Interpersonal Interaction and Cloud Computing', in Richard H. R. Harper (ed.), *Trust, Computing, and Society* (Cambridge: Cambridge University Press, 2014), pp. 172–98, at p. 179.
27 Put differently, the objection would imply that the truth conditions of 'I trusted her' were the same as the truth conditions for 'I trust her', only transposed to the past – those truth conditions being the facts of my mental condition – while the *assertability* conditions may have been different. 'I trust her' would, on this account, have been true all along but there would have been no way for me to *say* it without misleading.
28 Cf. Svend Brinkmann, 'Psychology in the Space of Reasons', *Journal for the Theory of Social Behaviour* 36 (2006), pp. 1–16.
29 See G. E. Moore, 'Proof of an External World', *Proceedings of the British Academy* 25 (1939), pp. 273–300. Reprinted in G. E. Moore, *Selected Writings*, Thomas Baldwin (ed.) (London: Routledge, 1993), pp. 147–70.
30 Malcolm relates these discussions between Wittgenstein, Moore and Malcolm in Norman Malcolm, *Ludwig Wittgenstein: A Memoir* (Oxford: Oxford University Press, 1984), at pp. 71–4.
31 Wittgenstein, *On Certainty*, § 151.
32 See Marie McGinn, *Sense and Certainty* (Oxford: Blackwell, 1989), p. 109.
33 See Elizabeth Wolgast, *Paradoxes of Knowledge* (Ithaca: Cornell University Press, 1977), p. 155 and *passim*.
34 Wittgenstein, *On Certainty*, § 468.
35 McGinn writes: 'the fact that Moore-type propositions cannot be the object of knowledge claims serves to emphasize their role as framework to our practice. Thus, Moore-type propositions represent a type of judgement which either we all make automatically, simply in virtue of being participants in the practice, or which will be affirmed and accepted without question, in cases where the relevant portion of the framework is something that we do not yet share' – McGinn, *Sense and Certainty*, p. 109.

36 Cf. Baier, 'Reply to Olli Lagerspetz', pp. 119–20. As she puts it (p. 120): 'Lagerspetz sees trust as in the eye of the beholder, as constituted by the disparity between observer's and agent's perspectives. If this were so, then a statement like "In God we trust" (on US banknotes) would be possible only to the extent that we are beholding each other, and would be generously construed as "In God the rest of you trust," or possibly as "In God we trusted". Why must there be a disparity between agent and observer? We are all soon self-observers, and as observers of others we are observers who can sympathize with the observed agents' perspectives.' (The phrase 'In God we trust', however, has problems of its own and I now leave it on one side; in any case Baier states elsewhere ['Trust and Antitrust', p. 242] that trust in God involves childlike dependence which makes it an unsuitable model for relations between mature adults.)

37 On this, see also Tage Kurtén, 'Suspicion Concerning World-views', in Tage Kurtén, *På väg mot det postsekulära. Tankar under femton år* (Uppsala: Acta Universitatis upsaliensis. Studies in Systematic Theology and Worldviews 2, 2014), pp. 71–88.

38 David Cockburn, 'Trust in Conversation'. *Nordic Wittgenstein Review* 3 (2014), pp. 47–67, at p. 65.

39 As my previous discussion has indicated, there is an important difference between these two kinds of criticism.

Communication, truthfulness, trust

1 Kohn, *Trust*, p. 40.
2 Richard Dawkins and John Krebs, 'Animal Signals: Information or Manipulation?', in John Krebs and Nicholas Davies (eds), *Behavioural Ecology: An Evolutionary Approach* (Oxford: Blackwell, 1978), pp. 380–402.
3 Kohn, *Trust*, p. 23; Dawkins and Krebs, 'Animal Signals: Information or Manipulation?', p. 283.
4 John R. Krebs and Richard Dawkins, 'Animal Signals: Mind-reading and Manipulation', in J. R. Krebs and N. B. Davies (eds), *Behavioural Ecology: An Evolutionary Approach*, 2nd edn (Sunderland, MA: Sinauer, 1984), pp. 380–402.
5 Dawkins and Krebs, 'Animal Signals: Information or Manipulation?', p. 309; Kohn, *Trust*, p. 24.

6 Hobbes, *Leviathan*, see esp. Pt I Ch 4, pp. [12–13]. Peter Winch originally drew my attention to the importance of Hobbes's understanding of language in his overall project, in Winch, 'Seminars on authority'.

7 Luciano Fadiga, 'Sensorimotor Processing of Speech and Language', Paper, *Dynamics of Active Perception: An Interdisciplinary Symposium on Perception and the Mind-Body Problem* (Helsinki Collegium for Advanced Studies, 15–16 May 2014).

8 It is not suggested here that any given thesis about the nature of linguistic communication can be established on the basis of empirical findings about mutual attunement in the development of language. This is first of all because *those* claims are not purely empirical either. Empirical discoveries (about the existence of mirror neurons, say) can be given a number of different roles in the overall account. Secondly, the mere fact that it is *possible* to take an alternative perspective here demonstrates already that the available facts do not force us to think of communication in Hobbesian terms.

9 Donald Davidson, *Inquiries into Truth and Interpretation* (Oxford: Clarendon Press, 1984). Cf. Richard Moran, 'Getting Told and Being Believed', *Philosophers' Imprint* 5 (2005), pp. 1–29, at p. 3. This argument is familiar from Davidson's work on radical interpretation, an argument to which Moran alludes (pp. 4, 15) without explicitly mentioning Davidson.

10 Moran, 'Getting Told and Being Believed', p. 4. The example also comes from this paper.

11 C. A. J. Coady, *Testimony: A Philosophical Study*; Angus Ross, 'Why do we Believe what we are Told?', *Ratio* 28 (1986), pp. 69–88; Moran, 'Getting Told and Being Believed'; Richard Moran, 'Problems of Sincerity', *Proceedings of the Aristotelian Society* 105 (2005), pp. 325–45; Edward Hinchman, 'Telling as Inviting to Trust', *Philosophy and Phenomenological Research* 70 (2005), pp. 562–87; Paul Faulkner, 'On Telling and Trusting', *Mind* 116 (2007), pp. 875–902; Paul Faulkner, *Knowledge on Trust*; McMyler, *Testimony, Trust and Authority*. In considering this debate, I have profited greatly from discussion with Jonas Ahlskog.

12 Moran, 'Getting Told and Being Believed', *passim*; McMyler, in *Testimony, Trust and Authority*, distinguishes between the *evidential* model, the *inheritance* model and the *second-personal* model, the last one corresponding to the Assurance View. See pp. 80–7, 87–91 and 91–4, respectively.

13 Moran, 'Getting Told and Being Believed', p. 5.

14 Moran, 'Getting Told and Being Believed', pp. 1–2, 9.
15 Moran, 'Getting Told and Being Believed', p. 6.
16 McMyler, *Testimony, Trust and Authority*, pp. 88–9, citing D. Owens, *Reason without Freedom* (New York: Routledge, 2000), p. 166.
17 Moran, 'Problems of Sincerity', p. 339.
18 McMyler, *Testimony, Trust and Authority*, pp. 61–4.
19 McMyler, *Testimony, Trust and Authority*, p. 94.
20 McMyler, *Testimony, Trust and Authority*, p. 94.
21 McMyler, *Testimony, Trust and Authority*, p. 137.
22 McMyler, *Testimony, Trust and Authority*, p. 100; Hinchman, 'Telling as inviting to trust'.
23 McMyler, *Testimony, Trust and Authority*, p. 149. McMyler makes, in this connection, an analogy with Hobbes's distinction between 'command' and 'counsel' (pp. 146–7). Cf. Hobbes, *Leviathan*, II: 25, pp. [131–2].
24 Julia Korkman, *How (not) to Interview Children: Interviews with Young Children in Sexual Abuse Investigations in Finland* (Åbo: Åbo Akademi University Press, 2006).
25 See especially McMyler, *Testimony, Trust and Authority*, pp. 10–44.
26 This apparently results from the fact that McMyler, like Moran, focuses on assurance and 'autonomy' as contrasting methods of *justification*, as two ways in which the hearer may deal with the utterance, while not considering the conditions of the meaningfulness of the utterance as such.
27 See Hertzberg, 'On Being Trusted', p. 198.
28 Peter Winch, 'Nature and Convention', in Peter Winch, *Ethics and Action* (London: Routledge & Kegan Paul, 1972), pp. 50–72, first published in *Proceedings of the Aristotelian Society* 60 (1960), pp. 231–52. Cf. R. F. Holland, 'Is Goodness a Mystery?', in R. F. Holland, *Against Empiricism* (Totowa, NJ: Barnes & Noble, 1980), pp. 94–109.
29 Winch, 'Nature and Convention', p. 61.
30 Winch, 'Nature and Convention', p. 62.
31 Winch, 'Nature and Convention', p. 67.
32 Winch, 'Nature and Convention', pp. 98–9.
33 Immanuel Kant, 'On a Supposed Right to tell lies from Benevolent Motives', in *Kant's Critique of Practical Reason and Other Works*

on the *Theory of Ethics,* trans. Thomas Kingsmill Abbott, 4th rev. edn (London: Longmans, Green and Co., 1889), pp. 361–6, at p. 362. Cf. Immanuel Kant, *Grounding for the Metaphysics of Morals* (Indianapolis: Hackett Publishing company, 1981), pp. 402–3; A similar argument was presented by St Thomas Aquinas; see Alasdair MacIntyre, 'The Privatization of Good'. *Review of Politics* 52 (1990), pp. 344–61, at pp. 356–7.

34 See also Mark Owen Webb, 'Why I Know about as Much as You: A Reply to Hardwig', *The Journal of Philosophy* 90 (1993), pp. 260–70, at pp. 269–70; C. A. J. Coady, 'Testimony and Observation', *American Philosophical Quarterly* 10 (1973), pp. 149–55, at pp. 152–4.

35 See also Oswald Hanfling, 'How We Trust One Another', *Philosophy* 83 (2008), pp. 161–77, at pp. 169–70.

36 Winch, 'Nature and Convention', p. 66.

37 See Alasdair MacIntyre, 'The Privatization of Good', p. 357.

38 Jokes with the object of ridiculing others have visible similarities with other practices of social exclusion. But they could not have been spread under the guise of *jokes,* including the typically bullying insistence that any protest by those chosen as the butts of the joke would just show their deficient sense of humour, unless the general norm was that jokes are essentially harmless.

39 Holland, 'Is Goodness a Mystery?', pp. 101–7.

40 Peter Winch, 'Introduction', in Peter Winch, *Ethics and Action* (London: Routledge & Kegan Paul, 1972), pp. 1–7, at pp. 4–5.

41 See Winch, 'Certainty and Authority'; Winch, 'How is Political Authority Possible?'.

42 Peter Winch, 'Authority', in A. Quinton (ed.), *Political Philosophy.* Oxford Readings in Philosophy. (Oxford: Oxford University Press, 1972), pp. 97–111, at p. 99, italics in the original. Originally published in *Proceedings of the Aristotelian Society* 32 (1958–9), pp. 235–40.

43 Peter Winch, *The Idea of a Social Science and Its Relation to Philosophy* (London: Routledge & Kegan Paul, 1958), p. 121.

44 Winch, 'Nature and Convention', p. 64.

45 Løgstrup, *Den etiske fordring,* p. 17. All quotes from this work are my translations.

46 Løgstrup, *Den etiske fordring,* p. 24.

47 Løgstrup, *Den etiske fordring,* p. 28.

48 Løgstrup, *Den etiske fordring*, p. 25.
49 Compare my discussion above of Garfinkel's experiment with 'trust' (Garfinkel, *Studies in Ethnomethodology*, p. 51).
50 Karin Boye writes in *Kallocain* (p. 175): 'All are not truthful enough to hear the truth, that's the sad thing. There could be a bridge between person and person – so long as it was voluntary, yes, so long as it was given as a gift and received as a gift. Isn't it strange how everything loses its value as soon as it stops being a gift – even the truth?'
51 Cockburn, 'Trust in Conversation', p. 63.
52 Cockburn, 'Trust in Conversation', p. 52.
53 Cockburn, 'Trust in Conversation', p. 58.
54 The conflict between Cockburn's and Weil's remarks (see below) is only apparent. Both speak of attending to the person herself rather than to her way of appearing in the plans and prejudices of others.
55 Cockburn, 'Trust in Conversation', p. 57.
56 *Billed*, plural: *billeder*: 'pictures', 'images'.
57 Løgstrup, *Den etiske fordring*, pp. 22–3.
58 Løgstrup, *Den etiske fordring*, pp. 20–3.
59 Fyodor Dostoevsky, *The Idiot*, trans. Constance Garnett (London: Heinemann, 1946), p. 171, Ch. XVI. Garnett translates *čelovek* (human being) as 'man'.
60 Origgi, *Qu'est-ce que la confiance?*, pp. 29–30, my translation. 'Mychkine [...] débarque à Saint-Pétersbourg dans une société mondaine, féroce et corrompue, avec un regard totalement naïf et bon sur le monde. [...] Cette confiance de Mychkine à l'endroit des autres, de tout le monde, est un sentiment désintéressé, basé plutôt sur la méconnaissance de la nature humaine, sur le regard pur et naïf qu'il porte sur le monde. Et pourtant sa confiance a le pouvoir thaumaturgique de transformer les gens qu'il rencontre, de leur révéler à eux-mêmes une dimension de leur nature qui ne leur était pas accessible.'
61 Dostoevsky, *The Idiot*, pp. 146–7, Ch. XIV.
62 Dostoevsky, *The Idiot*, p. 35, Ch. IV.
63 Dostoevsky, *The Idiot*, p. 37, Ch. IV.
64 Dostoevsky, *The Idiot*, p. 39, Ch. IV.
65 Dostoevsky, *The Idiot*, p. 120, Ch. XI.
66 Dostoevsky, *The Idiot*, p. 121, Ch. XI.

67 Simone Weil, 'Human Personality', trans. Richard Rees, in Siân Miles (ed.), *Simone Weil – An Anthology* (London: Virago Press, 1986), pp. 69–98; see also Peter Winch, *Simone Weil: 'The Just Balance'* (Cambridge: Cambridge University Press, 1989), pp. 203, 160.

68 Dostoevsky, *The Idiot*, p. 16, Ch. II.

69 Holland, 'Is Goodness a Mystery?', p. 107.

70 Moreover, it is conceivable to have different views about the correct place of truthfulness in life. Someone might say 'I have never set much store in the concern for truth' and mean it as a *moral* remark. It would, for instance, indicate the overriding importance of other values like kindness, of being there for those who need you.

71 Cockburn, 'Trust in Conversation', pp. 18–19, making a reference to Lagerspetz and Hertzberg, 'Trust in Wittgenstein'; see also Lagerspetz, *Trust*, pp. 135–6, 150.

72 Cockburn, 'Trust in Conversation', pp. 19–20.

73 On *On Certainty* and the sceptical argument, see Marie McGinn, *Sense and Certainty*.

74 Christopher C. Robinson, *Wittgenstein and Political Theory: The View from Somewhere* (Edinburgh: Edinburgh University Press, 2011), pp. 14, 18–19. The metaphor of language as a city is of course from Wittgenstein, *Philosophical Investigations*, I: § 18.

Basic trust

1 Giddens, *Modernity and Self-Identity*, p. 40.

2 Bernstein, 'Trust', pp. 396–9.

3 Govier, *Social Trust and Human Communities*, p. 32. Cf. Laurence Thomas, *Living Morally* (Philadelphia: Temple University Press, 1989).

4 Luhmann, *Trust and Power*, pp. 25, 4.

5 Lorraine Code, 'Second Persons', in Marsha Hanen and Kai Nielsen (eds), *Science, Morality, and Feminist Theory* (Calgary: University of Calgary Press, 1987), p. 377. Also see Trudy Govier, 'Trust, Distrust, and Feminist Theory', *Hypatia* 7 (1992), pp. 16–33.

6 Bernstein, 'Trust', p. 404.

7 Bernstein, 'Trust', pp. 404–5.

8 Bernstein, 'Trust', p. 404, fn 1.

9   Something similar was presented in earlier chapters of the present book. See my discussion of Rational Choice in Chapter 2 and of the 'dys-appearance' of trust in Chapter 5.
10 Bernstein, 'Trust', pp. 402–3; compare Karen Jones, 'Trust as an Affective Attitude'.
11 Bernstein, 'Trust', p. 403.
12 Bernstein, 'Trust', p. 405.
13 Bernstein, 'Trust', p. 409.
14 Baier, 'Trust and Antitrust', pp. 242, 244–5. See Bernstein, 'Trust', p. 408.
15 Baier, 'Trust and Antitrust', p. 244.
16 Baier, 'Trust and Antitrust', p. 242.
17 Giddens, *Modernity and Self-Identity*, p. 36; emphasis in the original. A discussion of basic trust and ontological security is also included in Anthony Giddens, *The Consequences of Modernity* (Cambridge: Polity Press, 1990), pp. 92–100.
18 Giddens, *Modernity and Self-Identity*, p. 40.
19 Giddens, *Modernity and Self-Identity*, p. 37, my emphasis; see also Giddens, *The Consequences of Modernity*, p. 98. In both works, Giddens appeals to Garfinkel's experiments for empirical confirmation of his view. On interpreting Garfinkel, see Chapter 5 above.
20 Giddens, *The Consequences of Modernity*, p. 100; emphases in the original.
21 Giddens, *Modernity and Self-Identity*, p. 40; see also pp. 38–42.
22 Bernstein, 'Trust', p. 398.
23 Bernstein, 'Trust', pp. 398–9.
24 See Chapter 3 above.
25 Bernstein, 'Trust', pp. 402, 401.
26 Raimond Gaita, *Good and Evil: An Absolute Conception* (Basingstoke: Macmillan, 1991), p. 314; my emphasis.
27 Gaita, *Good and Evil*, p. 315.
28 As argued in Chapter 4 above, *what* we take the 'data' to be is also already influenced by relations of trust and distrust.
29 Bernstein's expressions sometimes indicate openness to this wider understanding of 'reason'. Radical distrust, he suggests, can be seen as the practical equivalent of other minds' scepticism (Bernstein, 'Trust', p. 404), a position that cannot be logically refuted but which

at the same time cannot be practically or emotionally sustained. On this understanding, 'trust is best conceived of as a primitive and original relation to the other, how others first appear to us, and hence part of the original physiognomy of social interaction' (Bernstein, 'Trust', p. 405).

30 Ludwig Wittgenstein, *On Certainty*. See Hertzberg, 'On the Attitude of Trust'. See also Lagerspetz and Hertzberg, 'Wittgenstein on Trust'.

31 G. E. Moore, 'Proof of an External World'; G. E. Moore, 'A Defence of Common Sense', in J. H. Muirhead (ed.), *Contemporary British Philosophy, 2nd Series* (London: George Allen & Unwin, 1925), pp. 192–233; reprinted in G. E. Moore, *Selected Writings*, Thomas Baldwin (ed.) (London: Routledge, 1993), pp. 106–33.

32 Wittgenstein, *On Certainty*, § 151; see Marie McGinn, *Sense and Certainty*, pp. 144–5.

33 Moore, 'Defence...,' *Selected Writings*, p. 118; see also Wittgenstein, *On Certainty*, §§ 247–55.

34 Wittgenstein, *On Certainty*, § 103, § 105.

35 Cf. Wittgenstein, *On Certainty*, § 246.

36 Wittgenstein, *On Certainty*, § 152.

37 Wittgenstein, *On Certainty*, § 144.

38 Wittgenstein, *On Certainty*, § 162.

39 Wittgenstein, *On Certainty*, § 343.

40 An analogous point is possibly developed in R. G. Collingwood's *Essay on Metaphysics* (Oxford: Oxford University Press, 1979), in which he puts forward a conception of metaphysics as the study of the 'absolute presuppositions' of thought. Something is revealed as an absolute presupposition of a person's current thought not because it is impossible to construe a sceptical argument to question it, but because as things are, she would not be able to carry on with her thinking if she were to take the sceptical argument seriously. In that sense, for instance, the idea that every event has a cause constitutes a limiting case for natural science, a presupposition that must be left standing if a rational approach to natural processes is to be possible – insofar as such approaches involve asking questions like, 'What were the causes of this or that event?'.

41 Ludwig Wittgenstein, *On Certainty*, § 188; see also §§ 163, 182–92.

42 Also see Wittgenstein, *On Certainty*, §§ 96–9. For related reasons, Collingwood (in *Essay on Metaphysics*) describes the study of the absolute presuppositions of thinking as an essentially historical

investigation: those presuppositions will be different during different historical periods.

43 In his book on the genealogy of the concept of the visual record, Antony Fredriksson explores ways in which the putatively neutral documentary image, the persuasive power of which depends on its claim to represent reality, has historically *acquired* this role. The image has a claim to truth because it constitutes a bridge between subjects; the image shows to me not only what the other person sees but *how* she sees. See Antony Fredriksson, *Vision, Image, Record: A Cultivation of the Visual Field* (Åbo: Åbo Akademi University Press, 2014).

44 Wittgenstein, *On Certainty*, §§ 161, 160.

45 Wittgenstein, *On Certainty*, § 150, my emphasis.

46 Wittgenstein, *On Certainty*, § 509.

47 Wittgenstein, *Philosophical Investigations* II: xi, pp. 228–9.

48 Wittgenstein, *On Certainty*, §§ 160, 310.

49 See, for instance, Wittgenstein, *Blue Book,* p. 77; Wittgenstein, *Philosophical Investigations*, §§ 5–6, 157.

50 See Hertzberg, 'On the Attitude of Trust'; Bax, *Subjectivity after Wittgenstein*, pp. 121–41.

51 The suggestion of ethical relationships is arguably implicit in *On Certainty*, but they are not explicitly discussed. This may be related to Wittgenstein's general unwillingness to address questions of ethics in his avowedly philosophical writing.

52 Bernstein, 'Trust', p. 395.

53 Simone Weil, 'The "Iliad": Poem of Might', in Simone Weil, *Intimations of Christianity among the Ancient Greeks* (London: Ark Paperbacks, 1987), pp. 24–55, at p. 28. See Winch, *Simone Weil*, p. 148.

54 Weil, 'Waiting for God', quoted in Winch (1989), p. 205.

55 Note the Hobbesianism of this picture of human beings as obstacles.

56 Winch, *Simone Weil*, p. 190.

57 Winch, *Simone Weil*, p. 154.

58 Weil, 'The "Iliad"', p. 28. Also see the discussions of Winch, *Simone Weil*, pp. 105–13 and David Cockburn, *Other Human Beings* (Basingstoke: Macmillan, 1990), pp. 5–12.

59 Weil, 'The "Iliad"', p. 28.

60 Weil, 'The "Iliad"', p. 28.

61 Weil, 'Human Personality', p. 71.

62 Cf. Peter Winch, 'Who is my Neighbour?' in Peter Winch, *Trying to Make Sense* (Oxford: Blackwell, 1987), pp. 154–66.
63 Løgstrup, *Den etiske fordring*, pp. 25–6.
64 Løgstrup, *Den etiske fordring*, pp. 27–8.
65 Løgstrup, *Den etiske fordring*, p. 32.

BIBLIOGRAPHY

Adler, J. L., 'Testimony, Trust, Knowledge', *Journal of Philosophy* 91 (1994), pp. 264–75.
Ahlskog, J., '[Review of] Benjamin McMyler, *Testimony, Trust and Authority*', *Philosophical Investigations* 36 (2013), pp. 98–102.
Anderson, B., *Imagined Communities*, London: Verso, 1983.
Anscombe, G. E. M., *Intention*, Oxford: Basil Blackwell, 1957.
Armstrong, D. M. and Malcolm, N., *Consciousness and Causality*, Oxford: Basil Blackwell, 1984.
Ashworth, T., *Trench Warfare 1914–1918: The Live and Let Live System*, London: Pan, 2000.
Axelrod, R., *The Evolution of Cooperation*, New York: Basic Books, 1984.
Backström, J., *The Fear of Openness. An Essay on Friendship and the Roots of Morality*, Åbo: Åbo Akademi University Press, 2007.
Baier, A., 'Doing Things with Others: The Mental Commons', in L. Alanen, S. Heinämaa and T. Wallgren (eds), *Commonality and Particularity in Ethics*, Basingstoke: Macmillan, 1997.
—*Moral Prejudices: Essays on Ethics*, Cambridge, MA: Harvard University Press, 1994.
—'Reply to Olli Lagerspetz', in L. Alanen, S. Heinämaa and T. Wallgren (eds), *Commonality and Particularity in Ethics*, Basingstoke: Macmillan, 1997.
—'Trust and Antitrust', *Ethics* 96 (1986), pp. 231–60 (reprinted in Baier, A., *Moral Prejudices*).
Baker, J., 'Trust and Rationality', *Pacific Philosophical Quarterly* 68 (1987), pp. 1–13.
Bax, C., *Subjectivity after Wittgenstein. The Post-Cartesian Subject and the 'Death of Man'*, London: Bloomsbury, 2012.
Bernstein, J. M., 'Trust: On the Real, but Almost Always Unnoticed, Ever-changing Foundation of Ethical Life', *Metaphilosophy* 42 (2011), pp. 395–416.
Boye, K., *Kallocain*, Madison: University of Wisconsin Press, 1966, trans. Gustaf Lannestock. Original title: Boye, K., *Kallocain. Roman från 2000-talet*.

Brinkmann, S. 'Psychology in the Space of Reasons', *Journal for the Theory of Social Behaviour* 36 (2006), pp. 1–16.
Coady, C. A. J., *Testimony: A Philosophical Study*, Oxford: Clarendon Press, 1992.
—'Testimony and Observation', *American Philosophical Quarterly* 10 (1973), pp. 149–55.
Cockburn, D., *Other Human Beings*, Basingstoke: Macmillan, 1990.
—'Trust in conversation', *Nordic Wittgenstein Review* 3 (2014), pp. 47–67.
Code, L., 'Second Persons', in M. Hanen and K. Nielsen (eds), *Science, Morality, and Feminist Theory*, Calgary: University of Calgary Press, 1987.
Coleman, J., *Foundations of Social Theory*, Cambridge, MA: Belknap Press, 1990.
Collingwood, R. G., *Essay on Metaphysics*, Oxford: Oxford University Press, 1979.
—*The Idea of History*, Oxford: Oxford University Press, 1946.
Cudd, A., 'Game Theory and the History of Ideas About Rationality', *Economics and Philosophy* 9 (1993), pp. 101–33.
Dasgupta, P., 'Trust as a Commodity', in Gambetta, D. (ed.), *Trust: Making and Breaking Cooperative Relations*, Basil Blackwell, Oxford, 1990.
Davidson, D., *Inquiries into Truth and Interpretation*, Oxford: Clarendon Press, 1984.
Dawkins, R. and Krebs, J., 'Animal Signals: Information or Manipulation?' in J. Krebs and N. Davies (eds), *Behavioural Ecology: An Evolutionary Approach*, Oxford: Blackwell, 1978.
Dilman, İ., *Love and Human Separateness*, Oxford: Blackwell, 1987.
Dostoevsky, F. M., *The Brothers Karamazov*, New York: W. W. Norton, 1976.
—*The Idiot*, London: Heinemann, 1946.
Elias, N., *Über den Prozess der Zivilisation. Soziogenetische und psychogenetische Untersuchungen. Erster Band: Wandlungen des Verhaltens in den weltlichen Oberschichten des Abendlandes*, Frankfurt a.M.: Suhrkamp, 1981.
Elster, J., *Nuts and Bolts for the Social Sciences*, Cambridge: Cambridge University Press, 1989.
Fadiga, L., 'Sensorimotor Processing of Speech and Language', Paper, *Dynamics of Active Perception: An Interdisciplinary Symposium on Perception and the Mind-Body Problem*, Helsinki: Helsinki Collegium for Advanced Studies, May 15–16, 2014.
Faulkner, P., *Knowledge on Trust*, Oxford: Oxford University Press, 2011.
—'On telling and trusting', *Mind* 116 (2007), pp. 875–902.

Fredriksson, A., *Vision, Image, Record: A Cultivation of the Visual Field*, Åbo: Åbo Akademi University Press, 2014.
Fukuyama, F., *Trust: The Social Virtue and the Creation of Prosperity*, New York: Free Press, 1995.
Gaita, R., *Good and Evil: An Absolute Conception*, Basingstoke: Macmillan, 1991.
Gambetta, D., 'Can we Trust Trust?' in D. Gambetta (ed.), *Trust: Making and Breaking Cooperative Relations*, Oxford: Blackwell, 1990.
—(ed.), *Trust: Making and Breaking Cooperative Relations*, Oxford: Blackwell, 1990.
Garfinkel, H., 'A Conception of, and Experiments with, "Trust" as a Condition of Stable Concentrated Actions', in O. J. Harvey (ed.), *Motivation and Social Interaction*, New York: Roland Press, 1963.
—*Studies in Ethnomethodology*, Cambridge: Polity Press, 1996.
Gauthier, D., *Morals by Agreement*, New York: Oxford University Press, 1986.
Giddens, A., *The Consequences of Modernity*, Cambridge: Polity Press, 1990.
—*Modernity and Self-Identity*, Cambridge: Polity Press, 1991.
Good, D., 'Individuals, Interpersonal Relations, and Trust', in D. Gambetta (ed.), *Trust: Making and Breaking Cooperative Relations*, Oxford: Blackwell, 1990.
Govier, T., 'An Epistemology of Trust', *International Journal of Moral and Social Studies* 8 (1993), pp. 153–74.
—*Social Trust and Human Communities*, Montreal & Kingston: McGill-Queen's University Press, 1997.
—'Trust and Testimony: Nine Arguments on Testimonial Knowledge', *International Journal of Moral and Social Studies* 8 (1993), pp. 21–39.
—'Trust, Distrust, and Feminist Theory,' *Hypatia* 7 (1992), pp. 16–33.
Grant, R. G., 'The Politics of Equilibrium', *Inquiry* 35 (1993), pp. 423–46.
Hanfling, O., 'How We Trust One Another', *Philosophy* 83 (2008), pp. 161–77.
Hardin, R., 'Do we Need Trust in Government?', in M. E. Warren (ed.), *Democracy and Trust*, Cambridge: Cambridge University Press, 1999.
—*Trust and Trustworthiness*, New York: Russell Sage Foundation, 2002.
—'Trustworthiness', *Ethics* 107 (1996), pp. 26–42.
Hardwig, J., 'The Role of Trust in Knowledge', *The Journal of Philosophy* 88 (1991), pp. 693–708.
Harper, R. H. R. (ed.), *Trust, Computing, and Society*, New York: Cambridge University Press, 2014.

Hartmann, M., 'Einleitung', in M. Hartmann and C. Offe (eds), *Vertrauen: Die Grundlage des sozialen Zusammenhalts*, Frankfurt/New York: Campus Verlag, 2001.

Hawley, K., 'Trust, Distrust and Commitment', *Noûs* 48 (2014), pp. 1–20.

Hawthorn, G., 'Three Ironies in Trust', in D. Gambetta (ed.), *Trust: Making and Breaking Cooperative Relations*, Oxford: Basil Blackwell, 1990.

Hertzberg, L., *The Limits of Experience*, Helsinki: Acta Philosophica Fennica, 1994.

—'On the Attitude of Trust', in Lars Hertzberg, *The Limits of Experience*, Helsinki: Acta Philosophica Fennica, vol. 56, 1994; first published in *Inquiry* 31 (1988), pp. 307–22.

—'On Being Trusted', in A. Grøn and C. Welz (eds), *Trust, Sociality, Selfhood*, Tübingen: Mohr Siebeck, 2010.

Hinchman, E., 'Telling as Inviting to Trust', *Philosophy and Phenomenological Research* 70 (2005), pp. 562–87.

Hobbes, T., 'Human Nature', in *The English Works of Thomas Hobbes of Malmesbury*, vol. IV, London: John Bohn, 1840.

—*Leviathan*, London: Penguin, 1981.

Holland, R. F., *Against Empiricism*, Totowa, NJ: Barnes & Noble, 1980.

Hollis, M., *Trust Within Reason*, Cambridge: Cambridge University Press, 1998.

Hume, D., 'Enquiry Concerning Human Understanding', in D. Hume, *Enquiries Concerning Human Understanding and Concerning the Principles of Morals*, Oxford: Clarendon Press, 1902.

Jackson, J., *Truth, Trust and Medicine*, London: Routledge, 2001.

Johnson, P., *Frames of Deceit*, Cambridge: Cambridge University Press, 1993.

Johnsson, L., *Trust in Biobank Research: Meaning and Moral Significance*, Uppsala: Acta Universitatis Upsaliensis, 2013.

Johnsson, L., Helgesson, G., Hansson, M. G. and Eriksson, S., 'Adequate Trust Avails, Mistaken Trust Matters: On the Moral Responsibility of Doctors as Proxies for Patients' Trust in Biobank Research', *Bioethics* 27 (2013), pp. 485–92.

Jones, K., 'Trust as an Affective Attitude', *Ethics* 107 (1996), pp. 4–25.

—'Trusting Interpretations', in P. Mäkelä and C. Townley (eds), *Trust: Analytic and Applied Perspectives*, Amsterdam: Rodopi, 2013.

—'Trust: Philosophical Aspects', in N. Smelser and P. Bates (eds), *International Encyclopedia of the Social and Behavioral Sciences*, Elsevier Science, Amsterdam, 2002.

Kant, I., 'An Answer to the Question: What is Enlightenment?', in I. Kant, *The Cambridge Edition of the Works of Immanuel Kant:*

Practical Philosophy, trans. and ed. M. J. Gregor, Cambridge: Cambridge University Press, 1996.
—*Critique of the Power of Judgment*, Cambridge: Cambridge University Press, 2000.
—*Grounding for the Metaphysics of Morals*, Indianapolis: Hackett Publishing Company, 1981.
—'On a Supposed Right to Tell Lies from Benevolent Motives', in *Kant's Critique of Practical Reason and Other Works on the Theory of Ethics*, trans. Thomas Kingsmill Abbott, 4th rev. edn, London: Longmans, Green and Co., 1889.
Kohn, M., *Trust: Self-Interest and Common Good*, Oxford: Oxford University Press, 2009.
Korkman, J., *How (not) to Interview Children: Interviews with Young Children in Sexual Abuse Investigations in Finland*, Åbo: Åbo Akademi University Press, 2006.
Krebs, J. R. and Dawkins, R., 'Animal Signals: Mind-reading and Manipulation', in J. R. Krebs and N. B. Davies (eds), *Behavioural Ecology: An Evolutionary Approach*, 2nd edn, Sunderland, MA: Sinauer, 1984.
Kurtén, T., 'Suspicion Concerning World-views', in T. Kurtén, *På väg mot det postsekulära. Tankar under femton år*, Uppsala: Acta Universitatis Upsaliensis. Studies in Systematic Theology and Worldviews 2, 2014.
Lagerspetz, O., *Trust: The Tacit Demand*, Dordrecht: Kluwer, 1998.
—'Vertrauen als geistiges Phänomen', in M. Hartmann and C. Offe (eds), *Vertrauen: Die Grundlage des sozialen Zusammenhalts*, Frankfurt/New York: Campus Verlag, 2001.
Lagerspetz, O. and Hertzberg, L., 'Trust in Wittgenstein', in P. Mäkelä and C. Townley (eds), *Trust: Analytic and Applied Perspectives*, Amsterdam: Rodopi, 2013.
Leder, D., *The Absent Body*, Chicago: Chicago University Press, 1990.
Løgstrup, K. E., *Den etiske fordring*, København: Gyldendal, 1962. Published in English as *The Ethical Demand*, Notre Dame, IN: University of Notre Dame Press, 1997.
Luhmann, N., 'Familiarity, Confidence, Trust: Problems and Alternatives', in D. Gambetta (ed.), *Trust: Making and Breaking Cooperative Relations*, Oxford: Basil Blackwell, 1990.
—*Trust and Power*, Chichester: Wiley, 1979.
McGinn, M., *Sense and Certainty*, Oxford: Blackwell, 1989.
MacIntyre, A., *After Virtue*, Notre Dame, Indiana: Notre Dame University Press, 1981.
—'The Privatization of Good', *Review of Politics* 52 (1990), pp. 344–61.
McMyler, B., *Testimony, Trust, and Authority*, New York: Oxford University Press, 2011.

MacPherson, C. B., *The Political Theory of Possessive Individualism*, Oxford: Oxford University Press, 1962.
Malcolm, N., *Ludwig Wittgenstein: A Memoir*, Oxford: Oxford University Press, 1984.
Möllering, G., 'Rational, Institutional and Active Trust: Just do it?', in K. Bijsma-Frankena and R. K. Woolthuis (eds), *Trust Under Pressure: Empirical Investigations of Trust and Trust Building in Uncertain Circumstances*, Cheltenham, Glos.: Edward Elgar Publishing, 2005.
Moore, G. E., *Selected Writings*, Thomas Baldwin (ed.), London: Routledge, 1993.
Moran, R., 'Getting Told and Being Believed', *Philosophers' Imprint* 5 (2005), pp. 1–29.
—'Problems of Sincerity', *Proceedings of the Aristotelian Society* 105 (2005), pp. 325–45.
O'Neill, O., *A Question of Trust. Reith Lectures 2002* (BBC Radio 4) http://www.bbc.co.uk/radio4/reith2002/lecture2.shtm [accessed 18 August 2012].
Origgi, G., *Qu'est-ce que la confiance?*, Paris: Vrin, 2008.
Owens, D., *Reason without Freedom*, New York: Routledge, 2000.
Pagden, A., 'Trust in Eighteenth-century Naples', in D. Gambetta (ed.), *Trust: Making and Breaking Cooperative Relations*, Oxford: Blackwell, 1990.
Pascal, B., *Pensées de Blaise Pascal, Texte de Léon Brunschvicg*, Paris: Samizdat, 2010 http://www.samizdat.qc.ca/arts/lit/Pascal/Pensees_brunschvicg.pdf [accessed 29 December 2014].
Pedersen, E. O., 'A Kantian Conception of Trust', *Sats* 13 (2012), pp. 147–69.
Pettit, P., *Made with Words. Hobbes on Language, Mind, and Politics*, Princeton: Princeton University Press, 2008.
Plato, *Gorgias*, London: Penguin Books, 1971.
Putnam, R. D., *Bowling Alone: The Collapse and Revival of American Community*, New York: Simon & Schuster, 2000.
Rawls, J., *A Theory of Justice*, Cambridge, MA: Harvard University Press, 1971.
Robinson, C. C., *Wittgenstein and Political Theory: The View from Somewhere*, Edinburgh: Edinburgh University Press, 2011.
Ross, A., 'Why do we Believe what we are Told?', *Ratio* 28 (1986), pp. 69–88.
Rousseau, D. M., Sitkin, G. B., Burt, R. S. and Camerer, C., 'Not So Different After All: A Cross-discipline View of Trust', *Academy of Management Review* 23 (1998), pp. 393–404.
Schneier, B., *Liars and Outliers: Enabling the Trust That Society Needs to Thrive*, Indianapolis: John Wiley & Sons, 2012.

Shakespeare, W., 'Othello, the Moor of Venice', in *The Complete Works of William Shakespeare*, Chatham River Publishers, New York, 1987.
Simpson, E., 'Reasonable Trust', *European Journal of Philosophy* 21 (2011), pp. 402–23.
Simpson, T. W., 'Computing and the Search for Trust', in R. H. R. Harper (ed.), *Trust, Computing, and Society*, Cambridge: Cambridge University Press, 2014.
Skinner, Q., *Reason and Rhetoric in the Philosophy of Hobbes*, Cambridge: Cambridge University Press, 1996.
Skinner, Q., *Visions of Politics: Volume III: Hobbes and Civil Science*, Cambridge: Cambridge University Press, 2002.
Skirbekk, H., 'Et praktisk syn på tillit til velferdsstater. Intervju med Onora O'Neill', in H. Skirbekk and H. Grimen (eds), *Tillit i Norge*, Oslo: Res Publica, 2012.
—*The Patient's Trust – Theoretical Analyses of Trust and a Qualitative Study in General Practice Consultations*, Oslo: Faculty of Medicine, University of Oslo, 2008.
Stoutland, F., 'In Defence of a Non-psychologistic Account of Reasons for Action', in C. Gefwert and O. Lagerspetz (eds), *Wittgenstein and Philosophical Psychology. Essays in Honour of Lars Hertzberg*, Uppsala: Uppsala Philosophical Studies Vol. 55, 2009.
Sztompka, P., *Trust. A Sociological Theory*, Cambridge: Cambridge University Press, 1999.
Taddeo, M., 'Modelling Trust in Artificial Agents, A First Step Toward the Analysis of e-Trust', *Minds and Machines* 20 (2010), pp. 243–57.
—'The Role of e-Trust in Distributed Artificial Systems', in C. Ess and M. Thorseth (eds), *Trust and Virtual Worlds: Contemporary Perspectives*, New York: Peter Lang, 2011.
Thomas, L., *Living Morally*, Philadelphia: Temple University Press, 1989.
Travis, C., 'Pragmatics', in B. Hale and C. Wright (eds), *Companion to the Philosophy of Language*, Oxford: Blackwell Publishers, 1997.
Wanderer, J. and Townsend, L., 'Is it Rational to Trust?', *Philosophy Compass* 8 (2013), pp. 1–14.
Warren, M. E. (ed.), *Democracy and Trust*, Cambridge: Cambridge University Press, 1999.
Watson, R., 'Trust in Interpersonal Interaction and Cloud Computing', in R. H. R. Harper (ed.), *Trust, Computing, and Society*, Cambridge: Cambridge University Press, 2014.
Webb, M. O., 'Why I Know about as Much as you: A Reply to Hardwig', *The Journal of Philosophy* 90 (1993), pp. 260–70.
Weil, S., 'Human Personality', in Siân Miles (ed.), *Simone Weil – An Anthology*, London: Virago Press, 1986.

—'The "Iliad": Poem of Might', in S. Weil, *Intimations of Christianity among the Ancient Greeks*, London: Ark Paperbacks, 1987.
Williams, B., 'Formal Structures and Social Reality', in D. Gambetta (ed.), *Trust: Making and Breaking Cooperative Relations*, Oxford: Blackwell, 1990.
Winch, P., 'Authority', in A. Quinton (ed.), *Political Philosophy*, Oxford: Oxford University Press, 1972. Originally published in *Proceedings of the Aristotelian Society* 32 (1959), pp. 235–40.
—'Certainty and Authority', *Philosophy* (supplement) 1990, pp. 223–37. Republished in A. Phillips Griffiths (ed.), *Wittgenstein Centenary Essays*, Cambridge: Cambridge University Press, 1991.
—'How is Political Authority Possible?', ed. D. Z. Phillips, *Philosophical Investigations* 25 (2002), pp. 20–32.
—*Ethics and Action*, London: Routledge & Kegan Paul, 1972.
—*The Idea of a Social Science and Its Relation to Philosophy*, London: Routledge & Kegan Paul, 1958.
—'Lectures on Ethics and Value Theory at the University of Illinois, Urbana-Champaign, 1990' (notes by O. Lagerspetz, MS on file with the present author).
—'Seminars on Authority at the University of Illinois at Urbana-Champaign, 1991' (notes by O. Lagerspetz, MS on file with the present author).
—*Simone Weil: 'The Just Balance'*, Cambridge: Cambridge University Press, 1989.
—*Trying to Make Sense*, Oxford: Blackwell, 1987.
Wittgenstein, L., *The Blue and Brown Books*, New York: Harper & Row, 1965.
—*On Certainty*, New York: Harper & Row, 1972.
—*Philosophical Investigations*, Oxford, Basil Blackwell, 1953.
—*Zettel*, Berkeley: University of California Press, 1967.
Wolgast, E., *The Grammar of Justice*, Ithaca: Cornell University Press, 1987.
von Wright, G. H., *Explanation and Understanding*, New York: Cornell University Press, 1971.

INDEX

affective attitude 13, 82, 177 n. 36
agency 11, 14, 21–3, 45, 131–2, 153, 174 n. 3
Ahlskog, J. 160 n. 15, 182 n. 11
Anscombe, G. E. M. 174 n. 4
Aristotle 25
assurance view on testimony 113, 115–16, 182 n. 12, 183 n. 26
attunement 111, 182 n. 8
Augustine, St. 6
authority
   coercive 12, 27
   witness 114–15, 126, 145, 176 n. 27
autonomy
   epistemic 115–6, 183 n. 26
   personal 3, 50
Axelrod, R. 33–4, 36–8, 167 n. 37

Backström, J. 67
backward induction 167 n. 37
Baier, A.
   accepted vulnerability 22, 47–9, 54, 56–7, 59–60, 64–5, 67, 97, 171–2 n. 28
   basic trust 50, 135, 170 n. 10
   consciousness of trust 50–1, 92, 96–7, 172 n. 33, 173 n. 1, 176 n. 20, 181 n. 36
   critique of normativity 18–19
   critique of rationalism 47–9, 53, 171 n. 27
   entrusting model of trust 22, 47–54, 56, 134
   on marriage 10, 51–2, 62, 65
   normativity in 47, 49, 175 n. 14
   reliance vs. trust 15, 163 n. 43
   'Trust and Antitrust' 13, 48, 135, 170 n. 8
basic trust 23, 40, 50, 120, 131–53, 170 n. 10
Bax, C. 179 n. 13
Belief-Desire model 71–2
Bernstein, J. M. 97, 133–41, 147, 170 n. 8, 187–8 n. 29
betrayal
   vs. disappointment 15, 17–18, 55–6, 163 n. 48
   logically related to trust 8, 15–16, 18–20, 55–6, 65, 96–7, 100, 155, 163 n. 49, 173 n. 49
betting as a model for trust 7, 17–18, 31, 161 n. 25
bias in trusting 81–2, 84–5, 114, 177–8 n. 39
blind trust 2, 17, 50, 58, 124, 157, 170 n. 10
Boye, K. 22, 60–1, 64, 122, 185 n. 50
Brothers Karamazov, The (Dostoevsky) 38, 79–81

causal processes 25, 71
child-adult relations
  trust in 16–17, 19, 58, 67,
    135, 137–8, 170 n. 10, 181
    n. 36
  Wittgenstein on 145–6
Christie, A. 81
Coady, C. A. J. 5, 112
Cockburn, D. 105, 122, 126–7,
  179 n. 10, 185 n. 54
coercion 28, 33
cognitivism 49, 170 n. 9, 177 n.
  28
Coleman, J. 31, 166 n. 25
Collingwood, R. G. 174 n. 5, 188
  nn. 40, 42
commitment
  moral 11, 20, 28, 43, 74, 122,
    126, 161 n. 29, 167 n. 33
  to truthfulness 107, 118–20,
    126–7
communication *see also* language
  biological evolution of 108,
    110–12, 182 n. 8
  functions of 10, 108–10, 122
  moral relations in 23, 87, 107,
    121–3, 126–9
  in testimony 112, 115–16
  trust as condition of 120–3,
    126–9
  truthfulness as condition of 6,
    23, 107, 112, 116–19, 121,
    145
community 5, 41, 64, 119
context
  of inquiry 6–8, 11, 23, 104,
    115, 127, 139, 153, 156
  of interaction 30, 35, 106
  language use 161–2 n. 30
  social 15, 132, 142
  trust and distrust 13, 14
context-dependence
  of possibilities 57–8

  of psychological attributions
    10, 42, 79, 88–9, 97,
    105–6, 142, 179 n. 13
contractarianism 12–13, 49
conversation, trust in 98–9, 120,
  122, 127
cooperation
  biological evolution of 34–5
  game-theoretic approaches to
    29–40, 74–7, 166 n. 28
  Hobbes on 22, 25–9, 119, 138
  possibility of 4, 22, 26, 28–9,
    34–5
  probability of 30–1, 78–9, 166
    n. 28
courts of law 113, 115
Cudd, A. 164 n. 4

Dasgupta, P. 74, 78, 174 n. 9,
  175 n. 12
Davidson, D. 112
Dawkins, R. 108–10
deception 26, 108, 110, 117
decision to trust 63, 70, 78, 89
definitions of trust 6–8, 26,
  29–31, 54, 78, 106, 156,
  172 n. 29, 173 n. 49
Descartes, R. 2, 169 n. 1
desire, as a motivational source
  42–4, 70–3, 158, 164 n. 4,
  168 n. 52
Dilman, İ 80,
disease, illness 55, 96
Dostoevsky, F. M. 38–9, 79, 123
'dys-appearance' of trust 95–8,
  106, 187 n. 9

Elias, N. 66
Elster, J. 175 n. 11
emotional vs. strategic trust 163
  n. 48
Empiricism, Empiricist 14, 25, 71,
  113, 116, 128, 164 n. 4

encapsulated interest 37–9
Enlightenment 2, 3, 41, 169 n. 2
entrusting 22, 47–8, 50–4, 56, 134, 158, 171 nn. 22, 25
evidence
  basis of knowledge claims 2, 103, 143–4
  communicative behaviour as 110, 112–16
  context-sensitivity of 5, 22, 80–3, 177 n. 36
  in court cases 79, 81–2, 114–15
  in favour of trust or distrust 17, 80, 134, 173 n. 1, 176 n. 18, 177 n. 28
  meaning of 82
evidential view on testimony 113–16, 182 n. 12
expectation
  tacit, unself-conscious 8, 98–9, 133, 149, 152
  Wittgenstein on 93
explanation, of action or behaviour 42, 70–3, 174 n. 4

Faulkner, P. 8–9
feelings
  of betrayal 55–6
  as psychological states 88, 92–6, 99, 179 n. 13
  of trust 92, 95, 99, 132, 135, 152, 178 n. 2
Forster, E. M. 123
foundationalism 144
Fredriksson, A. 189 n. 43
friendship
  time dimension in 88
  vulnerability in 59–60

Gaita, R. 139–41
Gambetta, D. 12, 30–1, 34, 74, 78–9

game theory 12–13, 22, 31, 25–6, 39, 47, 75–6, 166 n. 29, 169 n. 56, 175 n. 11
Garfinkel, H. 87, 98–9, 187 n. 19
Gauthier, D. 169 n. 1
genuine duration 93–5, 179 n. 7
Giddens, A. 135–6, 178 n. 2, 187 nn. 17, 19
Gorgias (Plato) 44
Govier, T. 19, 77–8, 133, 139, 169 n. 2, 172 n. 29, 175 n. 14
Grant, R. 169 n. 56
Great War 34–7
grief, Wittgenstein on 88, 94–5, 97, 179 n. 13

Hardin, R. 18–9, 37–9, 160 n. 16, 161 n. 29, 163 n. 51, 173–4 n. 1
Hardwig, J. 2, 14
Hartmann, M. 7, 11, 13, 161 nn. 23, 25
Hertzberg, L. 14–16, 18, 40, 49, 65, 163 nn. 43, 49, 51, 168 n. 52, 176 n. 20, 178 n. 1
Hobbes, T.
  on communication 111, 182 n. 6, 183 n. 23
  interpretations of 165 nn. 16, 17
  on motivation 25, 27–8, 71, 164 n. 4, 174 n. 3
  rationality in 3, 119–20
  state of nature in 12, 26–8, 138
Hobbesian dilemma 12, 22, 26, 29, 32, 35, 45, 120
Hobbesianism 21, 127, 189 n. 55
Holland, R. F. 119, 126
Hollis, M. 2–3, 12, 41, 168 nn. 47, 50, 51, 169 n. 2, 175 nn. 12, 14

Hume, D. 1, 113
Huxley, A. 60

Idiot, The (Dostoevsky) 123–6, 132
image as impediment to communication 123, 126
individualism, methodological 88–9, 178 n. 42
individualist views on reason 2–3, 41
inheritance model of testimony 114, 182 n. 12
innocence 123–4
institutional constraints 36–7, 45
interest (self-interest)
  in Baier 48, 51, 56, 60, 171 n. 27
  encapsulated 37–9
  in evolutionary theory 108–11
  in game theory 12, 32–3, 39–40
  in Hobbes 26–8, 40, 111
  motivational source 42
interpretation as aspect of trusting 13, 80–3, 85–7
intimacy 17, 48–9, 55–6, 65–6, 170 n. 10

Johnsson, L. 20, 54–5
Jokes 119, 184 n. 38
Jones, K. 13, 22, 82–6, 169 n. 2, 170 n. 10, 175 n. 14, 176 n. 18, 177 n. 36
justification
  of behaviour 42–3, 72–3, 101–2, 174 n. 6
  of cooperation 4, 75
  of knowledge claims 2–3, 113–15
  of testimony 114–15, 160 n. 15, 176 n. 27, 183 n. 26
  of trust 4–5, 38, 40, 80, 127, 134, 139, 155–6, 169 n. 2, 175 n. 14, 176 n. 18

Kallocain (Boye) 22, 60–6, 185 n. 50
Kant, I. 3, 117–18, 16 n. 10, 170 n. 57
knowing a friend 79–80
Kohn, M. 34–7, 108
Krebs, J. 108–10

language *see also* communication; natural signs
  biological development of 107–12, 182 n. 8
  Hobbes on 182 n. 6
  ordinary 179 n. 13
  truthfulness as condition of 23, 112, 117
  Wittgenstein on 21, 91, 93, 128, 145
Leder, D. 23, 96
Løgstrup, K. E. 65, 120–3, 126, 128, 132, 147, 151–3
Luhmann, N. 29, 133, 163 n. 43, 173–4 n. 1

McCarthy, Senator J. 117
McGinn, M. 180 n. 35
MacIntyre, A. 36
McMyler, B. 49, 113–16, 126–7, 170 n. 9, 177 n. 28, 182 n. 12, 183 nn. 23, 26
Malcolm, N. 103, 179 n. 7, 180 n. 30
manipulation
  vs. trust 15, 19, 39–40
  in communication 109–10, 127
marriage
  vs. entrusting 51–3
  in *Kallocain* (Boye) 22, 61, 63, 65

INDEX   203

vulnerability in 65–7
mental state 97, 102, 105 see also
    psychological state, state of
    mind
mind-reading 108–10
Möllering, G. 30, 167 n. 37, 172
    n. 29
Moore, G.E. 103–4, 142–3
moral obligation 19, 27
moral relation 6, 18, 21, 23,
    126–7
Moran, R. 112–14, 126–7, 182 n.
    9, 183 n. 26
motivation, human 25, 28, 38,
    70, 76

natural signs 110–12
normality 37, 86–7, 120, 128,
    151
normative approaches to trust
    18–19, 47, 49, 69, 75,
    77–8, 155
normative expectation 20

On Certainty (Wittgenstein) 5,
    14, 103, 119, 128, 132,
    142, 144, 146–7, 163 n. 51
O'Neill, O. 17, 49, 170 n. 10
openness 17, 61, 67, 79, 122,
    151–2
Origgi, G. 48, 75, 123–4
Orwell, G. 60
Othello (Shakespeare) 83–5

paranoia 139–40
Pascal, B. 31, 167 n. 40
Pedersen, E. O. 160 n. 10
perspective
    disparity between, 59, 91, 100,
        105–6, 157, 181 n. 36
    of distrust 91, 140, 157
    moral, ethical 23, 65, 106,
        147, 152

neutral vs. engaged 85–6
    of reason 140
    reflexive vs. engaged 128
    role of 8, 10–11, 23, 67, 85,
        99, 107, 127, 138
    shift of 48, 64–5, 89
    of trust 18, 140
Pettit, P. 165 n. 16
Philosophical Investigations
    (Wittgenstein) 88, 92, 146
Plato 25, 44
possibility
    of betrayal 55–8, 96, 100, 105,
        139–40
    evoked in practical reasoning
        57–8
    meaning of 56–8, 137, 157
prediction 29, 35–6, 55, 70–1,
    110
predictive, trust as 12, 17, 20,
    40, 56
presence, human 123, 148–9, 151
Prisoners' Dilemma 31–7, 74–7,
    108, 167 n. 37
probability 30–1, 78–9, 166 n. 28
promising
    Dasgupta on 74
    Kant on 117
    meaning of 114, 118
    state of nature 27–8
psychological state 23, 88, 92–3,
    102, 158, 172 n. 29, 174
    n. 6

rational choice 12–13, 18, 30,
    64, 75, 77, 89, 157, 163 n.
    48 see also Game theory
rationalism 14, 47–8, 131, 139,
    153, 169 n. 1
rational trust 33, 37–8, 40, 157
rationality see also reason,
    reasoning
    first-personal 157

game-theoretic 35–6
ideas of 3–6, 22, 41–2, 44–5, 75, 131, 157–8
'normative' conception of 22, 111, 118–19, 132
Winch on 118–19
Rawls, J. 169 n. 1
realism about mental descriptions 102, 106
reason
    having a 97
    human 5, 132, 153, 158, 160 n. 10
reasoning
    dependent on perspective 85, 157
    meaning of 14, 40, 153
    practical 57, 71–2
reliance
    on testimony 115, 126
    vs. trust 15–18, 55–6, 134, 158, 163 nn. 43, 48, 172 n. 31
risk management 29, 47, 173 n. 49
risk, meaning of 57
risk taking 12, 29, 48, 53, 57
Robinson, C. 128, 177 n. 37

scepticism
    about communication 128
    attitude of, in interaction 98, 120, 140, 142
    default assumption of 3, 21, 131, 140
    external world 142
    other minds 187 n. 29
    philosophical 3, 14, 127–8, 132, 139, 144, 153
Shakespeare, W. 83, 85
Simpson, E. 163 n. 48
Skirbekk, H. 170 n. 10
snapshot conception (of agency, etc.) 71, 78, 88, 174 n. 6

social context 15, 132, 142
Socrates 44, 85
state
    meaning of 92
    of mind 11, 71, 92–5, 97, 109
    of nature 12, 26–8, 32, 35
    see also psychological state
Sztompka, P. 161 n. 25

testimony 4–5, 14, 23, 82, 112–16, 145, 160 n. 15, 176 n. 27
Thomas, L. 133
timelessness 70, 73, 74, 77, 88, 89
tone of voice 79, 120–2
Travis, C. 162 n. 30
truthfulness 6, 23, 107, 112, 116–23, 126–7, 186 n. 70

utility 3, 41, 48, 168 n. 47

vulnerability
    accepted 22, 30, 47–8, 54, 56, 64, 67, 172 n. 29
    ethical significance of 60, 65–7, 147
    meaning of 22, 47–8, 55, 64
    physical 54, 66
    in social life 133, 136–9

Wagner, R. 161 n. 29
Watson, R. 99
Weil, S. 125, 132, 147–53, 185 n. 54
Wells, H. G. 60
Winch, P. 25, 27, 116–20, 126, 128, 147–8, 168 n. 53, 182 n. 6
Wittgenstein, L.
    on community and reasoning 5, 14, 21, 132, 142, 146

ethics in 189 n. 51
on 'knowing' 103, 142–5
on language 21, 91, 128
on mental states and feelings
   88, 91–6, 179 n. 13
trust in 21, 128, 145, 153

see also individual entries
Wolgast, E. 3
World picture 143–4

Zettel (Wittgenstein) 93

www.ingramcontent.com/pod-product-compliance
Lightning Source LLC
Chambersburg PA
CBHW052042300426
44117CB00012B/1931